Symbolism in
Religion and Literature

Symbolism in
Religion and Literature

Edited and with an Introduction by

ROLLO MAY

George Braziller

NEW YORK   1960

The following essays were originally published in *Daedalus*, the Journal of the American Academy of Arts and Sciences, under the general editorship of Gerald Holton:

THE RELIGIOUS SYMBOL by Paul Tillich

THE CROSS: SOCIAL TRAUMA OR REDEMPTION by Amos N. Wilder

ON THE FIRST THREE CHAPTERS OF GENESIS by Kenneth Burke

THE PATTERN OF RELIGIOUS ORGANIZATION IN THE UNITED STATES by Talcott Parsons

THE SENSE OF POETRY: SHAKESPEARE'S "THE PHOENIX AND THE TURTLE," by I. A. Richards

THE REPRESENTATION OF NATURE IN CONTEMPORARY PHYSICS by Werner Heisenberg

Second Printing

Library of Congress Catalog Card Number: 59-8842

Printed in the United States of America

Contents

Of the essays in this volume, those by Paul Tillich, Amos N. Wilder, Kenneth Burke, Talcott Parsons, I. A. Richards, and Werner Heisenberg were originally published in DAEDALUS, the Journal of the American Academy of Arts and Sciences, in the issue devoted to "Symbolism in Religion and Literature" (Vol. 87, No. 3).

Introduction

The Significance of Symbols

ROLLO MAY

On undertaking to write this introductory chapter, I found myself in something of a dilemma: for obviously the distinguished essays in this book need no introduction. It then seemed, however, that the rich, concrete data that comes to the hand of the practicing psychoanalyst might make a contribution to the problems set by the book. Those of us in that profession have the privilege in our daily work of an especially advantageous position to observe the function and significance of symbols in the immediate existence of actual persons.

In this essay, therefore, I wish to deal with symbols as they come to us in psychoanalysis and psychology. After noting the present interest in symbols and myths in these fields, I shall give an example of a symbol in a dream. I wish, then, to present some general observations about symbols and the symbolizing process in psychoanalysis, and to discuss the Oedipus myth in the light of these observations. Finally, I propose to offer some implications about the healing power and function of symbols.

I

There has been a radical change during the past three decades in this country in the importance of symbols as subjects for discussion and inquiry in psychology and psychiatry. In the 1920's the tendency in these fields was to rule symbols out as much as

11

possible (except a few sign-symbols in science and mathematics), never to raise the topics of symbols or myths if it could be helped, and otherwise to regard symbols as temporary concessions to our ignorance in matters which we should soon be able to describe in clear, rational terms. We left these esoteric topics to the poets and literary critics. Neither term, symbol or myth, even appears in the index of the standard psychology textbook—written not by a Watsonian behaviorist but by a dynamic psychologist who was certainly enlightened and broad of interest—which my class and many similar classes studied in colleges throughout the country.[1] We tried to be "hard-headed" men, as Alfred North Whitehead put it in his essay cited in this volume, who "want facts and not symbols," and who therefore "push aside symbols as being mere make-believes, veiling and distorting that inner sanctuary of truth which reason claims as its own."[*]

This attitude brought with it a tendency to smile condescendingly at all the diverse meanings Freud claimed he found in so-called symbols in dreams and other subrational processes. In the edition of 1929, Woodworth writes, with amazing naivete to our —and no doubt to his—present ears, "A large share of dreams seem too fantastic to have any personal meaning. Yet they are interesting to the dreamer and they would be worth going to see if they could be reproduced and put on the stage. Isn't that sufficient excuse for them? May they not be simply a free play of imagination that gives interesting results just because of its freedom and vividness?"[1] Thus dreams, like symbols, may have an aesthetic, whimsical interest, but they are not for us realistic, tough-minded investigators!

This position in psychology was of course an understandable outcome of the proclivity for singling out for study those aspects of human behavior which overlapped with that of animals, and which could ultimately be described in physiological or stimulus-

* Page 233 below.

response terms. To the extent, indeed, that the psychologist does thus restrict himself, he *can* avoid the problem of symbols in his subjects; for as we shall indicate later, symbolizing and symbol-using are unique with human beings. Quite apart from the accuracy or inaccuracy of the above methods (these psychologists blandly evaded the highly intricate symbolic problem in the very concepts, such as S-R, they themselves used), the general upshot of this tendency was a widespread impoverishment and beggaring of our knowledge of man.*

The revolutionary change in the middle of our century with respect to psychological interest in symbols is due chiefly to the study of the inner, deeper levels of human experience by Freud, Jung and the other psychotherapists. It is ironic indeed that those psychologists who *really* had to be "hard-headed," that is, to deal with actual suffering people whose anxiety and distress would not be calmed by abstractions or theories, were the ones who could not escape becoming concerned with symbols. Once we were forced to see the patient in relation to his world—what Freud called his "fate" and "destiny," or what the existential

---

* This is why many of us made the odd discovery in those college days that we learned a good deal more about psychology—that is, man and his experience—from our literature courses than we did from our psychology itself. The reason, of course, was that literature could not avoid dealing with symbols and myths as the quintessential forms of man's expression and interpretation of himself and his experience. By the same token, when students now write to me stating that they wish ultimately to become psychoanalysts and asking my advice about what courses to take in college, I advise them to major in literature and the humanities rather than biology, psychology and pre-medical courses. There is time enough in the specialized graduate school to learn one's science and the special forms of scientific method; but if the student concentrates on these *before* he grasps the symbols and myths in man's self-interpretation in present and historical literature, he will be outfitted with a method which will do everything except help him to grasp his real data. Then his professional work as a psychoanalyst may well be boring to himself and might indeed be harmful (that is, limiting) to his patients. I speak of course in extreme terms; certainly many actual persons who become psychoanalysts already have some concern with the deeper symbolic and mythological dimensions of experience as a selective factor in their choosing to enter the field.

psychoanalysts were to call the "being-in-the-world"—we could
not overlook symbols, for they have their birth in just that relationship of the inner experience with the outer world, and are
indeed the very language of the patient's crises and distress.

II

Let us now ask what we mean by a symbol. The patient from
whom we take this example was a young lawyer who had come
for treatment because of recurrent sexual impotence, embarrass-
ing and uncontrollable blushing, and various psychosomatic ill-
nesses which had kept him out of professional school for long
periods of time. During the period I happened to be working on
this essay he brought in the following dream fragment:

> I was standing at the mouth of a cave, with one foot in and one out.
> The cave inside was dark, almost black. The floor in the center of the
> cave was a swampy bog, but it was firm on each side. I felt anxiety
> and a strong need to get out.

This symbol of the cave is less dramatic than dozens of other
symbols—"werewolf," "tarantula's web," *ad infinitum*—which
come up in the course of any one day's analytic sessions. We present this figure of the cave precisely because it is undramatic and
not at all unusual, and therefore cannot be relegated to some special literary imagination on the part of our patient. The dream
came during a period in his analysis when he was trying to work
on his difficulty in making dates with girls; it indeed occurred the
night after a day in which he had blushed a good deal, much to
his discomfort, felt envy of a colleague who could "pick up" girls,
and worried about his own possible homosexual trends. In the
session some of his associations to the dream were: "The darkness was like standing under the cables of Brooklyn Bridge,
where I kissed a girl the other night." "The middle of the cave
was like quicksand; it would suck you down." " 'Cave' reminds me

of Plato's story of the cave where men couldn't see reality." "The cave is like a kangeroo's pouch in which it carries the baby." And then, out of the blue, "I can't *stand* fat women!"

Since the meaning of the symbol of the cave was clear on the basis of these as well as numerous other data which he and I already had accumulated, I shall not give more associations. To him and to me this seemed the meaning: the cave is a womb and vagina symbol (the latter less central, for reasons I will not go into), a symbol which brought up before him the threat of being sucked into annihilation, absorbed by his own attachment to his mother (who, needless to say, is fat). The dream pictures him as now standing in a dilemma, wanting and needing the protection and warmth of the mother (the kangaroo's pouch) but realizing that this not only blocks him from seeing reality (Plato's cave) but threatens to suck him like quicksand into a smothering death.

We shall return to the more complex implications of the dream later. Here let us only note several characteristics of this symbol. First, the figure of the cave with its quicksand is infinitely more powerful than the specific words "womb" or "vagina" or such rational, positivistic statements as "I am afraid of being absorbed by my mother's womb," would be by themselves. Indeed, many patients in psychoanalysis try to phrase experiences in these rational statements precisely in order to avoid experiencing the vital power and immediate reality of their situation which the symbol would force them to confront.

The second thing we note about this symbol is that it brings together the various unconscious urges and desires, of both a personal depth on one hand and an archaic, archetypal depth on the other; and it unites these with conscious elements in the young man's day to day struggles with his problems. He would not have had a dream with a symbol which so clearly and force- fully showed his predicament except after several months of analysis. The symbols which arise in psychoanalysis are not, thus, to be viewed as special imaginative productions, but rather as the day-to-day language by which the patient communicates as a totality; he is able to say in the symbol not only what is present in the situation with respect to his problems, but to speak in the same symbol from unconscious depths as well.

In the third place, this symbol presents a picture in which some decision, some orientation toward movement, some action is called for; he has one foot in the cave and one out, and experiences anxiety in his urge to get out. We term this the *conative* element in the symbol.* In my judgment the distinguishing characteristic of genuine symbols which come up as the language of psychoanalysis is that they always involve this orientation toward action. It is not adequate to describe this as an expression of the "repressed wish" alone, or the expression of instinctual impulses from the "Id"; such descriptions refer only to one side of the picture. In its full form the symbol rather presents an existential situation in which the patient is asking himself the question, "In which direction shall I move?" It is not a question of how will "my wish" or "instinctual urge" or any other part of me move (except in sophisticated patients who have learned that by this language they can avoid the impact of their true symbols), but "in which direction shall *I* move?" This orientation toward movement obviously involves more than conscious levels of the self; it is by definition a function of the totality of the self; the "wish" from unconscious levels is related in complex, subtle fashion to the "will" from conscious levels, an interplay not to be oversimplified by saying that the former is the infantile, antisocial, and the latter the mature and social. Sometimes just the opposite is the case. Just as one cannot set out consciously to "construct" symbols, so one cannot confront a genuine symbol on merely conscious, rational levels. One must, like the patient in the dream, engage it and struggle with it on all levels of affect and willing. The commonly assumed idea in psychoanalysis that

---

* I have profited from a discussion by mail of this point and others in this paper with two other contributors to this volume, Amos Wilder and Erich Kahler, and wish to express my appreciation to them.

"willing" follows "wishing" is only half the truth, and thereby false in implication; it is just as true that the patient cannot become aware of "wishes" until he is ready to take some chance of "willing," and that he cannot let himself either dream or experience symbols, except as he has become ready in some way to confront the decision posed in the symbol. It may, of course, be many months and perhaps a couple of years—involving thousands of little decisions along the way—before our patient has fully moved beyond the threat of the annihilating maternal womb; but that should not lead us to overlook the fact that the symbol of the cave poses the issue demanding decision, and that some such element, no matter how minute, is present in all genuine symbols arising in psychotherapy.*

The final point we note in the young man's dream is that the symbol of the cave cannot be said always to mean "womb" or

---

* Whether or not *all* symbols can be said to involve this conative element, this orientation toward action on the part of the person who experiences the symbol, is a question which goes beyond my competence. My belief, however, is that this is true. It is true certainly of such classical symbols as the Christian Cross: like it or not, if you genuinely experience it, you must take some stand with regard to it; and the same is obviously true of such myths as Oedipus, Orestes and the Fall of Adam. It may also be true of the symbols we call words; every word which one genuinely experiences raises some affective response, some movement "toward" or "away." Nabokov has demonstrated in *Lolita* that practically all words can have an affective quality, a fact which is more obviously shown in poetry but which is also present in prose. I would go so far as to hypothesize that our point of the conative element in symbols is true even of the so-called "purely abstract" symbols such as those in mathematics, at least in their origin. If we look at the neolithic geometrical designs and forms on the vases of neolithic Egypt, for example, and sense at the same time how these were related to astronomical data, to the planting and harvesting of crops, and how they ultimately became geometrical symbols, we get some picture of how many affective and conative elements were and are present in the symbols, far beyond so-called "merely aesthetic"—if there is such a way of relating to reality—or merely "logical" aspects. Kahler speaks in his essay in this book of mathematical symbols as "communication with nature," which already implies some of the element of which we are speaking. I would suggest that the difference between a "sign" and a genuine "symbol" lies at this point: when a word retains its original power to grasp us, it is still a *symbol*, but when this is lost it deteriorates into being only a *sign*; and by the same token, when a *myth* loses its power to demand some stand from us, it has become only a *tale*.

"vagina" or what not; rather it is given its power and character as a symbol by the total situation of the patient's life at that moment. This patient might dream of a cave in another dream in which it would not be a symbol, or it might have any one of an infinite number of other meanings depending upon his existence at that time. This point is important to emphasize because of some tendency in psychoanalysis to equate given words and symbols with specific meanings. This is a literalistic, fundamental-istic approach, and in my judgment it is inaccurate. This is part of the reason Kahler holds that what Freud calls "symbols" in dreams are really "symptoms" expressed in images. Kahler goes on to say, in discussing Freud's and Jung's interpretation of symbols, "In all such cases, the actual 'symbolization' is done, not by the person in whose unconscious the image arises, but by the analyst through inferential interpretation. To him alone these images are meaningful, just as the physical symptom carries mean-ing only for somebody who looks for its cause."* Kahler's argu-ment is based upon his very important point that some conscious process must always be involved in a symbol. No image can have the power of a symbol if, as it is assumed in dreams, the patient himself is totally unconscious of its meaning. Kahler is right in holding that the equating of specific images and figures with spe-cific meanings is a process occurring in the analyst's mind and depends indeed upon his particular theoretical system.

But the critical issue here is that no symbol of which a patient dreams is ever completely "unconscious." This brings us to a development of our point raised above, namely that, contrary to popular assumption, *every dream has its conscious pole.* Indeed the matrix out of which the dream is born is precisely the inter-relation, often in struggle and conflict, between the conscious pole of the crises of the day and the unconscious depths within the person. Our young lawyer struggled during the day over his problem of embarrassment, immobilization and impotence with girls, and at night he constructed out of archaic and archetypal

* Page 59 below.

material the symbolic picture depicting what this immobilization consisted of. The dream is an "answer" from unconscious levels to a "question" posed by the patient's immediate existence. This is why we always ask, when interpreting a dream with a patient, what critical events occurred during the day or evening before the night of the dream; these events are almost invariably essential to our grasping what the dream seeks to tell us. The generally accepted idea that some chance happening "cues off" the dream (such a penetrating psychologist, in other ways, as Nietzsche, makes much of the chance physical events like posture in bed or what one eats before going to sleep) cannot be adequate. If so-called archaic, unconscious elements come up by such accidents, one would indeed be right in questioning whether they have more than whimsical, aesthetic interest! But the "unconscious" levels do not operate hit or miss. We find, in actuality, that the dream is an endeavor to work out some way of life, to get some perspective, to picture some "answer" to the issues which confront this person awake and asleep. And the dream has its particular blessing for us in that it is able to answer such questions posed by the patient's predicament by drawing upon the totality of levels of experience, whether we call these levels "subconscious," "preconscious," "unconscious," or what not. The symbol thus does not simply "surge up," as though it were carried within one like a foreign body with which one had no relation. Out of the matrix (or, as Rank would put it, dialectic) of conscious and unconscious the symbol is conceived, molded and born. The symbol is "mothered" by the archaic material in so-called unconscious depths, but "fathered" by the individual's conscious existence in his immediate struggles. Figures like our patient's cave, then, have the genuine meaning of a symbol in the patient's existence, providing we as analysts are able, with him, to read that meaning. Whether or not we can read this meaning does not depend on our theories; their constructive use is rather to show us the wide possible diversity of meanings. It depends rather upon our capacity to participate in his world and

to experience the symbol from the point of view of the questions
his existence poses for him.

III

A first observation which clinical work in psychoanalysis forces
upon us is that symbols and myths, far from being topics which
can be discarded in psychology, are rather in the very center of
our psychoanalytic understanding of men. Clinical data supports
the thesis that man is uniquely the symbol-using organism, and
is distinguished from the rest of nature and animal life by this
fact.

The research of the neuropsychiatrist, Kurt Goldstein, graphically demonstrates this point. As director of a large mental hospi-
tal in Germany during and after World War I, Goldstein studied
many patients with brain lesions, especially soldiers with parts
of the cerebral cortex shot away. He observed that these patients
could function adequately if their world were shrunken in space
and time to correspond to their limited capacities. These patients
kept their closets, for example, in compulsive order; if they were
placed in environments where objects surrounding them were in
disarray, they were at a loss to react adequately and showed
profound anxiety. When asked to write their names on a paper,
they would write in the extreme corner of the paper—any open
space (any "emptiness") representing a threat with which they
could not cope.

Now what had broken down in these patients was the capacity
for symbolic behavior, the capacity to relate to themselves and
their worlds *in terms of symbols*. They could no longer experience the self over, against, and in relation to, a world of objects.
To have a self and a world are correlates of the same capacity,
and it was precisely this capacity that in these patients was impaired. They lost the capacity, in Goldstein's words, *to transcend
the immediate concrete situation, to abstract, to think and live in
terms of "the possible."* Though we can never draw a one-to-one
relationship between a specific *part* of the neurophysical equip-

ment and a specific way of behaving (the organism reacts as a whole or it does not react at all) it is still significant, nevertheless, that the part of the organism which was impaired in these patients was the cerebral cortex. This is the part which most radically distinguishes man, the part which is present in considerable size in human beings but very small or not present at all in animals. Goldstein points out, furthermore, that these patients, in losing the capacity to transcend the concrete situation, lived in a radically shrunken range of possible reactions, and in proportion to this, they therefore lost their psychological freedom.

Another angle from which our point finds confirmation is the genetic. The capacity to use symbols, including language, emerges in the growing infant at the same time as the split between consciousness and unconsciousness and the capacity "to repress" which bulks so large in later psychotherapy. This split is not present at birth; the infant in the first months "knows neither guilt or shame," as Auden puts it. But sometime after the first couple of months we can detect the emerging of this capacity to experience himself as distinguished from the world of objects, separate from people around him, to know himself as the one who *has* a world. This is generally called "the emergence and development of the ego," I think a not entirely felicitous phrase. For our purposes here it suffices to say that this, when developed in maturity, is my capacity to experience myself as the being who exists and will exist in this world a limited number of months or years and will then die; but the being who, in this period of unknown length, can by virtue of this experience influence how I shall respond. Thus I can exercise some element of freedom and responsibility. Man, as Erwin Straus well puts it, is the being who can question his own being. Not only *can*, but *must;* as he must likewise ask questions of the world around him.

Symbols are the language of this capacity for self-consciousness, the ability to question which arises out of and is made necessary by the distinction of subject and object. As Erich Kahler points out, the symbol is a "bridging act," a bridging of the gap

between outer existence (the world) and inner meaning; and it
arose out of man's capacity to separate inner meaning and outer
existence. What is important to see is that a "hard fact" or a description of a "hard fact" can by itself never bridge that gap; all
the objective, intellectualized talk in the world with words which
have become signs and have lost their symbolic power about the
"dangers of morbid dependence on the mother," would not help
our young lawyer patient. The only thing that will help him is
some breaking through of an expression that will do justice *both*
to the objective situation and the subjective meaning within him.
This the symbol of the cave does for him. The psychological
essence of the symbol is that it has the power to grasp the person
as a totality as he immediately exists in his world.

It follows, thus, that an individual's self-image is built up of
symbols. Symbolizing is basic to such questions as personal
identity. For the individual *experiences himself as a self* in terms
of symbols which arise from three levels at once; those from
archaic and archetypal depths within himself, symbols arising
from the personal events of his psychological and biological experience, and the general symbols and values which obtain in
his culture.

A second observation impressed upon us by our psychoanalytic work is that *contemporary man suffers from the deteriora-
tion and breakdown of the central symbols in modern Western
culture.* I speak here mainly out of experience with neurotic
patients; but it will be self-evident that our patients in psychoanalysis are not suffering from some special ailment but show in
their symptoms the general, though not yet overt, predicament
in our society. The neurotic is characterized by the fact that his
defenses are not as firmly thrown up as those of the majority of
people, and he generally possesses some special sensitivities as
well as special needs which make him unable to "adjust" so
successfully. Therefore the neurotic problems of one decade
generally reflect underlying conflicts in the society which the
man in the street so far can defend himself against, but which

will come out endemically in the society of the next decade.

Now what we find typically in our patients in this decade is that no symbols seem to have compelling power and meaning to grip them any more—not "God" nor "father" nor the "stars and stripes." A decade or so ago the symbols related to "competitive success" and "love" did have power to grasp people and elicit their allegiance; but there is reason for believing that these symbols too have lost their power. Our patients do not have to be told that

> "The candles in the churches are out.
> The lights have gone out in the sky."[2]

But the bitterest aspect of their situation is that "blowing on the coals of the heart" also lacks efficacy for them. Since the symbols of love have largely been swallowed up by the needs for security, and the myths of success absorbed by the new myth of the organization man, even these time-honored Western symbols have lost their power. It is not, of course, that our patients have lost the capacity to symbolize, like Goldstein's organic patients; but rather that they have no available contents for their symbols which they can believe in wholeheartedly enough to make commitment of themselves possible. This is a central aspect of the "emptiness" experienced by so many contemporary sensitive persons; they can transcend the concrete situation indeed, but they land in a symbolic vacuum.

Nathan Scott is of course right in his discussion later in this book of the crisis of values in modern literature, that our present situation is that of a "broken center." As Robert and Helen Lynd pointed out in their discussion of the "chaos of conflicting patterns" in the typical American town of Middletown in the 1930's, every individual "is caught in a chaos of conflicting patterns, none of them wholly condemned, but no one of them clearly approved and free from confusion; or, where the group sanctions are clear in demanding a certain role of a man or woman, the individual encounters cultural requirements with no immediate

means of meeting them." [3] Since the 1930's the "chaos of conflicting patterns" seems to have developed toward an *absence* of patterns. We often observe in our patients that they cannot discover
any accepted symbol in their culture these days sufficiently accepted even to fight *against!* [*]

Let us now make clearer what we mean by the "central cultural symbols" and then refer to the case of our patient. In every
society there are certain formative principles which infuse every
aspect of that culture—art, science, education, religion. These
formative principles are expressed in certain basic symbols and
myths which lend form and unity to the culture. Such symbols
are the culture's form of transcending the immediate situation;
they will always be bound up with the fundamental values and
goals accepted in the society. Tillich uses the expression "style"
for these underlying unifying principles in a given culture; Mal-
inowski used to refer similarly to the "charter" of the society.
This "style" will always have a religious dimension since it points
to a meaning beyond the immediate situation of the culture. [*]

We may, for example, following Tillich, propose "circle" as a
symbol for classical Greek culture. We can see this "circular
form" resplendent in Greek sculpture (in radical contrast to the
later Gothic vertical lines and the Baroque horizontal lines). We
can find this "circle" in philosophy in the emphases on balance

---

[*] With most patients several decades ago (and with naive patients now),
we could assume, when they said they had nothing to believe in anymore,
that they were suffering from some unconscious conflict about symbols having to do, say, with "God and the authority of father," or "mother and
protectiveness" and so on. Our problem then was easier: we had only to
help them work through the conflict about their symbols in order that they
might choose their own; the dynamic was there. My point is that now, however, patients on a much broader scale seem to be reflecting the general
disintegration of cultural symbols, a disintegration that percolates down more
and more broadly into the members of society, and seems to be a lack of
transcendent symbols of any sort.

[*] We do not, of course, use the term "transcend" here in an otherworldly
or supernatural sense but refer to the fact that the symbols and myths pre-
suppose and point toward meaning and value not realized in the immediate
situation. This can be seen clearly in art and literature but I think it is as
much present in the science of a period.

and perfect eternal movement, and in such precepts as the golden mean and "nothing in excess." And it is so emblazoned in the spirit of Greek architecture that no one could possibly miss it. During several years of living in Greece I was continually struck by the circles of the islands rising out of the sea, the circular promontory of Salamis stretching away below Athens, the low round curves of the hills encircling Athens, all rising up in concentric circles to include the Acropolis and its Parthenon, a monument of dignity and magnificence that itself seemed to grow directly and organically out of the unending curves of the land and sea.

If we seek a geometric symbol for the Middle Ages, I would propose the "triangle." Mont St. Michel rises in a vast triangle, constructed partly by the rock of nature and partly by the marble hewn by man, ascending up from the ocean toward heaven. The triangle is reflected also in Gothic architecture in general and is present in the concept of the "trinity" so basic to medieval philosophy and theology.

When we ask what the central symbol is in the middle of the twentieth century, I do not have to hesitate long as I look out of the window of my office in the city of New York. I see a sea of skyscrapers, each one surging upward from its narrow base, utilizing nature not to be united with but simply to stand *upon,* each building rising upward not for spiritual purposes but for achievement, getting to "the top," the spirit of moving "onward and upward" every month and every year, surging on and on not to infinity or heaven but caught in the perpetual motion of the everlasting upward drive of finiteness. The skyscrapers outside my window are a beautiful form of art indeed, and I do not wish to disparage the marvelous use of concrete and steel and aluminum with such power and lace-like delicacy. But what is the underlying meaning of a symbol that "scrapes" a sky which is never there? This standing *on* nature in order to move forever *away from* nature, upward toward "a top" which never exists, is obviously parallel to the competitiveness in business life and is reflected in the mottos on the fronts of the churches among those skyscrapers, "How to Be Happier and Happier." It is revealed, too, in the restlessness, frustration, and often despair of our patients and countless other people living in the shadows of these vertical shafts of aluminum power.

The psychological symbols and values which go along with this are, of course, those of competitive success and achievement. In late decades, however, as Riesman in *The Lonely Crowd* classically demonstrated, the inherent contradictions in these values too became more and more evident. The ethical aspects of the modern "style" have been through the last four centuries associated with the humanistic and Hebrew-Christian traditions. Now these values, it is generally agreed, are in process of radical disintegration and transition. This makes the psychological task of modern man much more difficult as he struggles to find and work out not only symbols by which he can relate to his world but also symbols by which he can know himself and work out his own identity.*

When the transcendent symbols in the culture lose their cogency, furthermore, the individual's personal symbols, including

---

* Because of these emerging contradictions, the destructive aspects of modern individualism have become much more prominent. The individualistic character of the thought of the modern West and the factors compensating for it can be seen in Leibnitz. His basic doctrine of the "monads" is individualistic in the sense that the monads are unitary and separated; but the compensating element is given in his doctrine of "pre-established harmony." Tillich expresses this graphically, "In the system of harmony the metaphysical solitude of every individual is strongly emphasized by the doctrine that there are 'no doors and windows' from one 'monad' to the other one. Every single unit is lonely in itself, without any direct communication. The horror of this idea was overcome by the harmonistic presupposition that in every monad the whole world is potentially present and that the development of each individual is in a natural harmony with the development of all the others. This is the most profound metaphysical symbol for the situation in the early periods of bourgeois civilization. It fitted this situation because there was still a common world, in spite of the increasing social atomization." (Tillich, Paul, *The Protestant Era*, Chicago, 1948, p. 246. See also: May, Rollo, *The Meaning of Anxiety*, New York, 1950, pp. 17-22.)

biological and sexual symbols, seem to lose their power or be thrown into self-contradiction all down the line as well. Let us note again the cave symbol brought by our patient. The positive side of such a symbol would be the protection and warmth that one has a right to expect of the "womb," or the encompassing love associated with a loving mother's healthy relation to her child. When a typical patient from exurbia, let us say, exhibits in a psychotherapeutic session the desire for such mothering, we would ask the question, to ourselves if not to him, "Why not?" For we can assume that accepting the *healthy* aspect of this maternal form of love will proceed hand in hand with his capacity to get over the morbid dependency. In other words, what keeps him from being able to experience a cave without quicksand? But what we typically find is that our exurban executive fights, as though his life depended on it, *against* letting any woman, his wife included, mother him at all. This does not depend on whether or not the wife is dominating and exploitative (as was the mother of our lawyer patient) but rather upon the man's own inner inability to accept the mothering. The assertive, dominating roles are so often given to the woman in our culture (described variously as "momism," our "new matriarchy," and so on) that the exurban man does not know how to orient himself or by what standards and symbols to establish his own conviction of strength. Our young lawyer, for example, reported one day that he was impotent with a girl until he could hint to her that he had made a good deal of money recently on the stock market; then he became suddenly sexually potent. This confirmation of his strength as a competitive middle-class man enabled him to feel on an even level, at least for the time being, with the powerful woman "queen." But soon these values and symbols also no longer worked, for he discovered, as anyone must in our present decade of organization men, that it is now démodé to get ahead and that he encounters resentment and hostility from those below him, even from the women.* The symbols associated with love lose their power to give potency in a period when love is more and more identified with security. For how can one enjoy potency with the very woman who is also his source of security, and when sexual potency also is measured in terms not of his own joy and strength but of his power to satisfy the "queen" as gauged by her reaction to and "grading" of his efforts? This rough schema is related to many diverse problems which come up in psycho-analysis, from impotence and internalized aggression on one end to such psychosomatic symptoms as ulcers on the other.

What do modern people, using our patients for our data still, do when they experience this vacuum of symbols and values? By and large, they try to fill the vacuum with *tools* rather than *symbols.* They seize on signs and techniques borrowed from the scientific and mechanical spheres. It is not surprising, for example, that a plethora of books on sexual *technique* and *methods* comes out at just the time when people have difficulty experiencing the power of their own emotions and passions with the sexual partner. It makes sense to them to borrow technical symbols, for the symbols and values connected with science and technical prowess *seem* to most people in our day to be the least open to contradiction. True, tools and symbols have a somewhat analogous function. Tools are the method of communicating with nature, Kahler tells us; they are aids toward the transcending of the immediate situation with respect to nature. But the trouble from the psychological side is that when tools and techniques are substituted for genuine symbols, subjectivity is lost. The person may establish some power *over* nature (say, power over his own body, which our patients often desperately seek); but he

---

* David Riesman, et al, in *The Lonely Crowd* has made the point that modern students no longer accept or respect the standard of being *first* but prefer to be unobtrusively second or third down the competitive line. The whole problem of "outer directedness" of course raises serious problems for potency; the two are contradictory, for if your potency depends in the last analysis on something outside, you do not have psychological potency.

does so at the price of separating himself ever more fully from nature, including his own body. When emphasis beyond a certain point is placed upon technique in sexuality, the person finds that he has separated himself all the more from his own affects, from his own spontaneity and joy and the surging up of his own experience of potency. This means that the substituting of tools and techniques for symbols short-circuits his own search for potency; and in the long run adds to his feeling of emptiness.* In my judgment the most serious moral issue facing modern psychoanalysis is the tendency inherent in psychoanalysis itself to play into the patient's need—and our need in the whole society—to perceive ourselves and others in terms of the newly accepted psychological techniques, and to make ourselves over in the image of the machine.

Our third observation is that the *breakdown of these transcendent cultural symbols and values is fundamentally related to the emergence in our day of what we call psychoanalysis.* This point needs to be emphasized because of the tendency among many psychoanalysts, particularly of the central Freudian stream, to hold that psychoanalysis is to be understood as the discovery of a new method of diagnosis and a new method of treatment, roughly analogous to the way penicillin and the other antibiotics were discovered in the biological sciences. Granted the importance of Freud's great contribution in making the phenomena of dreams and other unconscious phenomena amenable to the methods of Western science and his revolutionary influence on the image of man,—contributions which will endure in literature and science—it is nevertheless true that psychoanalysis was called forth by certain historical crises. Chief among these was the disintegration of the symbols and myths in our age of transi-

* In his exceedingly penetrating essay in this volume on the relation of man to nature, Heisenberg points out the critical danger in the substitution of the technical attitude for science: "Technology thus fundamentally interferes with the relation of man with nature . . ." and the danger is that man becomes "uncertain in the impulses of his spirit."

tion which left the individual in the position in which he could
not orient himself or find his identity in accord with these
symbols or in rebellion against them.

When we look at other historical periods from this perspective,
we note that concern with such problems as anxiety, despair,
overt and endemic forms of neurotic guilt, and activities like
psychoanalysis designed to help individuals meet such problems,
emerge in the disintegrating, transitional phases of the historical
period and not in the phases when the symbols and myths of the
culture possess strength and unifying power. For example, in
reading Plato and Aristotle and other writers of the classical fifth
and fourth centuries in Greece, we find it almost impossible to
discover any references to anxiety as we know it today. Socrates
discusses death and fear of death in the *Apologia* and *Phaedo*, but
he is confident throughout that given moral virtue and the right
ideas death can be confronted without anxiety. Plato comes close
to describing anxiety in a passage in the *Republic* when he talks
of a man's lying awake at night in dread of dying; but he states as
though it were self-evident that if this man has no wrong on his
conscience, that is, has not cheated anybody in financial dealings,
he will have Hope and therefore no fear of dying and going on
into the next world. (And Alephas, who makes this speech in the
dialogue, adds that the chief value of having money is that you
are then able to avoid cheating others; to which Socrates agrees!)
We can find nothing here of modern *Angst* which falls on the
good man not only as much as, but often more than, the bad;
the rich man as well as the poor. Objective "fear" is present, to
be sure, and discussed by Plato and Aristotle; but such fear by
very definition is precisely *not* anxiety. The whole aura of these
times makes one know he is in a different psychological and
spiritual world from our own.

To be sure, anxiety, guilt and despair are presented in the
dramas, and hence we tend to see Aeschylus' Oresteia and
Sophocles' Oedipus from the point of view of our modern guilt

and conflict. But there is a radical difference, obvious to anyone who views the actual modern interpretations of these myths, say Sartre's *Flies* and Robinson Jeffers' *Tower Beyond Tragedy*. The difference is in the *aura of objectivity* in the Greek dramas, the assumption of the presence of accepted conditions of man's relation to himself, his fellows and the gods; and though Aeschylus and Sophocles, and the other creative spirits of their era, are engaged in molding the symbols, and changing, struggling and fighting against accepted attitudes and aspects of the myths, at least the symbols and myths were *there* to fight against in the first place.

Now in this classic phase of Greek culture we notice that the problems which are dealt with in psychoanalysis in our modern world seem to be taken care of by a kind of "normal" psychotherapy operating spontaneously through the accepted practices in Greek drama, religion, art and philosophy. It is not difficult for a modern psychoanalyst to imagine the great abreactive effect on some person burdened with guilt feelings because of hostility toward an exploitative mother, who watches, let us say, the public performance of the drama in which Orestes kills the mother who had destroyed his father, is then pursued over hill and dale by the punishing Erinyes (who, since they track evil-doers and inflict madness would seem psychologically to be symbols of guilt and remorse), and finally achieves peace when he is forgiven by the community and the gods. I do not mean, of course, that these therapeutic experiences would be consciously articulated by the citizen of Greece in the fifth century B.C. Indeed, our point is that just the opposite was true, that "therapy" was part of the normal, unarticulated functions of the drama, religion and other forms of communication of the day. One gets the impression in these classical periods of *education* rather than *re-education*, of normal development of the individual toward *integration* rather than desperate endeavors toward *re-integration*.

But in the subsequent decline of Hellenic culture, after the conquest of Greece by Alexander and later by the Romans and the dispersion of Greek culture to Asia Minor and Rome, we note a sharply different situation with respect to the problems of anxiety, despair, and guilt. In this Hellenistic period we find plenty of descriptions of anxiety; Plutarch paints a vivid picture of an anxious man which has entirely the ring of *Angst*. The numerous philosophical schools which had sprung up by that time—the Stoics, Epicureans, Cynics, Cyreniacs, Hedonists, along with the traditional Platonists and Aristotelians—not only now deal with the problems with which we are familiar in psychoanalysis but their concepts and manner of teaching have dramatic parallels to modern psychotherapy. Note, for example, the Epicurean doctrine of *Ataraxia*, a seeking to achieve tranquility of mind by rationally balancing one's pleasures, and the Stoic doctrine of *Apatheia*, the passionless calm attained by being above conflicts of emotion. Their teachings may not be good therapy from our modern cultural viewpoint, (the lectures of Hegesias in Alexandria had to be prohibited by Ptolemy because they caused so many suicides!) But content of "good" or "bad" is not the point; for the content of repressions, and therefore what needs to be brought out to achieve "wholeness," varies radically from culture to culture. What is significant about these diverse schools in the Hellenistic period is that they took the form of psychological and ethical systems designed to help the individual find some source of strength and integrity to enable him to stand securely and gain some happiness in a changing society which no longer lent him that security. The term "failure of nerve" which Gilbert Murray used for the second and first centuries B.C. could be used for any period which is in the throes of basic transition and change. This change and disunity is not primarily a political phenomenon. (Athens in the Hellenistic period had relative peace and the Golden Age, at least in its last thirty years when Athens and Sparta fought continuously, did not.) The question rather is whether the transcendent symbols, the "style" of the culture, move toward unity or are in the process of transition and disintegration.

A society furnishes means for its members to deal with excessive guilt, anxiety and despair in its symbols and myths. When no symbols have transcendent meaning, as in our day, the individual no longer has his specific aid to transcend his normal crises of life, such as chronic illness, loss of employment, war, death of loved ones and his own death, and the concomitant anxiety and guilt. In such periods he has an infinitely harder time dealing with his impulses and instinctual needs and drives, a much harder time finding his own identity, and is prey thus to *neurotic* guilt and anxiety.

My point is that our historical situation in the last of the nineteenth and twentieth centuries is likewise one of breakdown of transcendent symbols and has the above features. The emergence of psychoanalysis and its widespread popularity in America reflects this breakdown. Psychoanalysis is an activity which occurs in a culture when such symbols disintegrate; and it has the practical purpose of helping individuals endure, live, and hopefully fulfill their creative potentialities despite this situation. This does not deny that we may learn a great deal of basic truth about man in his times of crisis, his periods of being robbed of the protection of his symbols and myths. It does imply, however, that in a culture which attains some unity—in a *community* toward which, if we survive, many of us feel we are heading—the therapeutic functions will become more widely a normal and spontaneous function of education, religion and family life. This unity will be expressed in symbol and myth.

IV

Our thesis in this paper has been that symbols and myths are an expression of man's unique self-consciousness, his capacity to transcend the immediate concrete situation and see his life in terms of "the possible," and that this capacity is one aspect of his experiencing himself as a being having a world. We now wish to illustrate how symbols and myths do this through the myth of Oedipus.

The story of Oedipus is a myth rather than a symbol, but the two are very closely related. *Symbols* are specific acts or figures, such as the "cave" of our lawyer patient; while *myths* develop and elaborate these symbols into a story which contains characters and several episodes. The myth is thus more inclusive. But both symbol and myth have the same function psychologically; they are man's way of expressing the quintessence of his experience—his way of seeing his life, his self-image and his relations to the world of his fellow men and of nature—in a total figure which at the same moment carries the *vital meaning* of this experience. The myth of Adam is thus not just a tale of a man in paradise who eats an apple in disobedience to a command, but a story by which we confront the profound problem of the birth of human consciousness, the relation of man to authority, and moral self-knowledge in the sense symbolized by "the tree of the knowledge of good and evil." Thus true myths and symbols, so long as they retain their original power, always carry an element of ultimate meaning which illuminates but reaches beyond each individual man's concrete experience.

The Oedipus myth is particularly useful for our purposes since it is central both in psychoanalysis and literature. It is basic to the thinking and theoretical system of Freud, and is present in practically all other schools of psychoanalytic thought as well. Freud took it as a picture of the sexual attraction between the child and the parent of the opposite sex: the child experiences guilt thereby, fear of the parent of whom he is the rival, and, illustrated most clearly in the situation of boys, he then suffers castration anxiety. Other schools, like Adler's, deny the instinctual aspect of the Oedipal conflict and see it rather as a power struggle between child and parent; the neo-Freudian cultural schools likewise tend to view it, as does Fromm, in terms of the conflict with authority vested in the parent. In general it is accepted in American thought along the lines made popular by Freud, that the little boy wants to have sexual relations with and marry his mother, has concurrently the desire to kill and put out of the way his rival, the father, and experiences all the conflicts of repression, anxiety and guilt inherent in such a situation.

But there is a radical and very important difference between the approach of Freud to this myth and the meaning it is given in this country, including that by most orthodox psychoanalysts. Freud presupposed a view of the infant as destructive and driven by cannibalistic desires; the "innocence of the child consists of weakness of limb." For Freud, therefore, the Oedipus myth was genuinely tragic. But in this country we have an almost opposite attitude toward the infant, a Rousseau-esque attitude. The baby is essentially social, is called an "angel" by doting parents and viewed at least potentially, as an angel if only society—and these all-important mothers and fathers who, in the hey-day of this attitude, tried to discharge their impossibly heavy task by tiptoeing around on pins and needles when they weren't frantically reading books on child-care—does not frustrate the little angel's needs for nourishment too much. The significant point here is that Freud's emphasis on the genuine tragedy in the Oedipus myth was wiped out; the external form of the concept was kept, but its central meaning was lost. Recently one of the leading theorists of the orthodox psychoanalytic school remarked that the Oedipus myth only showed the "vicissitudes of the family relationship." Certainly it shows much more than that. This illustrates how the tragic aspects of Freud's theories—aspects which saved Freud from succumbing to the mechanistic implications inherent in his dynamics—are the first things thrown overboard when Freudianism crosses the Atlantic.

We believe that Freud's tragic view was closer to the truth, but that he was in error in interpreting the myth literalistically. One consequence of this literalistic interpretation was that the healing aspects of the myth are left out. We propose to demonstrate here that the myth transcends the literalistic problems of sex and aggression. Its tragic locus lies rather in the individual's self-

consciousness, his struggles with his fate, in self-knowledge and
self-consciousness.

When we read the actual drama of Oedipus, let us say as it
comes to Freud and to us from the pen of Sophocles,* we are
surprised to see that it has nothing to do with conflicts about
sexual desire or killing the father as such. These are all done
long in the past when the drama begins. Oedipus is a good king
("the mightiest head among us all," he is called) who has reigned
wisely and strongly in Thebes and has been for a number of
years happily married to Queen Jocasta. The only issue in the
drama is whether he will recognize what he has done. The tragic
issue is that of seeing the truth about one's self; it is the tragic
drama of the passionate relation to truth. Oedipus' tragic flaw is
his wrath against his own reality.

Thebes is suffering under a plague as the curtain rises. Word
has been brought from the oracle that the plague will be lifted
only when the murderer of King Laius is discovered. Oedipus
calls the old blind seer, Tiresias, and thereupon proceeds a grip-
ping and powerful unfolding step by step of Oedipus' self-knowledge, an unfolding replete with rage, anger at the truth and
those who are its bearers, and all other aspects of man's most
profound struggle with recognition of his own reality. Tiresias'
blindness seems to symbolize the fact that one can more insight-

* To the argument that we are taking Sophocles' *drama*, and that the
myth itself does have the *content* of killing the father and marrying the
mother, I would rejoin that the myth of Adam has the content of eating an
apple against a commandment. Then Anatole France could rightly remark,
"Tant de bruit pour une pomme" (so much noise over one apple). But
everyone would agree that such a literalistic, fundamentalistic interpretation
does not at all do justice to the profound truths and meaning of the Adam
myth. If we are to take the Oedipus myth literalistically, as a portrayal of
the growing boy's attachment to his mother, Oedipus would precisely *not*
have had this toward Jocasta; for he was thrown out on the hillside to die
as an infant before he scarcely saw his mother; his "Oedipus" would have
expressed itself toward the Queen of Corinth, who raised him. I wish by this
illustration of the "reductio ad absurdam" of the literalistic interpretation
to indicate that we must always go beyond such interpretations and ask the
meaning of the myth. Sophocles does this, and I think in a way faithful to
the inner consistency and truth of the myth.

fully grasp *inner* reality about human beings—gain *in*-sight—
if one is not so distracted by the impingement of external details.

Tiresias at first refuses to answer Oedipus' questioning as to
who is the guilty one with the words,

> "How terrible it is to know . . .
> Where no good comes from knowing! Of these matters
> I was full well aware, but let them slip me. . . ."[4]

In response to Oedipus' new demands and threats, he continues,

> "Let me go home; . . .
> So shalt thou bear thy load most easily."
> "Ye
> Are all unknowing; my say, in any sort,
> I will not say, lest I display my sorrow."[4]

The drama then unfolds as the progressive revelation of
Oedipus to himself, the source from which the truth proceeds
being not Oedipus himself but Tiresias.* The whole gamut of
psychoanalytic reactions like "resistance" and "projection" are
exhibited by Oedipus as the closer he gets to the truth, the more
violently he fights against it. He accuses Tiresias of planning to
betray the city; is this why he will not speak? The seer replies,

> "I will not bring remorse upon myself
> And upon you. Why do you search these matters?"

Then in a burst of angry projection Oedipus accuses Tiresias of
having killed Laius himself. And when Oedipus is finally told the
truth by the goaded seer, that he himself is the murderer of his
father, Oedipus turns upon Tiresias and Creon with the charge
that these words are inventions, part of their strategy to take
over the state. These forms of behavior termed "resistance" and
"projection" are an understandable part of every man's bitter
struggle against the impossibly heavy and painful burden of
responsibility in learning the truth about himself and of enduring

---

* A point made by Professor Paul Ricoeur of the Sorbonne, to whose
significant work in the interpreting of myths we shall refer presently.

the revolutionary impact on his self-image and identity. The
former, resistance, is an acting-out of the conviction "I cannot
bear to admit it is I, so I will not *see* it!" The latter, projection,
is a way of crying out, "If it is true, it is somebody else; not I!
not I!"

Jocasta tries to persuade Oedipus not to place any weight on
the seer's accusation,

> "Listen and learn, nothing in human life
> Turns on the soothsayer's art."[4]

But then, as he begins to sense that some portentous mystery
surrounds his birth, she, the mother whom he has married, now
herself becomes aware of the terrible knowledge that awaits him.
She tries desperately to dissuade him;

> " . . . But why should men be fearful,
> O'er whom Fortune is mistress, and foreknowledge
> Of nothing sure? Best take life easily,
> As a man may. For that maternal wedding,
> Have no fear; for many men ere now
> Have dreamed as much; but he who by such dreams
> Sets nothing, has the easiest time of it."[4]

When he still proclaims his resolve to face the truth whatever
it may be, she cries,

> "Don't seek it! I am sick, and that's enough . . .
> Wretch, what thou art O mightst thou never know!"[4]

It is fascinating to note here that Jocasta, in saying one should
not take dreams—or myths or symbols—too seriously, is sharing
the viewpoint we already saw in recent textbooks of psychology.
Her words above also express the concept of "adjustment" in
psychotherapy, an emphasis which tends always to creep into
psychology and psychoanalysis precisely because of the anxiety
and radical upheaval that goes with pursuing fully the truths
about one's self. Jocasta here enunciates the principle of accept-

ance of reality *without* the passionate, tragic relation to truth. Interestingly enough, this emphasis in this myth and many others is identified with the *feminine* principle. The mother or wife, the conserving biological function, is blamed for the tendency to hold the man back from the creative breaking through to truth. This tendency for the man to see the woman as the bearer of the temptation to "take life easily as a man may," the temptress leading him to turn against the possibilities of his emerging "better self," has been commented upon by C. G. Jung and Otto Rank in their depth-psychological studies of creativity. The most fruitful single line of explanation of this, in my judgment, is Rank's idea that all growth is a series of birth experiences and that every new view of truth or the creative act in life is a step in breaking out of the womb and gaining greater individuation. I would add that, since the original breaking out is from the actual womb of the mother, every subsequent act is a re-enactment both of fighting against the mother who now represents one's own fear of moving ahead, and an expression of anger and hostility at her for having ejected one in the first place.

Oedipus is not dissuaded, but insists that he must know what he is and where he came from. He must know and accept his own reality and his fate.

> "I will not hearken—not to know the whole,
> Break out what will, I shall not hesitate . . ."[4]

The old shepherd who rescued the infant Oedipus from death on the mountainside is finally brought, the one man who can provide the final link in the fateful story. "O, I am at the horror, now, to speak!" the shepherd cries. And Oedipus answers, "And I to hear. But I must hear—no less."

When Oedipus does learn the final, tragic truth, he cuts out his eyes. It is significant that he is not *castrated* nor does he castrate himself; he cuts out his eyes, the organ of *seeing*. (The tendency to call this a "symbolic castration" would miss the whole point, and would be another example of using a theory, *e.g.*, the pri-

macy of sexual prototypes—as a procrustean bed on which to
force the data.) His punishment is then *exile*, first self-imposed
but later, as in Colonus, imposed by Creon and the state. The
tragedy has now come full circle: he was originally exiled when
he was a few days old on his father's order; and his life at last
ends again in exile. The exile is a fascinating symbolic act from
our modern psychoanalytic viewpoint, for we have much data to
indicate that the greatest threat and greatest cause of anxiety for
Western man in the middle of the twentieth century is not
castration but *ostracism*, the terrible situation of being thrown
out of the group. Many a contemporary man, like our young
lawyer patient above, castrates himself or permits himself to be
castrated because of fear of being exiled if he doesn't. He re-
nounces his power and conforms under the greater threat and
peril of ostracism.

We now turn to the drama which reveals the healing, integrative
aspects of the Oedipus myth, namely *Oedipus in Colonus*. So far
as I know, this drama is never mentioned in psychoanalytic
literature at all, an amazing fact in itself. One reason for its
neglect is that discussion of the integrative functions of myths in
general tends to be omitted in psychoanalysis. But, more specifically, a consequence of the literalistic interpretation of the myth
as having to do with sex and killing the father requires that we
stop when these are worked through, punishment meted, and the
situation accepted as at the conclusion of *Oedipus Tyrannus*.
But viewing the myth as the presentation of man's struggle in
self-knowledge to know the reality about his own being, we must
indeed go on, as Sophocles does, to see how a man comes to
terms with the meaning of these acts. This subsequent drama is
Oedipus' stage of reconciliation with himself and with his fellow
men in the persons of Theseus and the Athenians, and it is a
reconciliation with the ultimate meaning in his life. "For the
gods who threw you down sustain you now," as his daughter
Ismene phrases it. In some ways this drama is more significant
than the first; and since it was written by Sophocles when he was

an old man of eighty-nine, it can be supposed to contain the wisdom of his old age as well.

One theme we find in the old Oedipus' meditation at Colonus is *guilt*—the difficult problem of the relation of ethical responsibility to self-consciousness. Is a man guilty if the act was unpremeditated, done unknowingly? In the course of his probing old Oedipus has come to terms with his guilt. He defends himself indignantly against the brash accusations of Creon,

"If then I came into the world—as I did come—
In wretchedness, and met my father in fight,
And knocked him down, not knowing that I killed him
Nor whom I killed—again, how could you find
Guilt in that unmeditated act? . . .

As for my mother—damn you, you have no shame,
Though you are her own brother,—

But neither of us knew the truth; and she
Bore my children also— . . .
While I would not have married her willingly
Nor willingly would I ever speak of it."[5]

Again, about his father he cries out that he has

"A just extenuation.
                    This:
I did not know him; and he wished to murder me.
Before the law—before God—I am innocent!"[5]

It is clear that Oedipus accepts and bears his responsibility; but he insists that the delicate and subtle interplay of conscious and unconscious factors (as we could call them) always makes any legalistic or pharisaic imputation of guilt inaccurate and wrong. It is a truism since Freud that the problem of guilt is as much within the heart as within the act. The play holds that the sins of meanness, of avarice and irreverence of Creon and Polyneices are "no less grave that those sins of passion for which Oedipus was punished; that in condemning them to the merciless justice soon to descend, Oedipus acts thoroughly in accord with a moral order which his own experience has enabled him to understand." [5]

In angry, vehement words, Oedipus refuses the tricky proposal of the cruel Creon, the present dictator of Thebes, who tries to get the exiled king to return by using Antigone as hostage; and Oedipus refuses likewise the entreaty of his son, Polyneices, though he knows the destruction of Thebes will result. Oedipus' maturity does not at all include the virtue of forgiveness of enemies, a later Christian idea he would no doubt have scorned. Nevertheless, the play does point toward a conclusion emphasized by modern existential psychologists, that because of this interplay of conscious and unconscious factors in guilt and the impossibility of legalistic blame, we are forced into an attitude of acceptance of the universal human situation and a recognition of the participation of every one of us in man's inhumanity to man. The words to Oedipus from the hero, King Theseus, who exhibits no inner conflict at all, are nevertheless poignant,

> " . . . for I
> Too was an exile . . .
> I know I am only a man; I have no more
> To hope for in the end than you have." [5]

Another theme in this integrative drama is the power of Oedipus—now that he has suffered through his terrible experiences and come to terms with them—*to impart grace.* As he himself says to the natives who find him with his daughter in the grove at Colonus,

> "For I come here as one endowed with grace,
> By those who are over Nature; and I bring
> Advantage to this race. . . ." [5]

Theseus accepts this: "Your presence, as you say, is a great blessing." This capacity to impart grace, assumedly, is connected with the maturity and other emotional and spiritual qualities which result from the courageous confronting of his shattering experiences. Says Oedipus,

> "One soul, I think, often can make atonement
> For many others, if it be devoted. . . ."[5]

But there is also a clear symbolic element to make the point of his grace unmistakable: the oracle has revealed that his body after death will ensure victory to the land and the ruler which possess him. The mere "presence" of his body has this power.

A last emphasis we mention in the outworking of the myth is *love*. The messenger who came back to the people to report the marvelous manner of Oedipus' death states that in his last words to his daughters he said

> " . . . And yet one word
> Frees us of all the weight and pain of life:
> That word is love."[5]

But Oedipus does not at all mean love as the absence of aggression or the strong affects of anger. His sharp and violent temper, present at that crossroads where he killed his father years before and exhibited in his sharp thrusts with Tiresias, is still much in evidence in this last drama, unsubdued by suffering or maturity. The fact that Sophocles does not see fit to remove or soften Oedipus' aggression and his anger—the fact, that is, that the "aggression" and the "angry affects" are not the "flaws" he has old Oedipus get over—lends support to our thesis above that the aggression involved in killing the father is not the central issue of the dramas. Oedipus' maturity is not at all a renouncing of passion to come to terms with society, not at all a learning to live "in accord with the reality requirements of civilization." It is a reconciliation with himself, with special persons he loves, and the religious meaning of his life.

Love, thus, is not the opposite of anger or aggression. Old Oedipus will love only those he chooses to love: his son, who has betrayed him, asks for mercy and remarks, "Compassion limits even the power of God,"[5] but Oedipus will have none of it. The love, rather, he bears his daughters, Antigone and Ismene, and

the love they have shown him during his exiled, blind wander-
ings, is the kind of love he chooses to bless.

And finally, describing Oedipus' miraculous death and burial,
the messenger says,

> "But some attendant from the train of Heaven
> Came for him; or else the underworld
> Opened in love the unlit door of earth.
> For he was taken without lamentation,
> Illness or suffering; indeed his end
> Was wonderful if mortal's ever was."[5]

This touching and beautiful death of a great character is magnificent as Sophocles presents it dramatically. As *Oedipus Tyrannus*
is the drama of the "unconscious," the struggle to confront the
reality of the dark, destructive forces in man, *Oedipus in Colonus*
may be said to be the drama of consciousness, the aspect of the
myth which is concerned with the search for meaning and reconciliation. Both together comprise the myth of man confronting
his own reality, a confronting that is made possible and inevitable by the unique structure of self-consciousness.*

---

* Robert Fitzgerald writes in his notes to the play, "It should be remembered that one of Oedipus' distinguishing qualities was, in the first place,
his intelligence. He saved Thebes once by solving the riddle of the Sphinx.
He saved the city again by solving with furious persistence the riddle of his
own birth. And in this play we see once more the working of that intellect,
driving this time toward a transcendence of the purely human." I think
Fitzgerald is wrong here in calling this "intelligence," though obviously he
is right in his general emphasis. This saving quality of Oedipus goes quite
beyond intellectual functions; his solving the riddle of the Sphinx (the word
"Sphinx" means "one who binds fast") is much more what we would call
"in-sight" and sensitivity than it is the purely rational functions. I believe
the term "self-consciousness" in the special way we have used it in this
paper, to refer to man's capacity for self-knowledge and self-transcendence
(rather than in the strictly Cartesian sense of consciousness) is what
Fitzgerald is referring to. It is, incidentally, an intriguing psychological
implication in the dramas as a whole that *that particular man* who lives
through his aggressive potentialities, who does not shrink from standing
against his father and consummating the sexual drives in his assertive way,
is just the man who solves the riddle and knows the answer "man" and the
one who, experiencing his tragic fate, goes on to be a bearer of grace and
salvation for others.

IV

The healing power of the symbol and myth has two aspects. This power resides, on one hand, in the fact that the symbol and myth elicit and bring into awareness the repressed, unconscious, archaic urges, longings, dreads and other psychic content. This is the *regressive* function of symbols and myths. But on the other hand, the symbol and myth reveal new goals, new ethical insights and possibilities; they are a breaking through of greater meaning which was not present before. The symbol and myth in this respect are ways of working out the problem on a higher level of integration. This we call the *progressive* function of symbols and myths.*

The tendency in Freudian psychoanalysis has been almost universally to reduce the latter to the former, and to treat myths in terms of regressive phenomena, which are then "projected" into ethical and other forms of meaning in the outside world. The upshot of this is that the integrative side of myths and symbols is lost. This is shown in the great emphasis on *Oedipus Tyrannus* and the total omission of *Oedipus at Colonus*.

Symbols and myths are means of discovery. They are a progressive revealing of structure in our relation to nature and our own existence, a revealing of new ethical forms. Symbols thus are *educative—e-ducatio*—and by drawing out inner reality they enable the person to experience greater reality in the outside world as well. We have shown in this paper that the inner reality is revealed by virtue of the fact that the symbol and myth are able to draw out content on the various levels of "preconscious," "subconscious," and "unconscious," and that this is done with the affects of these experiences united with their perceived, cognitive form. But now we want to emphasize the side that is generally

---

* I owe this semantic juxtaposition of "regressive" and "progressive" to Professor Paul Ricoeur, whose analyses of symbols and myths in relation to psychoanalysis I find of great value. Many of my own ideas run parallel to Ricoeur's.

overlooked, *that these symbols and myths discover for us a reality outside as well.* They are roads to universals beyond discrete concrete experience. For example, such supposedly simple symbols as geometric forms, triangles or parallelograms or what not, were at one time painted on the neolithic pottery because, we may assume, the forms had some relation to harmony and balance as the individual experienced it and therefore gave him some delight; but at the same time these geometric forms reflected nature in the relations of stars and sun and moon to earth, and were mathematical symbols by which secrets of nature were revealed.

To turn again to our patient's symbol of the cave before bidding it adieu, we can now see how his growing relation to this symbol would both draw out repressed aspects of his own psychic experience and would also reveal and make necessary new forms in his relations with the outside world. His confronting and experiencing of this symbol in psychoanalysis—his seeing "the cave" in fantasy, dwelling on it, turning it over in his contemplation with the disgust, anger, yearning, dread which could not be separated from it—would give him a greater awareness of his neurotic attachment to his mother and his desire to be carried by her as in a kangaroo's pouch. It would also give him greater awareness and experience of his neurotic anxiety connected with this: his fear of being sucked into annihilation in the quicksand bog. This kind of fantasy and the memories which go along with it often bring strong abreactive experiences in analysis; this is the point where Freud's idea of abreaction comes into its own and I have found it very useful. It is often good to help the patient live through as vividly as possible the great terror he must often have experienced in infancy and early years in this yearning to be encompassed by his mother but "knowing" (on subtle and certainly not centrally conscious levels) that this very desire would smother him and suck him into destruction.

Now the next steps in enlarged consciousness would be his

insight into the fact that his blushing is related to his desire to be sucked into the womb, which he both wants and dreads; and the insight that his impotence is a way of withdrawing from the vagina lest he be trapped for good. It is terribly painful to be impotent, but it is better to be impotent than dead. He is not afraid of castration in the sense that he would lose his penis; he would lose a lot more than that, namely his individuality and total existence in this absorption into the bog.

So far most analysts and therapists of various schools would roughly agree, though they would use their own terms. But now we must bring out that as the patient works the above experiences through, it becomes evident that he has never gotten, and does not now receive, the normal dependence, love and protection which every human being not only has a right to have but absolutely needs for his survival, particularly in the early years of infant development.* The question then arises as to why he is unable to let himself have warmth, protection, acceptance not only from new women (not the actual mother) but from other relationships in life itself. The possibility of his experiencing this question in self-consciousness—a step I would expect only some months after the first confrontation of the cave—already asks for some integration, some readiness for constructive steps. It is an error to view these stages in psychoanalysis as "automatic," or as results of "transference" or "relationship" or "communication" by themselves; I am convinced that as much attention needs to be paid to the integrative problems as to the regressive, and they are simultaneous, even though the latter may seem, at least on paper, to precede the former.

This *"accepting of acceptance"* is a very difficult task for modern man. It implies that he himself accepts others: our young

* The positive aspects of the figure of the cave can be seen in the pleasure all of us had as children in playing house by putting rugs over chairs; we make a cozy place, representing warmth, protection, belongingness and comfort, an experience that probably has a wealth of archaic and archetypal material behind it.

lawyer can scarcely permit himself to accept and enjoy the warmth and protective qualities of love if he continues to view all women as prostitutes. So the symbol of the cave now implies the problem of *Mitwelt*, the reciprocity of attitudes in relation to one's fellowmen—what Paul Ricoeur calls "the problem of justice." But the patient does not stop even here. The side of the symbol relating to normal, constructive warmth and acceptance brings with it *ultimate assumptions about existence itself:* to what extent can one's existence be trusted, to what extent are we "thrown," to what extent inseparably strangers to each other? I do not at all mean the patient will discuss philosophy or theology; if he does this very much, the odds are that some "resistance" is in process. I only mean that he cannot avoid coming to terms with ultimate considerations in his relation to his own existence, and willynilly he chooses for himself some essential presuppositions. This would be the "faith" on the basis of which he proposes to leap, to take his chances in love and other aspects of life from here on out. It is only on the basis of some such faith that the individual can genuinely accept and overcome the earlier infantile deprivations without the continued harboring of resentment all through life, which has the effect of holding him back in the future. In this sense the past can be accepted and does not block the future.

There are infinite subtleties and critical contradictions in this process, and every individual, certainly every patient, needs to make the journey in his own unique way. A concomitant process all along the way will be that his neurotic anxiety is transmitted into normal anxiety, his neurotic guilt into normal, existential guilt. And in this form both can be used constructively as a broadening of consciousness and sensitivity. We have sought to show that the journey is made by means of symbols and myths, and that the symbol and myth thus have not only an archaic, regressive side but an integrative, progressive, normative side as well.

REFERENCES

1. WOODWORTH, Robert S., *Psychology* (New York: Holt, 1929).
2. MACLEISH, Archibald, *J. B.* (Boston: Houghton Mifflin, 1958).
3. LYND, Robert S., and Helen Merrell, *Middletown in Transition* (New York: Harcourt Brace, 1937).
4. SOPHOCLES, "Oedipus Tyrannus," *Dramas*, translated by Sir George Young (New York: E. P. Dutton, Everyman's Library).
5. SOPHOCLES, "Oedipus at Colonus," *The Oedipus Cycle*, translated by Dudley Fitts and Robert Fitzgerald (New York: Harcourt Brace, 1949).

1. The Nature of the Symbol

ERICH KAHLER

I

ALL UTTERANCE, be it expression or communication, be it "language" or shaping of objects, tends to expand and eventually to split the being from which it comes. Plain, solid existence is mute.

The most rudimentary, inarticulate form of utterance in sound or gesture is mere *expression*, that is to say, a reaction to the stimuli of pain or joy, want or fear. But even the cry of a hunted animal, the groan of a suffering or starving creature, is a *symptom* of something, it is a *sign* of some motivated feeling. It is, however, only a sign *of* something, not, or not necessarily, a sign made *to* and intended *for* somebody; and it is so close to its actuating source that we still feel it one with the being itself.

Utterance turns into language when contact with the environment is sought and, through sound or gesture, some kind of *communication* occurs. Communication is directed expression. The wooing song and warning cries of birds, though roused by elementary urges, are addressed to mates and fellow creatures; they are *signals*. The "wagging dance" of pilot bees goes a step further; it transmits detailed factual information. In all these cases the emphasis has shifted from mere expression to communication. Something new is introduced; the utterance carries a meaning, a meaning for someone else. A sheer symptom, an unintentional, undirected sound or gesture, has no meaning, it has a cause; more precisely, it has a meaning only for someone who wants to discover the cause. (Or, on the subliminal, physiological level, a symptom, like pain, may be said to carry a warning of organic disturbance from the body to consciousness.) An intentionally communicative utterance, however, is not simply a sign *of* an experience; it *signi-fies* something, it *is* not, it *makes* a sign.

Through communication the living being is carried beyond its sheer existence, much farther than by pure expression. It has found a target, indeed an anchorage, in the environment. A partner, a counterpart has come into play, that will respond to, occasionally counter, and by this challenge reflect on, the correspondent's existence. And in the course of this developing dialogue the means of communication unfold, a vast world of multifarious and multilevel articulation, of words and concepts and universes of discourse, all of which, growing weightier and weightier, ever more objectified and autonomous, come increasingly to split existence into different sections and layers.

The same thing happens in the development of *tools* which, like language, are a means of communication between the living creature and its surrounding world. To be sure, the objects and materials of nature to which tools are addressed are not partners in the same sense as living correspondents of language are. Resisting or complying, they respond passively; not directly to the maker or user, but to the impersonal function of the tool. They do respond, however, and particularly in the higher technical stages they are induced to answer questions which are put to them through experiments. Here, in the use of tools and machines, communication has assumed the character of conformation, conformation of objective material to the human being and, retroactively, of the human being to objective material.

The most primitive tools, ant-hills, birds' nests, beavers' dams, artificial arrangements for breeding and dwelling, are an "accommodation," an adaption of environment, a special kind of dealing with the elements of nature. The long history of these objectified procedures, from such initial contrivances as artificial dwelling places to the overwhelming machinery of modern technology, shows, more evidently still, the same features as the evolution of language. A huge realm of apparatus evolved between the human being and nature, which stretched his existence to such an extent as to divide it into manifold strata. The human being came to reside in different spheres at once; and on the broadening and lengthening way of his getting acquainted with ever wider surroundings, the direction of his communication slowly shifted from the immediate to the intermediate; practical means turned into, or brought forth, theoretical ends. So it happens today that the human being, in his capacity as an individual, corresponds with other individuals and uses the complex products of an elaborate communication with nature in a personal way, for the personal ends of his living; and at the same time, in his work and even as a consuming participant in technological achievement, he also lives in the realm of generalized apparatus. Inasmuch as the human being has come to extend his existence over manifold spheres, his communication with his outer world turns into a communication with his self, of his practical with his theoretical mind, and—since the outer expansion reflexively involved an inner, psychic, expansion—of his Ego with his Id, with the lighted depths of his unconscious.

The use of language and the use of tools are deeply interrelated and differ only in their media and points of emergence. Words and concepts can be seen as instruments, not merely to reach an accord with fellow men, but to assimilate and integrate ever wider ranges of objective reality and of the expanded self. Tools, conversely, may appear as means of conformation with the world of objects. Concepts are tools; tools and machines (which are more elaborate and rarefied tools) are materialized concepts. Both kinds of communication mutually supplement and support each other.

Even *art* in its beginning was the use of magic as a tool to appropriate other creatures or to influence animate powers. And here again, communication with living forces eventually turned into a discourse with objective reality, visual or psychic, a venture into the depths of outer and inner reality. Art, however, has preserved that original character of magic even in its most advanced and perfected works, it has remained an act of conjuration even in the stage when it has lost its patently magic or cultic intent. Both science and art evolved in expanding communication, which means, expanding the reach of human existence; both became, at least provisionally, self-sufficient: theory for theory's sake, art for art's sake. Science developed words, which are rudimentary concepts, into more complex, theoretical concepts; concepts into formulas, which are intellectual tools; and thus, in its means of communication, it quite explicitly maintained an instrumental character. Art transformed words and tools into organically consistent, representational forms, i.e. images, magic into *"imagic."* While this implies basic differences of approach in dealing with the objective world, it should not blind us to the fact that both scientific formulation and artistic figuration are exploratory ways to get acquainted with the nature of reality. Science proceeds in a direct manner, through analysis and quantitative reduction of reality itself, art indirectly, through imagical representation of coherent existences, or existential coherences. By establishing such independent exemplary entities, art introduces a third mode of utterance: *creation.* In art, communication proceeds by creation.

II

It is against the background of this evolutionary process that we can best understand the nature and development of the *symbol.* The symbol originates in the split of existence, the confrontation and communication of an inner with an outer reality, whereby a meaning detaches itself from sheer existence. Com-

ication starts with signs, with *made signs,* and, as has been
d before, only made signs are signi-fications, that is, carry a
meaning. This simple fact that a sound or gesture carries a meaning implies a first, original establishment of two levels of existence and also of two distinct spheres, the inner sphere of motivation and the outer sphere that is asked to answer, to satisfy this
motivation; it establishes them by bridging them.

Any made sign is a bridging act, an act of pointing to something or somebody. In the distinctive mating or warning *signal*
of an animal species it appears in a somewhat stabilized form,
but it has not parted with the living creature and settled down
as a separate entity. The word, however, the articulate name of a
person or of a thing, is an objectified fixation of the act of "calling" him or "de-signating" it; it is a *frozen* act. It inaugurates
what Alfred Korzibsky has called the time-binding capacity of
the human being; it bridges not only spatial but also temporal
spheres. This fixation, this consolidation and extension of the
bridging act, this settling down of the meaning as a separate
entity and established junction of diverse spheres of existence,
marks the actual beginning of the *symbol.*

The linguistic sign as established in words (and perpetuated
in writing) carries a magic spell which was strongly felt in previous ages. The word was not limited to sheer designation, but an
aura of influence went with it. The bare name of a deity constituted an invocation, and contained in the bud the *magic formula*
in all its variations and stages. The formal prayer, the liturgy, the
litany, all of them are ritually hardened acts of bridging through
incantation and cultic service. (Greek *leitourgia* derives from
leitos, public or voluntary, and *ergon,* work.) Their literal meaning is mostly forgotten or overgrown, it is solidified, contracted,
and thereby transformed into a verbal instrument of communication with divine powers.

Thus, in the magic formula the act of bridging turns into an
act of abridgment, of contraction. It is still, however, an uninten-

tional contraction, the result of a long ritual practice of repetition. Subsequently, the broadening communication of man with his surrounding world, this ceaseless questioning and seeking answers, engendered wider and deeper questions and exfoliated new spheres and levels of existence. The increasing distances between these spheres produced new forms of contraction, *intentional contraction of reality,* needed to make man's communication—with his fellow men, with his self, and with nature—more manageable. Such fully conscious, deliberate contraction is *abstraction,* which gained its overwhelming importance when man was confronted with a fundamental change in the nature of his surrounding world.

In dealing with daemonic or divine powers, man faced animate beings of a somehow familiar, organic character, on his own level as it were, inasmuch as these powers were believed to respond in the same way, with the same will and the same feeling, as man himself; they were indeed projections of man's own forms of existence and therefore accessible to magic influence. When the domain of these powers was gradually pushed back through the broadening of secular experience, there emerged a realm of objective reality, essentially different from the nature of the human being. In this vast, unbounded realm it seemed quite uncertain with what entities man would have to deal. Effects were cut off from animate sources. Loose, impersonal energies appeared to be functioning autonomously. Directing its exploratory questions to these forces, the human mind was lured into dimensions far exceeding the bounds of man's organic equals—be it fellow man, living creature, or deity. Such far-reaching, impersonal forces could not be met through magical, i.e. personal, contact. They called for a rational, "nomothetic" approach toward certain regularities which were brought into view by the new suprahuman perspective, the disproportionate relation of the human to the cosmic forms. These regularities, which promised predictability, appeared as the only possible media of communication with the forces of nature, and they could only be comprehended through abstraction, an abbreviating act of thought which again consolidated in various forms.

The most elementary abstraction is *number*. The conception of number presupposes a twofold capacity: to distinguish different single events as set against the mere recurrence of one and the same event and to isolate common likenesses from the variety of single events and phenomena. Only likenesses, or entities connected by some identical property, can be numbered.

Number was established in the dim past, far back in the age of cultic communication, and like the word it has carried a charge of magic potencies. (It may even have come to the primitive mind originally through visual configurations to which magical power was attributed.) But its great role began when in the face of an inanimate universe words proved incapable of dealing with impersonal and boundless forces which could be approached only by way of their regularities and common properties. The adequate vehicle of correspondence was number. Being initially abstraction, it contained the seed of unlimited further abstraction. The relationship of numerical abstractions, the study of numbers, "arithmetic" (from Greek *arithmós*, number) was generalized, i.e. abstracted again, through the substitution of letters, "algebra" (from Arabic *jabara*, to bind together, to combine). Calculus, the theories of functions, of aggregates, of probability, etc. are so many extensions and rarefications of numerical abstraction. The operation of combinatory and abstractive thought was reduced to pure, general form by logic in its sundry varieties. Along with all such abstracting operations which were built up over one another in intensified degrees, and raised to an ever higher power, there evolved the *modern, rational formula*, the conceptual tool that helped the natural sciences in their steadily expanding correspondence with the forces of nature. The rational formula, just like the magic formula, is the fixation of an act of bridging, but a bridging of ever widening distances through ever more condensing abbreviation. The "law of nature," finally, in that it establishes samenesses in the functionings of natural forces, is the statement of the conclusive act of quantitative abbreviation, opening up a way for man's theoretical and technological communication with nature.

III

We have traced the genetic line from the *symptom* (undirected sign) through the *signal* (the made sign and the stabilized sign) to the fixed sign, the actual inception of the *symbol*. The signal marks the transition from expression to communication; and all the various kinds and stages of the symbol which we have considered so far, the word, the tool, the number, the magic and the rational formula, the law of nature, all of them are frozen acts of communication—communication, first through bridging, and later through abridgment, contracting and abstracting abridgment.

But anything fixed, anything settled in a steady form, tends to become autonomous; it starts on a life of its own. So any act of designation, as soon as it is firmly established, no longer merely points to, or "points out," something, it gradually comes to represent the thing it points to. If stabilization of a sign may be seen as the preliminary, and fixation of the sign as the first stage, of the symbol, *representation* is its second and final stage.

In common language, in formulas, magic or rational, the character of active communication, of designation and bridging, predominates. Language always moves toward a human partner, be it even the self, to whom it carries a message. A formula is concerned with, it is "instrumental" in, establishing relations. But when, in our memory or in theoretical contemplation, a name or a concept engenders an *image*, the emphasis shifts from communication to representation; or, to be more exact, communication is effected by representation. So the second stage of symbolization, the stage of representation, implies the formation of an image, which is *simultaneity of meaning*—meaning, not as relation, but as substance.

The capacity to form images, "imagination," is deeply rooted in the human psyche, probably even in the psyche of animals.[*] Its subliminal, spontaneous operation in dreams has become a focus of attention of *psychoanalysis* which uses the term "symbolize" for the unconscious translation of a personal or archetypal "dream thought" into a distinct dream image ("dream element," in the terminology of Freud) and calls the resulting images "symbols." They are, however, it seems to me, rather symptoms than accomplished symbols (i.e., *made* signs or representations), symptoms emerging in images instead of sounds or gestures. If,

[*] The psychiatrist Silvano Arieti[1] rightly assumes that animals have images: "They seem to dream, and if they dream, they must do so with some kind of images. However, animals do not seem to have the capacity to evoke or reproduce images when they want to, and, of course, they are incapable of expressing them to others. . . ." Then, he raises the question whether animals are capable of the next step: making images into symbols. He writes: "The comparative psychologist, Kellogg, reports, that his little chimpanzee, Gua, was so attached to him that whenever he left the house she became very despondent. She would go into a tantrum of terror and grief. If, however, he gave her his coverall at the time of his departure, she seemed placated, showed no emotional displeasure, and carried the coverall around her as a fetish. As [Susanne] Langer points out, this fact is extremely important. This is probably one of the first manifestations of high symbolization of which animals are capable. The coverall represented the master . . . it replaced the master . . . it was a symbol, but it was a symbol which was identified with the object it symbolized. Possibly the ape was able to evoke the image of his master at the sight of the coverall, or the coverall reproduced the image of the master plus coverall, or the ape really accepted the coverall not as a coverall, but as an emotional equivalent of his master. . . ." These interpretations of Susanne Langer, with which Dr. Arieti seems to agree, appear to me highly anthropomorphic, or better, logomorphic. Similar experiences I have had with dogs lead me to believe that what went on in the psyche of the chimpanzee was of a very different nature: The coverall was not a symbol, but rather a real piece of the master, a share of his presence, which probably was conveyed to the animal through smell combined with associative sensations of touch and vision. Even among certain primitive humans we find the assumption that objects of personal property are parts, or extensions, of the body of their owners. In any case, the chimpanzee did not perform a conscious act of substitution, which alone could be called symbolization.

as Freud tells us, parents in dreams take the shape of emperor and empress, and children that of little animals or vermin, if being born is pictured as plunging into water, and dying as departing by train,[2] such a process of transformation appears to be a kind of reflex, an automatic projection of inner urges or discomforts into whatever visual material is at hand in the outer world. This is even more evident in archetypal images, where the visual material is not taken from the outer, but from the inner world. C. G. Jung relates a dream of a seventeen-year-old girl, in which she saw her mother "hanging from the chandelier and swinging to and fro in a cold wind that blows in through the open windows." This dream had nothing whatever to do with her mother, but turned out to be the symptom of an organic disease of the girl herself. The mother image expressed something going on in her physical depths, for it is, as Jung says, "archetypal and refers to . . . that which passively creates, hence . . . to material nature, the lower body (womb) and the vegetative functions . . . the 'mother' is also a vessel, the hollow form (uterus) that carries and nourishes. . . ." Indeed, the mother image "points to a darker meaning which eludes conceptual formulation and can only be vaguely apprehended as the hidden, nature-bound life of the body. . . . All this is dream-content, but it is nothing which the . . . girl has acquired in her individual existence; it is rather a bequest from the past."[3] Likewise, the Mandāla image, a circle with a tendency to combine with a square, which Jung found recurring in dreams, drawings, dances of his patients who could "say very little of the meaning of the symbols," appears as a kind of organic geometry deriving from the inmost form of the living being. Jung sees in it "the archetype of wholeness."

In all such cases, the actual "symbolization" is done, not by the person in whose unconscious the image arises, but by the analyst through inferential interpretation. To him alone these images are meaningful, just as the physical symptom carries a meaning only for somebody who looks for its cause.

Only consciously formed images are real symbols. To be sure, borderlines between unconscious and conscious operation, between sheer expression and intentional representation, are fluid, and, as Jung has amply demonstrated, archetypal patterns, which operate in the unconscious, pass over into the conscious work of artists, poets, thinkers, who create cultic images. These images, being *made* as means of communication with divine powers and their worshippers, are actual symbols, capable even of embodying complex doctrines.

Science, particularly the basic natural science, physics, in its exploratory advances, has gone beyond the sphere of the visually "imaginable"; it progresses by way of mathematical conceptions verifiable through very complicated instrumental questions and reactions, whereby observation itself is achieved only in an inferential, somehow abstractive manner. The natural sciences, however, make use of certain auxiliary images: *geometrical figures* and *diagrams,* pictorial abstractions which are the equivalent, in the visual domain, of arithmetical abstractions with which they combine or in which they result; and *models,* such as the age-old, now obsolete, "ether," or the field concept, or Bohr's atom model. In all these kinds of images the instrumental, mediatorial element predominates; none of them is meant actually to represent reality. Geometrical figures are a means to convey and manipulate the proportions and relations of spatial structures. Diagrams are used to clarify phenomenal or rational complexities through exemplary visual reduction; they are a sort of pictorial metaphor. A model, being just a *modulus,* a measure of the real thing, will never permit us to forget its provisional, hypothetical nature; it can never stand for an established reality.

IV

It is only in *art* that representation comes to prevail over the signi-fying act. Here, the act merges in the accomplished form.

Ultimately, the image is no longer merely a road to re⟨...⟩ the very figuration of reality—more than that, it is in its⟨...⟩ independent reality.

In the development of such accomplished symbolization, the *religious image,* plainly or artistically shaped, has an intermediate role: it is real representation, but at the same time it remains predominantly a sign.

Religious and artistic imagery arose in common. Earliest images, prehistoric cave paintings, are not symbols as yet, they are virtual acts of seizure; they do not signi-fy or represent, they actually *are* the creatures represented. They do not point to prototypes, they are pointed at with the points of arrows. Similarly, the original totemistic idol, as long as the deity is believed to be actually present in the image, is not a likeness of the worshipped being, it is the being itself. Only when a difference is felt between the visually present idol and a remote, or temporarily absent, deity, when the image turns into a mere residue or residence of the deity, only then does the image become a symbol.

Of course, any divine image always tends to evoke the imagined presence of the deity through a mystomagical connection. In Holy Mass, the host and the wine in the chalice, symbolic residues of the body and blood of Jesus Christ, are, through the magic process of transubstantiation, turned into the very presence of Christ. Insofar as this happens, the symbol-character of the image is abolished.

All cultic symbols, though representing accepted reality, are still, just like formulas, instituted acts of bridging distances between different existential spheres. They may be seen as imagic formulas, formulas, not discursive or "discoursive," but contracted into simultaneous, embodied meaning. Frequently, they present a *pars pro toto,* that is to say, they signify a sacred being by a characteristic part of it, which may be a mythical or legendary happening, a peculiar divine quality or domain. Or they may use a homologous abstraction of a total form.

The crucifix, for instance, points to Jesus' sacrificial death— even the magic act of apotropaic conjuration is still present in a person's making the sign of the cross. The Indian symbol of the multiheaded snake, called the Remainder, the Residue, signifies "the residue that remained after the earth, the upper and infernal regions, and all their beings, had been shaped out of the cosmic waters of the abyss."[4] The Phallus, or Lingam, originally a deity in itself, later recalls the creative capacity of Greek chthonic gods like Dionysos and the Cabiri (Kabeiroi), or the Indian Shiva. The she-bear or hind of the huntress Artemis indicates her nature and natural sphere. The wheel or hooked cross (swastika) represents the dynamic shape of the worshipped sun-god.

All these forms of symbolic contraction passed over from hieratic to profane uses, from religious cult to the cult of tradition. Royal, official, national insignia, heraldic emblems and coats of arms, point to the origins, the dominions, the aims and claims, of rulers or families or places. The ball or "apple" surmounted by a cross, which a medieval emperor carried at ceremonial occasions, signified, as its name "orb" or "mound" indicates, the catholic globe under his control. The fifty stars in the American flag symbolize the united states. The apothecary pills in the Medici coat of arms picture, along with the name of the family, their medical beginnings.

A beautiful example of an immediate, personal message conveyed through an abbreviating image-symbol, a veritable act of poetry, has been related to us by Marie de France (12th century) in her poem Chèvrefoil: Tristram, exiled by King Mark, wants to indicate to Iseult on her ride to the castle of Tintagel, that he is hiding in the woods to get a glimpse of her. He lays a hazel-twig on her path, from which she will know that he is near. For "both of them were like the hazel-bush and the honeysuckle that clings to it; interlaced they fare well, but parting they both die. So it

is with us, beloved one, not you without me, not I without you."
The sacred being that is here represented in a contracted form is
love, absolute, total love between two human beings, of which
the story of Tristram and Iseult is the first instance in European
tradition—love seizing upon, devouring the whole of existence,
disregarding convention and morality, disregarding life itself.
Such impassioned, life-transcending celebration of a supreme, if
mundane, power is a lived cult.

V

All forms of cultic representation, religious or traditional, are
intended to carry on and revive the communication, indeed communion, of present man with his mythical or perennial sources of
life. Communication, the sign-character, still looms saliently in
cultic representation, not merely where it indicates a whole by a
part, but also where it portrays the whole in full, as in paintings,
statues, or stories.

Cultic images are made to conjure up historical or canonically
sanctioned actuality, which means that representation is not
entirely free. The substratum of plastic or poetic depiction is
furnished by something outside the creative range, by figures and
happenings that are believed to have existed, or be existent, as
such. Mythography and narration only elaborated and adorned
them; those who re-lived the events in their tales or pictures were
probably vaguely convinced that the vivid additions of their
fantasy were true, just as devout medieval painters, while em-
pathically penetrating into the destinies and attitudes of their
saints, must have come to think that this could not have happened
otherwise. Creative imagination clustered around a core of reality
pre-established by old-age events or by long grown incarnations
of true emotions and drives in the human being.

We know today that Ilion existed and was destroyed several
times, we know of Mycenae and the migrations of Hellenic tribes.

The princes of the *Iliad* are probably ancestral projections of tribal lords in the Homeric age. Likewise, the Nordic *Edda* fused mythical elements with accounts of early Burgundian and Hunnish campaigns. To a still higher degree the Biblical stories may be seen as historical documents. Thus, the early epics are by no means pure fiction; they are, all of them, based on happenings, either attested as real by historical memory, or sanctioned as real by a long, anonymous process of mythogenesis. (Myths, in their original form, were accounts of the beginning of things, of the deeds and destinies of gods or heroic demi-gods; and their magic rested on people's belief that they were true. This is confirmed by the violent opposition of Greek philosophy to the mythographic epics of the "lies" they tell the people.)

Cultic images, then, are symbols inasmuch as they are signs; they are not, however, wholly accomplished symbolic representation. A fully representational symbol may be called a plastic or literary depiction that is not designed foremost to revive the human relationship to some cultic reality, but that is *intended* and *created*, from the outset and in its full extent, as a symbolic representation. Just as, in the initial stage, the sign turns into a symbol only when it is a *made* sign, carrying a meaning for somebody, so an image attains its full representational meaning only when it is created in its entirety by the conscious imagination of an artist—when the artist freely *invents* symbols by selecting, or synthesizing, from the immense diversity of life specific "representative" figures and configurations apt to stand for something generally human, or to clarify a commonly human situation.

The transition, in art, from the sign-image to the fully representational image is a result of the same process that turned man from magic to science: the widening and deepening of secular experience, and the depersonalization of the forces that determine human life. Less and less were human destinies derived from divine and mythical sources, more and more from the nature and condition of man himself. Communication with external powers changed into communication with internal dispositions, into communication with the human self, i.e., self-representation.

Yet, reading the great works of the cultic ages we sense a kind of symbolism not unlike that of the artistic creations of our modern era. Whether we are believers or not, we do not read the Biblical stories simply as an account of some remote happenings. We do not read the Homeric epics as we would read any ordinary adventure or travel story. We feel *ourselves,* our own lives, deeply involved in all these doings and sufferings. So these great tales seem to fit exactly the pattern of accomplished symbolic representation; they present in singular figures and destinies matters of common human purport.

There is, however, a crucial difference between the representational symbolism of these ancient works and that of modern works of art, a difference which is due precisely to the dependence of the ancient works on pre-established reality.

We have to distinguish between two kinds of representational symbolism: *descending* and *ascending* symbolism.

Descending I would call all symbolism in which symbolic representation detaches itself, descends to us, from a prior and higher reality, a reality determining, and therefore superior to, its symbolic meaning. That is to say, genuinely mythical and cultic works are not intended as symbolic representation, they are meant to describe real happenings. It is *we* who, a posteriori, derive a symbolic meaning from them. In the early ages, when all of life moves under cultic or mythical guidance, reality is so monumentally plain, so naturally comprehensive, undisclosed like a bud, that it holds for us a dormant wealth of meaning, all but inexhaustible. This is what makes for the grandeur of that primordial actuality. The ancient divine or mythical beings are by no means, as our modern rational thinking would have it, plainly and fully individual figures made to represent something common or general. They are, for all their characteristic personal singularity, inherently generic existences: the Greek gods, daemons, heroes constitute tribes or localities incarnate; the patriarchs of the Bible, the sons of Jacob, *are* their respective clans. They are not products of symbolic representation, they are real beings comprising their progeny.

This intricate difference may be illustrated by the somehow related difference between the Platonic idea and our modern scientific concept. Like the deities which they replaced, the Platonic ideas were not conceived as man-made terms designating general likenesses in a group of phenomena; they were meant to be quasi-divine absolute entities, not generalizations derived from the divers material of empirical reality, but the pre-existent realities of which empirical forms are mere shadowy replicas. Accordingly, they were not attained through inductive abstraction, but through a process of mental *maiōsis*, i.e., midwifery. The medieval controversy between the "realists," who contended that universals, "generalities," are real entities, and the "nominalists," who considered them *nomina*, conceptual fabrications, marks the decisive clash between the ancient and the modern view, between the divinely pre-established "idea" and what was to become the scientifically developed concept.

Jesus, in all his capacities, as Messiah, God's messenger, or as God the Son, or "Son of Man," is, unlike the patriarchs, a fully and genuinely individual person, but he too was for original Christianity a thoroughly real, not a symbolic, figure. He was seen to be God's actual descent to man, His very real deed of salvation. Accordingly, Jesus' taking upon himself the expiation of man's sinfulness through his sacrificial death was a real, unique act, which it is believed to be again whenever it is repeated in Holy Mass. The potential overabundance of symbolism that was contained in this event has been unfolded only by post-Pauline theologians and thinkers. Up to this very day, Catholic dogma considers Adam and Eve as the actual ancestors of mankind, who hereditarily transmitted their original sin to all later generations. In this Biblical story of the fall of man, so simple and concrete, so strikingly palpable, we see today an account of the intrinsic genesis of man, that is, the rise of consciousness through freedom of choice, the feeling of shame, and labor. But to become aware of this vast symbolism, we needed the accumulated human experience up to Hegel[5] and Heinrich von Kleist.[6] The legend of Parsifal was assembled by Chrétien de Troyes quite naively from unknown folklore sources; it was not told as symbolic fiction. But afterwards a symbolic meaning has been gathered from it. The grail, *gradalis*, was originally a precious plate on which venison was served at princely carousals. Only later it was turned into a chalice holding divine grace, and as such it became the goal of a quest.

In contradistinction to such descending symbolism that detaches itself for the interpreting mind from a religious, mythical, or historical reality, *ascending* symbolism is a new creation entirely, springing from artistic imagination. Here, no external, preexistent material is furnished to the artist; no longer is he guided by cultic patterns. He is free to create images which, though being unique, singular forms, imply something commonly human.* In such works the symbol reaches the stage of consummate representation. To be sure, even in such creations the symbol is not completely divested of its sign-quality, for they too are intended to convey a message, they too signify something to somebody. But the strained care that such work of free imagination requires, the growing awareness of artistic means, the artistic consciousness and conscience which it has developed, all this keeps the artist's attention focused on the effort to render his vision with utmost preciseness, to such a degree that the communicative purpose is wholly absorbed by the task of representation. The addressee of the message has become an ideal respond-

---

* Wherever modern authors, as for instance Gide, Thomas Mann, Giraudoux, Sartre, use Biblical or mythical motifs to elucidate problems of our age, they do so in a completely independent manner. To them these motifs are no longer a true superior reality to be followed, but raw material like any other from which they build their symbols.

ent, a postulate, an inner figure, of the artist; the demand of the artist's vision shapes him so that he almost belongs within the work itself.*

* *Music* is a language of its own, it is the complex articulation of inarticulate sound. The articulation consists in the differentiation of pitch, the rhythmical division of differentiated pitch, i. e. of tones, and the interplay of the different grades of pitch and their sequences. While even the simplest word carries a meaning in that it is a sign designating something beyond itself, the simplest unit of music, the tone, has in itself no meaning, it receives a meaning only through a sequence or group of tones. A word, therefore, is itself a symbol; a tone becomes a symbol only within its sequence or group. The special, dynamic nature of the musical symbol has been most lucidly described by Victor Zuckerkandl.[7] "The key to understanding the processes that made the tones of this melody a melody at all, a piece of music, we found not in the relation of the tones to any particular feeling, but in the relation of the tone e to the tone d. That the dynamic qualities of tone . . . have nothing to do with the expression of feeling, or with the expression of anything whatsoever, follows from the mere fact that they clearly appear even where absolutely nothing is meant to be expressed or stated, namely, when a scala is played . . . The word and its meaning are independent things. *Here* is the word—a complex of sounds or signs; *there* is what it means. The two are separable; each exists by itself, the word without the thing, the thing without the word. The same thing is designated in different languages by different words . . . The tone and its meaning, on the other hand, are connected in a far more intimate way. The acoustical event and its musical meaning are in no sense two independent phenomena, existing by themselves. They cannot be imagined separate. To be sure, it is possible to imagine a tone that means nothing, that is simply an acoustical phenomenon; but it is impossible to imagine the musical meaning of a tone, its dynamic quality, without the tone . . . What tones mean musically is completely one with them, can only be represented through them, exists only in them . . . tones must themselves create what they mean. Hence it is possible to translate from one language into another, but not from one music into another—for example from Western into Chinese music . . . Tones too indicate, *point to* something. The meaning of a tone, however, lies not in what it points to but *in the pointing itself;* more precisely, in the different way, in the individual gesture, with which each tone points toward the same place. The meaning is not the thing indicated but the manner of indicating . . . Words lead away from themselves, but tones lead into themselves . . . Tones . . . have completely absorbed their meaning into themselves and discharge it upon the hearer directly in their sound." So while the musical symbol appears to be identical with the act of pointing, or, more precisely, with pointing in action, while it is thus a signifying per se and *in perpetuo*, it still can reach, in the strictly organized "composition" of a fugue, a sonata, a symphony, a peculiar kind of image, an image of pure form as it were: The dynamism coincides with the simultaneity of perfected wholeness.

VI

Ascending symbolism, having originated in profane art, starts
from a fully and purely secular plane of existences which have no
factual, but only vicarious reality, which are created for the very
purpose of vicarious representation. Inversely, what makes
a wholly devised image into a work of art is precisely its quality
of symbolic representation. Only when we feel that a story tells
us more than just some peculiar happening, that it shows us
through the singular story a generally human or epochal condition, when, by its piercing vividness, it touches the human core
in us; only when a picture, even a portrait, reaches through the
individual form into a conception of the structure of the phenomenal world *—only then do these images attain to the sphere of
art.

This, in itself implies another, an ultimate degree of symbolism
that goes beyond mere representation. For truly artistic representation is not possible without an inherent dynamic quality,
which is a drive toward the unknown, the hitherto unseen and
unexpressed. Whatever moves us in a work of art, the overwhelming surprise of a suprarational, "imagical" revelation, the intensity
and authenticity of vision, the penetration beyond the surface
aspects of our life; whatever carries us along with it and kindles
in us a feeling of human communion—all this is due to the vital
power of the artist to experience reality *for the first time,* and
that means to discover new reality. This "for the first time," this
immediacy of perception that pushes beyond the stale appear-
ances and unearths a virgin truth beneath, this is an essential,
indispensable part of artistic quality. It comprises what goes
under such vague names as "freshness," "vigor," "originality"; it
is precisely what distinguishes a master from a disciple. The

---

* This quality also makes works of cultic representation into works of art.
Indeed, insofar as they achieve in their cultic depiction a fresh revelation of
the phenomenal form, just so far do they too gain the stage of full
representation.

history of art is nothing else than the history of such conquests, and inasmuch as artistic representation is not just *mimesis,* the rendering of an already patent reality, but rather an evocation of a latent, heretofore unseen reality, it carries out in its artistic performance a supra-artistic, a human deed of the greatest consequence: *the creation of a new form of reality.* Such coincidence, indeed identity, of the artistic and the human act, is the supreme reach of the symbol.

VII

It may, finally, be of some help to understanding the nature of the symbol to contrast it with other forms of representational imagery: *allegory* and *metaphor.*

Between allegory and symbol the borderlines are not always easily discernible, and therefore their difference is frequently blurred in common terminology. The reason for this is their aiming at the same goal from opposite ends. The *symbol* is something concrete and specific that is intended to convey something spiritual or general, either as an indicating sign, i.e., an act of pointing, or as an actual representation in which the dynamic division of the sign is abolished: that which points, that which it points to, and the act of pointing, have become one and the same. The Greek word *symballein,* from which "symbol" derives, means: "to bring together," or, "to come together." The symbolic *sign* brings together, the symbolic *representation* is a coming together, to the point of complete fusion, of the concrete and the spiritual, the specific and the general.

Allegory, conversely, starts from something primarily general and abstract, a purely conceptual entity, which it clothes in a concrete body.* Allegory is a rather late product, it presupposes

* Related distinctions between allegory and symbol have been made by Goethe and Coleridge. Goethe: "Allegory transforms the phenomenon *(Erscheinung)* into an abstract concept *(Begriff),* the concept into an image, but in such a way that the concept can still be expressed and beheld in the image in a clearly circumscribed and complete form. Symbolism transforms the phenomenon into an idea, the idea into an image, in such a way that

fully developed reflection, indeed an incipient separation of mind and body. Accordingly, its high period is the Christian era. In a certain respect, Plato's replacing divine personalities by divinified thought-images is the inauguration of allegory; and a further advance in this direction may be seen in the doctrine of Philo of Alexandria, which is a synthesis of Judaism and Stoic, Neo-platonic, and Neopythagorean thinking. To Philo, the hypostases, i.e., the powers mediating between God and man, are attributive faculties of God (as for instance justice, grace, etc.,) but at the same time they are real angels. Their head and archangel, the Logos, is God's rational power, His thought and creative word, but simultaneously His "first son," His "shadow," the paraclete in corporeal person. What distinguishes the Platonic and Philonic substitutions from allegory proper is the fact that these incarnations of thought were believed to be real entities, indeed *the* true reality, whereas the figures in a perfected allegory, as for instance Good-will, Faith, Piety, etc. in Bunyan's *Pilgrim's Progress*, are sheer means of presentation.

Dante's *Divina Commedia* is a historical junction-point of allegory and symbol, of descending and ascending symbolism. Its design is the structure of the Christian universe which the individual man, Dante, traverses. This dogmatic universe with its purgatorial, infernal, and celestial regions and subregions is a suprahistorical sphere of absolute, pre-existent reality, which

---

the idea remains for ever infinitely active and unreachable in the image and, even if expressed in all languages, still inexpressible." (*Maximen und Reflexionen*. Aus dem Nachlass) "We may speak of true symbolism, when the particular represents the more general, not as a dream, or shadow, but as a living instantaneous revelation of the inscrutable." (*Maximen und Reflexionen*. Aus Kunst und Altertum 1826.) Coleridge: Allegory is merely "a translation of abstract notions into a picture language, which is itself nothing but an abstraction from objects of the senses . . ." a symbol "is characterized by a translucence of the special [the species] in the individual, or of the general [genus] in the special . . .; above all by the translucence of the eternal through and in the temporal." (*The Statesman's Manual*, quoted by René Wellek and Austin Warren in *Theory of Literature*, New York 1949 pp. 193 ff.)

is symbolically interpreted down to the minutest details. This is descending symbolism. But Dante, on the other hand, the individual person, wandering through the cosmic zones and arriving at his heavenly haven, represents man with his earthly history which is elaborately displayed in its memorable figures and destinies, and thus an ascending symbolism is built in, encompassed in descending symbolism. Likewise, allegory is included in the picture to serve the universal symbolism, and in some places it actually coincides with the symbol. It can hardly be made out for instance whether Reason is embodied in Virgil, which would be an allegory, or whether the historical person, Virgil, represents reason, which would be a symbol. This example shows how difficult it is sometimes to distinguish allegory and symbol.

The *metaphor* (from Greek *metaphorá*, transference) is neither a sign, nor the representational unity of duality, but paraphrase, parallelism, "simile." Commonly, it is meant to elucidate an abstraction by visualizing it, transferring it into an image; this, however, not in the manner of allegory, through personifying incarnation, but rather by way of analogy.

Our daily language abounds with such "figurative" uses: words and idioms rendering supravisual circumstances by plain, corporeal images. Expressions of this kind have become elements of our daily linguistic commerce without our being aware any longer that they are metaphors. A transfiguration of bodily images into abstract meanings has been growing in an age-old anonymous process, along with the increasing complexity and intellectualization of human life. Its residues are concealed in etymology. Who would still connect "management" with Latin *manus,* hand; indeed even "handling" with hand? Who would still recognize in the word "demand" the Latin *de-mandare* (i.e., *manum dare*) which means in a physically literal sense "to hand over" (to one's charge), or in "differ" the original *dis-ferre*, "to carry apart?" In idioms, as for instance when we say that something "goes hand in hand" with something else, or that "this has a bearing on that," the metaphor is of course quite evident.

What poets do is exactly the reverse of the anonymous linguistic process; they transfer the intricate, intellectualized and spiritualized, experience of modern man into imagery, either through comparison and paraphrase, or, as in our days, through immediate transmutation, which is implicitly a condensation. A subtle interaction takes place between the flaring image and the experience that kindled it, whereby the image is capable of driving the experience farther, that is, of creating new experience. In such a process of intercreation metaphor and symbol merge.

REFERENCES

1. Arieti, Silvano, *Interpretation of Schizophrenia* (New York: Basic Books, 1955), pp. 282 ff.
2. Freud, Sigmund, *Introductory Lectures on Psycho-analysis*, second edition (London, 1949, Tenth Lecture: Symbolism in Dreams) pp. 128 ff.
3. Jung, C. G., *Modern Man in Search of a Soul* (New York: Harcourt, Brace, 1933), pp. 27 ff.
4. Zimmer, Heinrich, *Myths and Symbols in Indian Art and Civilization* (New York: Pantheon, 1946), p. 62.
5. Hegel, Georg Wilhelm Friedrich, *The Logic of Hegel*, translated by William Wallace (Oxford, 1874), Ch. II pp. 46 f.
6. Kleist, Heinrich von, "Essays on the Marionettes," in *Vertical* a yearbook for the Romantic-Mystic Ascensions, edited by Eugène Jolas (New York: Gotham, 1941).
7. Zuckerkandl, Victor, *Sound and Symbol: Music and the External World* (New York: Pantheon, 1956), pp. 56 ff: The Dynamic Symbol.

2. The Religious Symbol*

PAUL TILLICH

I. THE SYMBOL

THE RELIGIOUS SYMBOL combines the general characteristics of the symbol with the peculiar characteristics it possesses as a religious symbol.

The first and basic characteristic of the symbol is its figurative quality. This implies that the inner attitude which is oriented to the symbol does not have the symbol itself in view but rather that which is symbolized in it. Moreover, that which is symbolized can itself in turn be a symbol for something of a higher rank. Hence, the written character can be called a symbol for the word and the word a symbol for its meaning. Devotion to the crucifix is really directed to the crucifixion on Golgotha and devotion to the latter is in reality intended for the redemptive action of God, which is itself a symbolic expression for an experience of what concerns us ultimately.

The second characteristic of the symbol is its perceptibility. This implies that something which is intrinsically invisible, ideal, or transcendent is made perceptible in the symbol and is in this way given objectivity. The perceptibility of the symbol need not

* Based on an article with the same title in *The Journal of Liberal Religion*, Vol. II (1940), pp. 13-33, translated by James Luther Adams, with the assistance of Ernst Fraenkel.

It can just as well be something imaginatively con-
in the example already given of the crucifixion or as in
gures. Even abstract concepts can become symbols if their
volves a perceptible element. Thus perhaps the concept of
plus value" as a symbol of economic exploitation in the consciousness of the proletariat or the idea of the "Supreme Being"
as a symbol of the ultimate concern in the consciousness of the
religious community may serve as examples.

The third characteristic of the symbol is its innate power. This
implies that the symbol has a power inherent within it that distinguishes it from the mere sign which is impotent in itself. This
characteristic is the most important one. It gives to the symbol
the reality which it has almost lost in ordinary usage, as the
phrase "only a symbol" shows. This characteristic is decisive for
the distinction between a sign and a symbol. The sign is interchangeable at will. It does not arise from necessity, for it has no
inner power. The symbol, however, does possess a necessary
character. It cannot be exchanged. It can only disappear when,
through dissolution, it loses its inner power. Nor can it be merely
constructed; it can only be created. Words and signs originally
had a symbolic character. They conveyed the meaning which they
expressed, with an inherent power of their own. In the course of
evolution and as a result of the transition from the mystical to
the technical view of the world, they have lost their symbolic
character, though not entirely. Once having lost their innate
power they became signs. The pictorial symbols of religious art
were originally charged with a magical power, with the loss of
which they became a conventional sign-language and almost for-
feited their genuine symbolic character.

The fourth characteristic of the symbol is its acceptability as
such. This implies that the symbol is socially rooted and socially
supported. Hence it is not correct to say that a thing is first a
symbol and then gains acceptance; the process of becoming a
symbol and the acceptance of it as a symbol belong together. The

act by which a symbol is created is a social act, even though it first springs forth in an individual. The individual can devise signs for his own private needs; he cannot make symbols. If something becomes a symbol for him, it is always so in relation to the community which in turn can recognize itself in it. This fact is clearly evident in creedal symbols which at first are merely the signs by means of which the members of the group recognize each other. "Symbolics" is the science of the distinctive marks of the different churches, that is, the science of creedal distinctions. But all other symbols could also be considered in this light. Thus universal "symbolics" is conceivable as a general science of the self expressions of all groups, tendencies, and communities.

These general characteristics of the symbol hold for the religious symbol also, as the various examples show. Religious symbols are distinguished from others by the fact that they are a representation of that which is unconditionally beyond the conceptual sphere, they point to the ultimate reality implied in the religious act, to what concerns us ultimately. All other symbols either stand for something that has also an unsymbolic objective existence aside from its ideal significance, as, for example, a flag can represent a king, and the king in turn represents the state; or they are the forms giving expression to an invisible thing that has no existence except in its symbols, as for example, cultural creations like works of art, scientific concepts, and legal forms. It is only in symbolic fashion that such intangible things as these can be given expression at all.

The situation is essentially different with religious symbols. They must express an object that by its very nature transcends everything in the world that is split into subjectivity and objectivity. A real symbol points to an object which never can become an object. Religious symbols represent the transcendent but do not make the transcendent immanent. They do not make God a part of the empirical world.

II. THEORIES OF THE RELIGIOUS SYMBOL

The theories of the religious symbol are valid also in many respects for the symbol in general. In the consideration of these theories, however, we shall always come to a point where the independent and specific problems of the religious symbol will arise and require a solution. The theories of the symbol can be classified into negative and positive theories. The negative theories are those that interpret the symbol as reflecting an aspect of reality that is not consciously intended in the symbol. They deny that the symbol has an objective reference and attribute to it merely a subjective character. A definite subjective state and not the actual facts referred to in the symbol is expressed in the symbol. These theories are especially dangerous for religious symbols, since the latter do not refer to a world of objects, yet they intend to express a reality and not merely the subjective character of a religious individual.

On scientific and systematic grounds these theories are ultimately reducible to two types: the psychological and the sociological theory of the symbol. Both types have acquired historical significance because they have effectively, though one-sidedly, recognized one aspect of the development of symbols: they have shown that the psychological and social situation is decisive for the selection of symbols in all spheres. Going beyond this, they attempt also to show that symbols have no other reality than to serve as an expression of the psychological and social situation; that is, these negative theories set forth a genetic theory of the symbol itself. The two prophetic personalities of the nineteenth century, Nietzsche and Marx, gave the decisive impulse to this tendency.[1] This fact indicates that these theories are devised for combat and that they aim to do away with something, to destroy a symbol-complex. The object of their attack is the symbolism of bourgeois society including that of the churches supported by bourgeois society. The means employed in their attack is the argument that these symbols are an expression of a definite will to power and have no other reality than that which is conferred upon them by this will to power.

Marx used the expression "ideology" to describe this function of symbols and he made it into an unprecedentedly powerful political symbol. Symbols are ideologies. The intellectual content, that is, the objective reference of symbols, or that which is expressed in them, is a political subterfuge that is consciously or unconsciously created for the sake of dominance. This thesis has not, to be sure, been followed up by a tested application in the various fields of symbolism. Wherever this has been attempted (and it was not done in the writings of Marx), the result has been a complete failure.

Wherever there has been a discussion of the inherent character of symbols and of their effect upon the social situation, the more rigid theory has been relinquished and the objective reference of symbols has been recognized. This retreat is unavoidable, for a consistent carrying through of the theory would brand the theory along with its political symbolical power as itself an ideology that could only make the claim to be an expression of the proletarian social situation, but by no means an expression of real relationships. Thus the symbol "ideology" would itself be an ideology. It would also remain inconceivable how the will to power could make use of different kinds of symbols, if a cogent relevance to the facts were not inherent in the symbols.[2]

The theory of symbols deriving from Nietzsche has in our day received substantial support from the psychology of the unconscious (depth psychology). The Freudian analysis of the unconscious in a similar way interprets cultural and religious symbols as arising out of unconscious processes. The obscure and mysterious realm of dreams is held to be a symbol area of the first order. When we examine the unconscious, we see the no less mysterious symbols of mythology in a clearer light. All symbols are interpreted as sublimations of vital and instinctive impulses which have been repressed. This interpretation has been employed with greatest success in connection with those symbols that are lacking in any objective foundations, like the dream and the myth. In this way they are deprived of their objective reference.

But this theory has not been carried out consistently either. In the concept of sublimation the problem is concealed rather than solved; for this conception implies not only a pointing up or refining of the instinctive impulses but also a turning of the impulses towards areas of reality that, so far as their content is concerned, have nothing to do with impulses. Therefore an earnest attempt at carrying out the theory has never been made so far as it concerns the symbols that have objective reference. This holds especially for the science of psychoanalysis whose own inherent character is all too clearly the basis that supports the whole theory. Before it one always comes to a halt—and just for the same reason as obtains for the theory of ideology. All the more insistently, however, the question is raised by the psychology of the unconscious, concerning those symbols that have no objective empirical basis.

When psychoanalysis, for example, interprets the use of the father symbol in reference to God as an expression of the analytical father-complex (just as sociology on its part interprets it as an indication of the dominance of the male), we must raise the question as to how far the significance of this explanation extends. Obviously no further than its next assertion: that the *selection* of this symbol is to be explained by the father-complex. But the interpretation that in general the setting up of religious symbols is determined by complexes, is not valid. In other words, a theory of the religious symbol is not given but rather a theory as to how religious symbols are selected. Nor is anything more than this possible; for the positing of an unconditioned transcendent can by no means be explained on the basis of the conditioned and immanent impulses of the unconscious. But the final thing has not yet been said on the question of the selection of religious symbols; the possibility has not been taken into account that the vital impulses which induce the selection of the father symbol are themselves the operation of a primordial shaping of life, and therefore the intuition of the Unconditioned in this symbol expresses a truth which, though limited, is yet an ultimate, and therefore a religious, truth. The same thing would hold also for the sociological theory of the selection of symbols. Psychological and social impulses control the selection; but they can themselves be viewed as symbols for an ultimate metaphysical structure of existence. This consideration deprives these theories of their negative implications even when they are correct, namely, in their explanation of the *selection* of symbols.

With the consideration of the cultural-morphological interpretation of symbols we make a transition from the negative to the positive theories. In common with the negative theories, they make the selection of symbols dependent upon a subjective factor, the soul of the culture. But this factor is not, as it is asserted to be by the negative theories, unrelated to the objective reference of the symbols, but rather has an essential relation to it. Indeed, it is by means of this relationship that the subjective factor is defined as "the soul of the culture." The vital and the cultural are not separate from each other, but rather they constitute a unity within the creative, formative principle of a culture. All cultural creations are symbols for a definite, psychic, formative principle. This symbolic character does not, however, negate its objectivity.

The central phenomenon of the cultural-morphological theory is "style." In the style of works of art, concepts, legal forms, and the like, the soul of the culture from which they derive, finds expression. By means of this conception of style all aspects or forms of cultural life become symbols.* The morphologist of culture is

---

* Thus we can speak of a "style of thought" and conceive of the history of philosophy as a history partly of a typical, partly of a changing, style of thought. This can lead to important insights if it is carried out with due attention to the singularity of historical events and to the claim to validity asserted by every philosophical idea.

concerned with style and not with the precise details of the development of a culture. Thus he will incur the strictures we have associated with the negative theory. Indeed, he must do so, if he looks upon morphology as an absolute principle, that is, if he denies all objective connection between the creations of the different cultural epochs. In this theory he exposes himself to the danger that his theory will itself be interpreted only as a symbol for a psychological-cultural situation. At least when dealing with his own science he too must come to a halt.

The symbols that are most of all threatened by this theory are those symbols that possess no objective references and can be interpreted as immediate forms of expression of the soul of the culture and as such can be interpreted as detached from every realm of fact. Against this threat we must assert: the fact that the soul must express itself religiously when it expresses itself immediately, cannot be explained in any other way than by the fact that the soul is religious, that the relation to the unconditioned transcendent is essential or constitutive for it. The fact that religious symbols are distinguished from all others in power of expression and immediacy, can be explained only by the fact that that which pertains to the soul, and this holds also for the soul of a culture, must be defined precisely by the relation to the unconditioned transcendent. When this "soul"—apart from all objective, empirical relations—expresses itself, it does so religiously. It is in this context that the connection between the vital and the cultural elements in the "soul" can be understood, namely, from the fact that each element, in transcending itself, meets the other at the point of transcendence: the vital element, by breaking through its own immediacy (for which perhaps the instinct of death, as maintained by Freud, is an expression, although it is absolutely incomprehensible on the basis of the vital); the cultural element, insofar as none of its forms can be exempt from the crisis that they encounter as a result of the demands of the objective world as well as of the meaning of life itself. This fact explains how a "style" of culture possesses a symbolic power that has religious significance. Insofar as the psychic element or the "soul" is expressed in the style, the relation to the unconditioned transcendent is expressed in it. The sphere of religion insofar as it is expressed in symbols embraces the whole autonomous culture.[3] Thus a science of the symbolics of culture worked out from the religious point of view, becomes a necessary task. Naturally this consideration has to do with only one side of culture. The various independent spheres of things remain intact; the symbolic character of cultural creation is "broken" by its objective, empirical character. The symbolism of style is a "broken," indirectly religious symbolism. But it is for this very reason that it has a fundamental significance for the understanding of the religious symbol in general.

We have presupposed the difference between the symbolic and the objective character of cultural creations. This conception, however, is opposed by the critical-idealistic theory of the symbol. The latter identifies the symbolic and the objective character and thereby gives to the concept of the symbol a new form and a tremendous extension. As a result of the work of Cassirer, this conception today stands in the foreground of symbol theory. We shall combine the exposition and criticism of this theory with an exposition and criticism of Cassirer's theory of mythical symbols.

The myth is viewed as a definite form of the cultural interpretation of existence and thus, in accordance with idealistic presuppositions, it is viewed as an objective creation. A symbolic reality is attributed to the laws according to which myths are formed. The myth is classified along with the other cultural spheres that are also manifested in symbols, such as language, philosophy, art, etc. The subject-matter of myth is therefore not to be considered as in any special way symbolic. It has a symbolic element in common with all cultural creations; for a cultural life exists only in symbols. To be sure, a pre-cultural and pre-symbolic world of intuition does exist, but not a reality transcendent to symbols. Cultural reality is in its essence symbolic reality; not because in itself it reflects a reality but rather because, being free from the relation to any thing-in-itself beyond the empirical, it creates a world of cultural objects. At this point we shall turn aside from the epistemological problem and raise the question as to how mythical and religious symbolism are related to each other. The answer given by critical idealism is that originally mythical and religious symbolism are interfused. But gradually religious symbolism rises above mythical symbolism, struggles against it and overcomes it. This answer grasps the problem and formulates it. But it does not contain the solution: if mythology is in its essence a cultural creation like science, art, law, it is difficult to understand why it should be destroyed, indeed it is impossible that it should decline, for it has its own proper and necessary place in the meaningful structure of cultural life. If religion, on the other hand, is an autonomous area of meaning, we must ask how it is possible that it was originally embedded in myth. In short, the evolutionary and the transcendental conceptions of the myth contradict each other.

This tension is resolved as soon as it is pointed out that the myth, far from having disappeared, has only altered its form. Thus the conflict between religion and myth would not be a conflict with myth as such but rather of one particular myth with another. And this is what appears to me to be the case. The struggle of the Jewish prophets against pagan mythology was a struggle of the ethical henotheism of the old religion of the desert against the ecstatic polytheism of agrarian religion, a struggle of Jahwism against Baalism. But the mythical element is just as active in the religion of Jahwe as in the religion of Baal. To be sure, something has happened to bring in question the myth in its immediacy: the Jahwe is an historical myth, that is, it is related to the empirical realities of history. It has the realism of the historical. Yet transcendence has in a radical fashion insinuated itself into the mythical figure of Jahwe. Jahwe acquires the unconditionedness which is intended in the religious act. But the myth is not thereby removed. Empirical history remains always related to a super-empirical, a transcendent history, which extends from the primitive period of innocence on beyond Jahwe's choice of his people to the end of history. Unconditioned transcendence as such is not perceptible. If it is to be perceived— and it must be so in religion—it can be done only in mythical conceptions. Of course these mythical ideas thereby lose their immediate meaning, they point beyond themselves, just as, conversely, history, when interpreted mythically, always remains real history demanding actual decisions. Nor does mysticism eliminate the myth, though it has broken the immediately mythical consciousness, for example, in India. The highest concept of even an abstractly transcendent mysticism has necessarily a mythical element still within it. The lower forms of the myth are not negated but are rather deprived of their ultimate reality just as all real facts are deprived of their actuality. The mythical consciousness can therefore be either broken or unbroken; in any case, it does not disappear. If one decides to characterize only the unbroken mythical mentality as mythical, then of course the myth is overcome in religion and it is shown to be non-essential. If, on the other hand, one calls every intuition of transcendence mythical, then there is no such thing as an unmythical attitude and the myth is shown to be essential. The usage is unsettled, presumably not because of the lack of scientific clarification but because of the inner dialectic that characterizes the concept of myth.

The objects of mythical intuition are at the same time the objects of scientific and philosophical investigation. With the appearance of science they enter as such into a new dialectic. There begins a transformation of the objects of mythical intuition into objects of mere empirical experience. A separate objective world arises and confronts the rational, perceiving subject. As a result,

the subjective factor which is adapted to all immediately mythical data, the inner living connection of the consciousness with
everything existing and with the inwardness of everything real,
disappears or is repressed. Insofar as science thus builds up its
own world of objects, it repels the myth. But, for the purpose of
constructing this world of "things," science needs concepts that
are transcendent to reality. In this way science comes into a new
mythical situation and itself becomes myth-creative; thus concepts like evolution, will to power, life, etc., have a mythical
character. They no longer serve only for the construction of the
empirical order, but rather indicate the transcendent presuppositions of this order. But since the element of the Unconditioned
is firmly implanted in each of these presuppositions, and since
the presupposition of all thinking (which is below the "abyss of
being"), signifies both the limits and the abyss of objectification,
there comes into science an element of the religious, mythical
mentality. Hence, it is possible for the ultimate presuppositions
of science to be classed with the highest concepts of abstract
mysticism or of abstract monotheism. In this way there arises an
abstract myth that is no less a myth than a concrete one, even if
it is broken in its immediacy. Indeed, the living meaning of
creative metaphysics is that it involves just such an abstract myth.
And from this fact it derives both its doubtful character as a
science and its religious power.

Under these circumstances one must reject the classification of
mythology as an independent type of symbol-creation different
from science and religion. In both science and religion mythology
is an element that cannot be eliminated, even though it may be
broken. Plato recognizes this when on the one hand he puts
science in opposition to myth and on the other must acknowledge the indispensability of myth to science. All metaphysics reaches a point where its concepts are myths not only in
fact but even in the sound of its words. The myth is, therefore,
an essential element of everything in the intellectual and cultural

sphere. Nevertheless it is necessary to distinguish between the unbroken and the broken form of the myth. In the unbroken myth three elements are linked together: the religious, the scientific, and the truly mythical elements: the religious element as relatedness to the unconditioned transcendent, the scientific as relatedness to objective reality, the truly mythical as an objectification of the transcendent through the medium of intuitions and conceptions of reality. This unity was possible only so long as the unconditionedness of the religious transcendent and the rationality of the world of things were hidden from consciousness. Thus the creations of the mythical consciousness could appear as satisfying both the religious and the scientific claim (of course, the contrast between religion and science as such was not evident at that time). This situation could not continue indefinitely. The breaking down of this unity signifies a transition into an autonomous religion and into an autonomous science, and thus it signifies the breaking down of the original mythical mentality. At the same time, however, the mythical stands forth in its purity and in its true character, as a necessary element in the construction of a meaningful reality. Thus it becomes clear that the myth is the central concept of those symbols in which the unconditioned transcendent is envisaged either mediately or immediately.

On this basis not only the original connection of the myth with religion and with a general awareness and understanding of the world becomes intelligible, but also the fact that the myth by its very nature must always strive to achieve again this original unity. Wherever the objective world is recognized in its relatedness to the unconditioned transcendent, and wherever the unconditioned transcendent is interpreted from the point of view of the objective world, the unity of religion with the desire to understand the world is restored in the mythical symbol. Thus science becomes a myth despite its rational autonomy, and religion absorbs certain aspects of the understanding and knowledge of the world, despite its own transcendent autonomy, in order in these ways to sense the transcendent. In our time, however, this development is more a tendency than a reality. Its success would involve a thoroughgoing transformation of both the scientific and the religious mentality.*

It must not be supposed that mythical symbols constitute one sphere of symbols beside other spheres. For, in contrast to the others they are "unfounded" symbols, that is, they are determined essentially by their symbolic character. If it is presupposed in accordance with critical idealism that cultural creations do not give expression to a thing-in-itself, but rather that reality is the cultural and objective sphere constituted by these creations, then it is quite clear that the world of mythical objects has an imaginary and figurative character entirely different from that of the world of artistic objects. The work of art expresses wholly intrinsically the reality that it aims to express. The work of art as a figurative thing does not point beyond itself to a reality of a different order. When it tries to do so, as in symbolic art, a special intention is present, the peculiarity of which shows that art as such does not create symbols but rather a meaningful reality of its own. In so far as it has a symbolic character, it acquires a mythical character also. It surrenders its own character as pure art in order to express a transcendent meaning. The same thing is true for science. The attempt to present a historical figure as a symbol raises this figure to the mythical level and gives to the empirically historical a certain figurative character in favor of its transcendent meaning. The fact that the view here alluded to is advocated only by a small group of historians (the school of the poet Stefan George) again indicates that science, although it does create its own peculiar structures of meaning, does not create symbols. (The secondary level of linguistic and written sign-symbols does not come into consideration for our question.) If,

---

* All the talk about the "new myth" is an indication of how remote the new myth is in actuality. A myth that is sought for as myth is for that very reason repelled. Only when one's thinking has objective reference can a truly mythical element pulsate through it.

nevertheless, the meaning structures of art and science are called symbols, no other objection can be made to this usage than that one must search for a new word for symbol in the narrower sense. The category of the mythical, therefore, includes essentially that of the symbolic, and that in distinction from the other areas of meaning which include the symbolic exactly to the degree that they are subservient to the mythical. That this connection is never completely absent has been shown by the discussion of the symbolic character of "style."

The fact that mythical symbols are from the objective, empirical point of view without a basis—even when cultural creations are involved—and the fact that they are for this reason symbols in the genuine sense, indicates the inadequacy of critical idealism. In its place we propose a transcendent realism. The thing referred to in the mythical symbol is the unconditioned transcendent, the source of both existence and meaning, which transcends being-in-itself as well as being-for-us. On the basis of this presupposition, which cannot be further dealt with here, the ensuing discussion of the religious symbol will proceed.

III. TYPES OF RELIGIOUS SYMBOLS

We distinguish two levels of religious symbols, a supporting level in which religious objectivity is established and which is based in itself; and a level supported by it and pointing to objects of the other level. Accordingly we call the symbols of the first level the "objective religious symbols" and those of the second level, the "self-transcending religious symbols." The objective religious symbols will occupy the central place in our discussion. Indeed, all the previous discussion has been concerned with them. They are themselves to be subdivided into several groups.

The first and basic level of objective religious symbolism is the world of divine beings which, after the "breaking" of the myth, is "the Supreme Being," God. The divine beings and the Supreme

Being, God, are representations of that which is ultimately referred to in the religious act. They are representations, for the
unconditioned transcendent surpasses every possible conception
of a being, including even the conception of a Supreme Being. In
so far as any such being is assumed as existent, it is again annihi-
lated in the religious act. In this annihilation, in this atheism, immanent in the religious act, the profoundest aspect of the religious act is manifest. Wherever this aspect is lost sight of, there
results an objectification of the Unconditioned (which is in essence opposed to objectification), a result which is destructive
of the religious as well as of the cultural life. Thus God is made
into a "thing" that is not a real thing but a contradiction in terms
and an absurdity; demanding belief in such a thing is demanding a religious "work," a sacrifice, an act of asceticism and the
self-destruction of the human mind. It is the religious function
of atheism ever to remind us that the religious act has to do with
the unconditioned transcendent, and that the representations of
the Unconditioned are not objects concerning whose existence
or non-existence a discussion would be possible.

This oscillation between the setting up and the destruction of
the religion object expresses itself immediately in the living idea
of God. It is indeed true that the religious act really signifies
what it refers to: it signifies God. But the word "God" involves
a double meaning: it connotes the unconditioned transcendent,
the ultimate, and also an object somehow endowed with qualities
and actions. The first is not figurative or symbolic, but is rather
in the strictest sense what it is said to be. The second, however,
is really symbolic, figurative. It is the second that is the object
envisaged by the religious consciousness. The idea of a Supreme
Being possessing certain definite qualities is present in the consciousness. But the religious consciousness is also aware of the
fact that when the word "God" is heard, this idea is figurative,
that it does not signify an object, that is, it must be transcendent.

The word "God" produces a contradiction in the consciousness,

it involves something figurative that is present in the consciousness and something not figurative that we really have in mind
and that is represented by this idea. In the word "God" is contained at the same time that which actually functions as a representation and also the idea that it is *only* a representation. It
has the peculiarity of transcending its own conceptual content:
upon this depends the numinous character that the word has in
science and in life in spite of every misuse through false objectification. God as an object is a representation of the reality ultimately referred to in the religious act, but in the word "God"
this objectivity is negated and at the same time its representative
character is asserted.

The second group of objective religious symbols has to do with
characterizations of the nature and actions of God. Here God is
presupposed as an object. And yet these characterizations have an
element in them that indicates the figurative character of that presupposition. Religiously and theologically, this fact is expressed
in the awareness that all knowledge of God has a symbolic
character. The question concerning the reality and the real differentiation of the attributes of God likewise indicates that we are
concerned with symbols here. But this by no means signifies that
these statements are lacking in truth or that these symbols are
interchangeable at will. Genuine symbols are not interchangeable at all, and real symbols provide no objective knowledge, but
yet a true awareness. Therefore, the religious consciousness does
not doubt the possibility of a true awareness of God. The criterion of the truth of a symbol naturally cannot be the comparison of it with the reality to which it refers, just because this
reality is absolutely beyond human comprehension. The truth of
a symbol depends on its inner necessity for the symbol-creating
consciousness. Doubts concerning its truth show a change of
mentality, a new attitude toward the unconditioned transcendent. The only criterion that is at all relevant is this: that the
Unconditioned is clearly grasped in its unconditionedness. A

symbol that does not meet this requirement and that elevates a conditioned thing to the dignity of the Unconditioned, even if it should not be false, is demonic.

The third group of objective symbols are the natural and historical objects that are drawn as holy objects into the sphere of religious objects and thus become religious symbols. In the foreground stand the historical personalities that have become the object of a religious act. It would of course be entirely contradictory to the religious consciousness if one characterized these personalities, or what they did and what happened to them, as symbols. For the peculiarity of this kind of object of the religious consciousness depends precisely upon their historical reality, their reality in the objective sense. The use of symbolism with regard to this world in which the holy is supposed to be really present would involve a denial of its presence and hence the destruction of its existence. And yet this denial is inevitable as soon as these holy realities are looked upon as being rationally objective. For in the context of the rational world of concrete objects they have no place. And if it were possible to give them such a place, for instance, with the help of occultism, the thing aimed at in the religious act, that is, the intuition of the unconditioned transcendent, would not be grasped. These historical personalities, insofar as they are considered as symbols, therefore, have no place in the objective world. More than this, they cannot have such a place even though it be to their advantage as historical figures. This signifies, however, that these objects that possess a holy character are not empirical, even if they can only be conceived of as existing in the empirical order. This means that they are symbols, they represent the presence of the unconditioned transcendent in the empirical order. That this presence is viewed as an empirical event (for example, the resurrection), indicates the figurative character that attaches to every objectification of the transcendent. It is therefore correct to say that Christ or the Buddha, for example, in so far as the unconditioned transcendent is envisaged in them, are symbols. But they are symbols that have at the same time an empirical, historical aspect, and in whose symbolic meaning the empirical is involved. Therefore both aspects, the empirical and the transcendent, are manifest in this kind of symbols and their symbolic power depends upon this fact. The same thing holds for them as for the name of God: all of these are symbolic, and in such a way that in both cases the unsymbolic reality is expressed—in the one case, the empirical, in the other, the transcendent. It is the task of historical criticism, which runs along parallel to atheistic criticism, to prevent these groups of symbols from degenerating into false objectifications. Religion is greatly indebted to modern research on the life of Jesus, in that it has accomplished this task by recognizing the problematic character of the empirical element and by emphasizing the importance of the symbolic element. It is never possible, however, to alter or to re-create a symbol by means of historical criticism. This group of symbols can also be measured by the standard of how effectively the unconditioned transcendent is expressed in them. The rise and decline of symbols is a matter of the religious and not of the scientific mentality.

The third group of objective religious symbols involves the level of symbols that we have characterized as "pointing" symbols. It is the immensely large class of signs and actions of a special significance that contain a reference to religious objects of the first level. This whole class of symbols can be divided into actions on the one hand and objects on the other that symbolize the religious attitude. In the first category belong, for example, all cultic gestures, to the second, all illustrative symbols, such as the cross, arrows and the like. An elaboration of this class of symbols would be tantamount to working out a theory of the phenomena of religion in general. This is not at the moment feasible. Only one point significant for the principle in question may be mentioned here. All these symbols can be conceived as objective symbols of the third group reduced to a lower power. They all had originally more than "pointing" significance. They were holy objects or actions laden with magical sacramental power. To the degree in which their magical-sacramental power was reduced in favor of the unconditioned transcendent on the one side, and in the direction of the objectification of their reality on the other, they were brought down to the level of the "pointing" symbol. This process is never wholly completed. Even in radically critical religions like Judaism and Protestantism the conservatism of the religious mentality has preserved the magical-sacramental attitude toward reality. Concerning the other great forms of religion it is much better to be silent. Even in the mere "pointing" symbols, so long as they are living, there remains a residue of their original sacral power. If this is wholly lost, it is no longer justifiable to speak of symbols; the symbol is now replaced by conventional idioms which may then be raised by means of religious art into the purely esthetic sphere. And this can happen not only to divine signs and attributes but also to the divine beings themselves, as history has demonstrated. This observation leads to the conclusion that the second level of religious symbols, the "pointing" symbols, are transitional in character. And this is based on the nature of things. So long as symbols are imbued with sacral power the religious act is orientated toward them. When the religious act is no longer oriented toward them, that is, when they lose their sacral power, they degenerate into mere signs. This transition, however, involves so large an area of the religious life that one is justified in assigning to it a special place. At all events, this one conclusion is evident, that the real religious symbol is the objective symbol, which in its three groups represents the unconditioned transcendent.

IV. THE RISE AND DECLINE OF RELIGIOUS SYMBOLS

Religious symbols are created in the course of the historical process of religion. The inner impulse of this historical process has been made clear through the consideration of the myth. It is a tendency that is two-fold, toward religious transcendence and toward cultural objectification. Religious criticism manifests itself in the opposition of the divine and the demonic. As a result of this criticism religious symbols are forced inevitably into the status of the demonic. At first their reality is not destroyed, but it is weakened; the real symbolic power lives on in the sphere of the divine. The thus weakened demonic symbols can still have a long life; eventually, however, they tend to withdraw and become mere signs, or wholly to disappear.* Scientific criticism does not in itself have the power to make religious symbols disappear. Wherever it seems to have this power, a deflection in the religious consciousness has already taken place. Wherever scientific criticism is effective, it leads not to a demonization, but rather to a profanization of the symbols. The decisive means for bringing about the profanization of symbols is the exposing of their symbolic character. For this reason the religious consciousness always protests against the characterization of its objects as symbols. In this respect nothing is changed by proving that reality can, indeed must be embraced in the symbol. The shimmering quality that attaches to all objects to which the concept of the symbol is applied can, by the peculiarly religious sense for reality, be recognized only as a negation of its reality. Thus the question arises as to what can be or become a religious symbol in the cultural situation of our day.

On the whole the situation is such that the contents of categories

---

* The Calvinist criticism of the mass (as "accursed idolatry") forces it into the demonic and makes the eucharist a mere "pointing" symbol: the beginning of its disappearance. The question may be raised—and it has been raised by critics of this essay—whether every religious symbol is necessarily subject to the process of destruction. This question cannot be decided *in abstracto*. The possibility that a symbol, freeing itself from all its demonizations and profanizations, will come to life again through the power inherent in it, is always a real possibility *in abstracto*. Whether it becomes a reality depends upon the actual faith of the time, whose ways are not to be determined *a priori* nor on the basis of something extraneous to it.

arising out of the scientific and philosophic mode of creating concepts have the immediate persuasive power that fits them to
become symbols. The fact that in the most highly educated
circles the attitude of certainty towards scientific concepts is
shattered and that the mythical character of these concepts is
recognized, does not even in these circles greatly affect the self-
evident symbolic power of these concepts. The idea of God illustrates the kind of change to which religious symbols have been
subjected. The idea of God has by misuse through objectification
lost its symbolic power in such measure that it serves largely as
a concealment of the unconditioned transcendent rather than as
a symbol for it. The recognition of this, its unobjective, symbolic
character, has a chance of influence only insofar as the "ring" of
the unconditioned transcendent can still be heard in the word
"God." Where this is not the case, the proof that the intellectual
content of the idea of God is symbolic can only hasten its loss of
power.

This situation with regard to religious symbols, a situation
which is fraught with great danger, may give rise to the desire
to treat that which is referred to in the symbol without using
symbols. Of course this cannot mean that beyond all symbols the
unconditioned transcendent should be directly intuited. Rather it
signifies that reality should no longer be used as material for
symbols. It signifies that reality itself should be looked at immediately and be spoken of in such a way that its position in and
before the unconditioned transcendent would receive direct expression. Undoubtedly, it might well be the highest aim of theology to find the point where reality speaks simultaneously of itself
and of the Unconditioned in an unsymbolic fashion, to find the
point where the unsymbolic reality itself becomes a symbol, where
the contrast between reality and symbol is suspended. If this
were really possible, the deepest demand of the religious consciousness would be fulfilled: religion would no longer be a

separate thing. This in no way signifies, however, that religion should be reduced to an artistic or scientific approach to reality. It signifies rather an immediate concern with things in so far as they confront us unconditionally, that is, in so far as they stand in the transcendent.

But against this idea, which would involve especially in our day a great unburdening of the religious consciousness, an emancipation from the burden of a symbolism that has lost its self-evident character, there arises a serious objection: the idea rests on the presupposition that an unmythical treatment of the unconditioned transcendent provides the religious possibility of fully penetrating reality. This possibility, however, presupposes that reality stands in God, that is, that reality is eschatological and not present. In our time the idea prevails that certain realities with symbolic power must be placed above other realities without symbolic power; this very fact indicates that reality as a whole is separated from what it ought to be, and is not transparent of its ultimate meaning. Only insofar as this were the case, would reality itself acquire symbolic power and thus the realm of special symbols would become unnecessary: reality and symbol would become identical.*

---

* This section is the most important and the most questionable of the entire essay. In my essay on "Belief-ful Realism" I have attempted to accomplish the same thing, namely, a language without symbols. Perhaps it is a sign of the maturity of our religious development that its prophetic word— so far as any such is used—grasps the transcendent without symbol, just as it is a sign of the genius of great poets that they have at their command words that are both unsymbolic and precise and nevertheless penetrate into the deepest levels of our existence. Examples of this may perhaps be found in the later poems of Rilke and in some of the writings of Werfel. The word "unsymbolic" here signifies, without a transcendent, objective symbol.

The idea is that if God is all in all, there is no more need to speak of God in special symbols and even to use the word God. Speaking of things would mean speaking of the depth in which things are rooted and of the heights to which they are elevated. For me the greatest religious utterances are those in which this type of non-symbolic speaking is more or less reached. But they are rather rare and they must be rare, because our real situation is that of distance from God and not of God being all in all.

REFERENCES

1. Cf. my book *The Religious Situation,* trans. H. Richard Niebuhr
   (New York: Henry Holt and Company, 1932), for an estimate of
   Nietzsche and Marx.
2. Cf. the general epistemological treatment of the concept of ideology in Karl Mannheim's book, *Ideology and Utopia,* and my
   review of this book in the October 1929 number of *Gesellschaft.*
3. This is the basic thesis of my *Philosophy of Religion;* cf. my ad-
   dress "Ueber die Idee einer Theologie der Kultur," *Vortraege der
   Kantstudien,* 2nd ed. 1921, and my *Religionsphilosophie* in Des-
   soir's *Lehrbuch der Philosophie,* 1925.

3. The Cross: Social Trauma or Redemption*

AMOS N. WILDER

Odour of blood when Christ was slain
Made all Platonic tolerance vain,
And vain all Doric discipline.

> W. B. YEATS, *"Two Songs from a Play"*[1]

We think that this long night,
This cold eclipse, is shade cast from Christ's cross.

> ELDER OLSON, *The Cock of Heaven*[2]

IN ANY discussion of symbolism the religious category may well receive attention. All the issues that arise in the study of cultural symbols appear here and with additional dimensions. If cultural symbols are both community-building and time-binding, religious symbols have an additional ultimacy of reference which adds to their power. If the media and vehicles of cultural self-identification undergo mutation, exhaustion, or renewal, these features of religious symbols have special interest. Of particular importance in connection with the latter is the way in which they lose touch

---

* This chapter is largely based on the author's book and is reprinted by permission of the publishers from Amos N. Wilder, *Theology and Modern Literature* (Cambridge, Massachusetts: Harvard University Press, Copyright 1958 by the President and Fellows of Harvard College).

99

with ongoing actuality and the consequences that follow both
for the symbol and for the society in question. Also of interest is
the new meaning that is often put into old religious symbols. In
such cases we may have a radical revision in the understanding
of the religious tradition, one which may be viewed ambiguously
as either "heresy" or reformation. It is hoped that the following
discussion of one of the major Christian symbols may illuminate
some of these considerations.

CHRIST AND THE PSYCHOLOGISTS

When poets and novelists deal with the Christ-story and the
scenes and personages of the Gospels, they unconsciously modern-
ize just as historians and theologians do and even more freely.
They see Christ in their own image or in the image of their pre-
ferred life-ideal and make the Gospels a sounding board for their
own philosophy and ethic. Churchmen do the same thing, but
they are to some extent controlled by their training in the evan-
gelical history and by their own particular patterns of sectarian
tradition. Such patterns, diverse and dated as they often are,
nevertheless rule out some forms of fanciful freewheeling.

There is, indeed, a sense in which every significant portrayal of
Christ must be a modernization. The "distance" between Nazareth and Detroit, between the first century and the twentieth,
must be bridged. But re-portrayal should not be betrayal. Christ
in modern dress is rarely convincing, though he has his incog-
nitos in all times. The best attempts to present him on the
modern scene are the most indirect, as in the case of Georges
Duhamel's superlative short story "Élévation et mort d'Armand
Branche."[3] Here we have an allusive suggestion of Christ in the
trenches in World War I which is all the more effective because
it is not pressed. But the poet-Christ of Renan or of William
Ellery Leonard, the antinomian oracle of Nietzsche and of Gide,
the "man of genius" of Middleton Murray, the "Comrade Jesus"
of some Marxists, the esoteric initiate of George Moore and now

of Robert Graves, and the pacifist-anarchist of Faulkner's *Fable:* all such are modernizations which only show how we are led to delineate the past (as the future), each in terms of his own contemporary urgency. The unhappy result of this perennial practice is that in every decade men instruct Christ as to what he was and is instead of allowing themselves to be instructed by him.

The literary interpreter of the life of Christ, as one who waives usually both the relevant historical study and the theological tradition, is doubly vulnerable to the contemporary *Zeitgeist* in all spiritual matters. As an intellectual this means that he is more or less captive to the particular reigning science and its popularizers: in the current situation, psychology. As Darwinism produced its interpreters of Jesus and his influence, so more recently Freudianism has done the same thing, usually in conjunction with the influence of Sir James Frazer. First came the clinical demonstrations of the insanity of Jesus which Albert Schweitzer answered definitely in his doctoral dissertation at Strasbourg. Then came the portrayals of the Nazarene healer as the first psychiatrist. More generally his saving death and resurrection have been fitted into a slot in this or that schema of redeemer-archetypes provided by cultural studies in myth and ritual, and so evacuated of any distinctive significance. The layman, including the most sophisticated philosophers and social scientists, notes that the terminology of seasonal fertility rites and the symbols of gnostic regeneration occur in the New Testament. But they have not recognized the decisive underlying difference between faith based on revelation through historical experience and religion based on nature or on nature and the soul. What the cosmos can tell us about ultimates—whether the constellations or the fertility-cycles of living forms—is very little compared with what man's social and moral experience can teach him. And what the psyche and the spirit can teach in whatever form of mysticism or seizure, exalting as it may be, is again little as compared with the tuition of the heart and its loyalties.

Thus the most common occasion for misconception of Christ today among intellectuals lies in the new psychology, especially in social psychology. This confusion is, however, abetted by the wide prevalence of morbid forms of Christianity which justify the social psychologist at many points.

These observations are preliminary to an examination of one modern literary presentation of Christ, that of the poet Robinson Jeffers in his poetic drama, *Dear Judas*.[4] We are interested here in one particular slant which the poet gives to the Gospel story, namely, his emphasis on suffering as the clue to the appeal of Christ and of Christianity. It is at this point that we may identify a preoccupation on the part of the interpreter derived from modern psychology. But we are also concerned with what to some extent justifies Jeffers' emphasis on this point: a widespread heresy of Christians evident in exaggeration of and even obsession with the Cross in its aspect of pain.

Through the centuries Christians have recurrently fallen into this kind of error. They have all too easily identified the Cross or the blood of Christ with mere suffering or let this motif play too large a part. What psychology sees on the one hand as masochism or on the other as sadism usurps an undue place in our understanding of the central event of Christianity. The consequences are seen in Christian art and ritual. Such a displacement of the real import of the Cross has its corollaries in various forms of sub-Christian asceticism, punitive attitudes or self-punishment, and orgiastic religious exercises. The dangers are not absent from forms of the faith which we think of as refined.

This question of the Christian's attitude to suffering is a fundamental one. What is at stake can be discussed in terms of contemporary literature. Jeffers presents the plausible but surely mistaken view—and the thesis in the work under examination can be found in his other writings—that Christ's empire over the hearts of men through the centuries rests upon the sheer fascination of agony and upon men's thinly veiled obsession with cruelty.

Yet this writer and others may be partly excused for this view in the light of a good deal of Christian history. In any case the topic looked at in literary works offers the possibility of some significant Christian discriminations.

A MODERN LUCRETIUS

We take *Dear Judas* as our main text but we may well give some prior attention to the work of this poet as a whole. Various factors combine to obscure the significance of his writing. Many readers are alienated by the violence and cruelty of the subject matter of his narrative poems. His unpopular political opinions openly voiced in his poetry have disaffected others. His art stands apart, moreover, from the kinds of poetry most appreciated in our period. Perhaps one feature of this isolation is to be found in his lack of inhibition in expressing a view and speaking in his own voice whether with respect to things political or more ultimate moralities. A reader of Jeffers should first free himself from any too limited definition of the art of verse, especially from the prestige of current critical opinion. He should then give his attention to the best of the narratives, which can be distinguished from those that are less successful. In the case of Jeffers this commonplace takes on a special importance. Finally the reader should allow himself to be interested in the philosophy of this poet, at least as an interesting option in our century for those who cannot accept the prevailing religious traditions but who are equally indisposed toward materialism and negation.

The position of Jeffers has, indeed, been identified with nihilism. This characterization is only proper if it is recognized that he only rejects and denies in order to carry out his main role of celebrant all the more effectively. His affirmation is in terms of a kind of cosmic mysticism which must be distinguished from all usual forms of pantheism, an attitude which he calls Inhumanism. The final appeal of his often perplexing narratives lies in their dramatization of triumph, triumph of some life-principle or world-principle through wounds, mutilation, and agony. The best of them take on the character, at least in their climaxes, of hymns of salvation.[5]

The reputation of this twentieth-century Cassandra waned after the twenties, when he won extravagant testimonies from a number of outstanding critics. Attention was again drawn to him after World War II by his version of the *Medea* of Euripides, which enjoyed a significant success in its New York production. A valuable new study of the poet has recently been published, *The Loyalties of Robinson Jeffers*, by Radcliffe Squires,[6] of the English Department of the University of Michigan. This book, to which we are particularly indebted, dissipates many confusions about this Californian Titan and his work, gives order to the various views that have been held about him and the influences that have been at work in his writing, draws clear lines between the better and the worse in the total output, and discusses reasonably the more controversial aspects of Jeffers' poetry and views.

There is no question that we have here an enormously talented writer and that as a figure in the cultural scene his stance and attitudes repay scrutiny. He illustrates the thesis that our nation will continue to produce its rebels and primitivists, its individualists of the frontiers (Jeffers identifies himself with "the West of the West") or the Big Woods or the Open Road, its new avatars of the American Adam uninitiated into law or church or restive under law and church, its Thoreaus and Whitmans, in every age. When this impulse is found in one so strongly marked with a Calvinist lineage it is doubly interesting. Radcliffe Squires' final category for Jeffers is that of a modern Lucretius, and this typing is illuminating especially as it identifies well both the kind of cosmic *mystique* which finds expression in him and his scientific and rationalist leanings.

This writer's narrative poems are filled with violent actions, with unnatural crimes and with disgust of civilization. He sees the disorder of his characters as a dramatization of our fallen condition. He proclaims his gospel of Inhumanism—the glory of inhuman things which we also may share. He states his case as follows:

It seems time that our race began to think as an adult does, rather than like an egocentric baby or insane person. This manner of thought and feeling is neither misanthropic nor pessimist, though two or three people have said so and may again. It involves no falsehoods, and is a means of maintaining sanity in slippery times; it has objective truth and human value. It offers a reasonable detachment as a rule of conduct, instead of love, hate and envy. It neutralizes fanaticism and wild hopes; but it provides magnificence for the religious instinct, and satisfies our need to admire greatness and rejoice in beauty.[7]

Jeffers' father was a professor of Old Testament literature in the Western Theological Seminary in Pittsburgh (Presbyterian). How many sons of talent born in the church have departed from the family faith in our time, yet always with some remaining indebtedness and distress! Jeffers' sonnet "To His Father"[8] contrasts movingly his own lacerated lot with the serenity of the parent:

> Christ was your lord and captain all your life,
> He fails the world but you he did not fail,
> He led you through all forms of grief and strife
> Intact, a man full-armed, he let prevail
> Nor outward malice not the worse-fanged snake,
> That coils in one's own brain against your calm,
> That great rich jewel well guarded for his sake
> With coronal age and death like quieting balm.
> I Father having followed other guides
> And oftener to my hurt no leader at all,
> Through years nailed up like dripping panther hides
> For trophies on a savage temple wall
> Hardly anticipate that reverend stage
> Of life, the snow-wreathed honor of extreme age.

Mr. Squires suggests that the grievous repudiation of what his father had stood for plays its part in the deeper imagery of the poems, especially that of "the destroying prodigal." The relation to the church today of its alienated sons is marked by ambivalence and is full of creative stress. Even when Jeffers writes what reads like a parody on the Gospel, namely his *Dear Judas,* it carries with it a profound homage to the Christ.

Like many agnostics of today, Jeffers' thought has been influenced by writers like Spengler. He sees the western world as well-advanced on a final phase of emptiness and internecine destruction. Civilization to him means death and has as its fruits both such sanguinary perversions and crimes of individuals as abound in his tales and modern war on a world scale as we have known it. His political poems castigate the loss of freedom and of deep-rooted religious integrity of the citizen. The poem "Shine, Perishing Republic"[9] offers a good illustration:

> But for my children, I would have them keep their
> distance from the thickening center; corruption
> Never has been compulsory, when the cities lie at
> the monster's feet there are left the mountains.
>
> And boys, be in nothing so moderate as in love of man,
> a clever servant, insufferable master.
> There is the trap that catches noblest spirits, that
> caught—they say—God, when he walked the earth.

In such passages we seem to hear the voice of the author's Calvinist father. The doctrine of the fall of man is indeed no stranger to modern literature. We know that in some disguise or other it recurs in writers like Faulkner, Eliot, Auden, and Robert Penn Warren. Recognition of the deceitfulness of the heart and its perennial masks of egotism is a condition of salvation, personal and political. This disabused view of man is one of the major distinctions between western Christendom and Communism. But it is important that the arraignment of man be based on our own self-knowledge rather than upon embittered contempt for others. And everything depends also upon how the Fall is understood—whether as a morbid dogma or as a realistic appraisal.

Jeffers appears to see the evil in the world as conditioned by cycles. We live in the fall of an age, though men are not therefore excusable. Salvation is to be attained by "escaping the net," by transcending the common lot. Symbols of the life of God are found in aspects of nature that are wild and magnificent, alien and untouched by man. For Jeffers, as for many men without religious belief in the usual sense, a door opens now and then beyond human disgust and anguish upon an august reality, an "all-heal," glimpsed especially in the ongoings of nature. The poems celebrate such moments with impressive power. For the rest, life is lived in a stoic endurance which purges itself not only of hatred and envy but also of the love of man. From the shorter lyrics or sketches, "Their Beauty Has More Meaning" [10] may be taken as representative.

> Yesterday morning enormous the moon hung low on the ocean,
> Round and yellow-rose in the glow of dawn;
> The night herons flapping home wore dawn on their wings.
>   Today
> Black is the ocean, black and sulphur the sky,
> And white seas leap. I honestly do not know which day is
>   more beautiful.
> I know that tomorrow or next year or in twenty years
> I shall not see these things—and it does not matter,
>   it does not hurt;
> They will be here. And when the whole human race
> Has been like me rubbed out, they will still be here: storms,
>   moon and ocean,
> Dawn and birds. And I say this: their beauty has more meaning
> Than the whole human race and the race of birds.

JEFFERS' *DEAR JUDAS*

Our main interest here, however, has to do with Jeffers' attitude toward Christ. We have seen in the poem "Shine, Perishing

Republic" that he refers to Christ as one who was caught, like
many of the "noblest spirits," in the trap of the love of man. In
Dear Judas we get the same theme. Jesus is caught by the love
of man. He thinks that as the Son of God he will be able to save
men by supernatural means. Lazarus, returned from the dead,
bids him disregard the lot of men, which will only involve him
in disaster. But Jesus perseveres. Lazarus, at the end of the poem,
says to Mary (page 48):

> Your son has done what men are not able to do;
> He has chosen and made his own fate. The Roman
>   Caesar will call your son his master and
>   his God; the floods
> That wash away Caesar and divide the booty,
>   shall worship your son. The unconjectured
>   selvages
> And closed orbits of the ocean ends of the earth
>   shall hear of him.

It is Judas' role in the poem to betray Christ lest he occasion a
Jewish uprising and a terrible Roman reprisal. Later Jesus com-
forts the conscious-stricken Judas by saying (page 39):

> Dear Judas, it is God drives us.
> It is not shameful to be duped by God. I have
>   known his glory in my lifetime, I
>   have *been* his glory, I know
> Beyond illusion the enormous beauty of the
>   torch in which our agonies and all
>   are particles of fire.

But it is Jeffers' final view, as stated in one of his shorter
poems,[11] that Christ's way, his "insane solution," had

> . . . stained an age; nearly two thousand years are
> one vast poem drunk with the wine of his blood.

This reminds us of a recurrent view that the idea of the crucifixion, so deeply lodged in the Western consciousness, has given the Western people a lust for blood. We meet this idea in Yeats; in his poem "The Second Coming," [12] for example:

> But now I know
> That twenty centuries of stony sleep
> Were vexed to nightmare by a rocking cradle.

And Yeats refers again to this theme in the lines we have cited in our praescript from "Two Songs from a Play": [13] *

> Odour of blood when Christ was slain
> Made all Platonic tolerance vain,
> And vain all Doric discipline.

Now what we have here is a very fundamental issue. There are not a few modern intellectuals who genuinely believe that Christianity, centering as it does in the Cross, has exerted its power by an appeal to, and indeed a secret stimulus to, man's hidden obsession with suffering and even blood-lust. They point to the popular piety and art forms of the centuries—crucifixes, paintings, and sculpture representing specifically the tortured Christ, as well as hymns, poems, and homilies dwelling in an ambigious way upon the blood of Christ. It is not surprising that such observers find it difficult to draw the line between the healthy and the morbid. Psychology appears to speak all too relevantly of masochism and sadism. Social psychology speaks of repressions and ritual compensations and of ancient archetypes of the atoning victim.

---

* Note the context of the lines: a new cycle of ages, a new *magnus annus*, is introduced by the death of Christ. This cycle is marked by "Galilean turbulence." The star of the Magi and the child of the "fierce virgin" initiate a sanguinary age of disorder:

> *The Babylonian starlight brought*
> *A fabulous, formless darkness in.*

On such a view the crucifixion of Christ, like a blasting vision, was so vividly implanted in the imagination of believers that it has had a morbid effect on his followers in all generations; it disturbed what Yeats calls "Platonic tolerance," or the natural sanity of the Hellenic and humanist ideal; it acted as a kind of social or cultural trauma in the life of the West. Among the sophisticated such a thesis would be related to deeper patterns of the scapegoat or sacrificial victim in ancient rites inspired by sanguinary delusions. The drama of the Cross would be seen as a main link in a long chain of enormities which testify to man's fatal propensity toward blood-lust or self-destruction.

It is not only in Yeats and Jeffers that one finds a connection established between the Cross and the sanguinary history of the Christian West. In Book VII of Elder Olson's cycle of poems, *The Cock of Heaven,* we read: [14]

> We think that this long night,
> This cold eclipse, is shade cast from Christ's cross.

And further:

Cries one, 'I study the hanged staring Man
    Strung like a hanged worm in spider-string;
    Foretell, thus, foulness; foul braves for Nero and Charlemagne,
Crowned Frederick, gowned Gregory, Dolfuss, Fey, Stalin.'

Jesus as presented in Jeffers' *Dear Judas* recognizes that the power over mankind which will be his will be achieved through suffering and men's secret affinity for cruelty (page 33):

Oh, power
Bought at the price of these hands and feet,—and all
    this body perishing in torture will pay—is holy.
Their minds love terror, their souls cry to be
    sacrificed for: pain's almost the God
Of doubtful men, who tremble expecting to
    endure it, their cruelty sublimed. And I
    think the brute cross itself

Hewn down to a gibbet now, has been worshipped;
  it stands yet for an idol of life and
  power in the dreaming
Soul of the world. . . .
  I frightfully
Lifted up drawing all men to my feet: I go a
  stranger passage to a greater dominion
More tyrannous, more terrible, more true, than
  Caesar or any subduer of the earth
  before him has dared to dream of.

And Christ predicts the "wasted valor of ten thousand martyrs"
that will come after him (page 38):

  And men will imagine hells
  and go mad with terror, for so I have
  feathered the arrows
Of persuasion with fire, and men will put out
  the eyes of their minds, lest faith
Become impossible being looked at, and their
  souls perish.

There are many who, like Jeffers, see in what they call Cross-tianity a morbid ideal. One finds another example in Bernard Shaw. In the little book he wrote about the Bible called *The Adventures of the Black Girl in Her Search for God*,[15] Shaw charges the disciples with superstition and a "masochist Puritanism" which prepared the way for "all the later horrors of the wars of religion, the Jew burnings of Torquemada" and other atrocities. The crucifixion of Jesus, moreover, had, as he writes (page 72) the

hideous result that the cross and the other instruments of his torture were made the symbols of the faith legally established in his name three hundred years later. They are still accepted as such throughout Christendom. The crucifixion thus became to the churches what the chamber of horrors is to a waxwork: the irresistible attraction for children and for the crudest adult worshippers.

The theologian is confronted in all such views with a major challenge. The scandal of the Cross is sharp enough without adding to it this unnecessary element. But there are undoubtedly many discerning men and women who misunderstand the Christian faith just at this point. They find it tainted with morbidity and they are abetted in their error by widely current Christian attitudes and practices. It is, of course, true that the Christian faith relates itself to a horrendous episode, the crucifixion of Jesus of Nazareth, and that the event carries shock and revulsion at many levels. It is true that there is a profound relation between the theme of vicarious sacrifice in the Gospel and ancient rites and myths dealing with expiation. It is true also that Christianity has its own proper forms of asceticism and world-denial.

But the theologian can also make clear that there is no proper foothold in the Christian story for man's persistent or recurrent morbidity, his impulse to give pain or to endure pain, his propensity for mortification and maceration. If such traits have attached themselves to Christianity in any of its forms, Catholic, Orthodox, or Protestant, they are excrescences. Most often they represent survivals of pre-Christian patterns, outcroppings of primitive legacies, or corruptions of Christian piety occasioned by contemporary cultural factors. Dr. John Mackay has well documented this fact in connection with Latin-American Catholic practices, as well as in some forms of Spanish Catholic art and mysticism. Writing about Miguel de Unamuno, he says: [16]

"[Unamuno] makes the luminous suggestion that in the Spanish religious tradition there have been two representative views of Christ. . . . One Christ is the 'Recumbent Christ of Palencia,' who is utterly dead; the other is the 'Crucified Christ of Velásquez,' who never ceases to agonize. The Recumbent Christ of Palencia . . . is an utterly dead figure, a veritable mass of death. The gruesome image represents Christ taken down from the cross, gory and pallid. 'This Christ . . . will never rise again.' On the other hand, there is in the Spanish religious tradition what Unamuno would call the *Agonizing Christ of Velásquez*. . . . His viewpoint recalls that of Pascal for whom Christ 'will continue to be in agony until the end of the world.' . . . The Christ of Velásquez, like the cross which Unamuno drew across his heart, is the symbol of his endless struggle. . . . As a follower of this Christ, he does not ask for light or peace, but only for water, water from the abyss, to give him strength to maintain the struggle. The only peace he asks for is 'peace in Christ's struggle,' 'peace in the midst of war'."*

The cases of Pascal and Unamuno (appealing to Velásquez) indicate that there is an irreproachable sense in which the suffering of Christ can be stressed and even be viewed as lasting to the end of time. As one moment or station in the contemplation of Christ this concentration on the agony may be seen as essentially Christian, provided always that it gives way promptly to the theme of resurrection and victory. A hyperbolic or baroque artistic expression of this moment of the agony may well be expected in the Spanish mystical tradition. At the same time, such forms of piety are overstrained and easily pass over into forms that are more than suspect, as is evident in other aspects of Spanish Catholicism and especially in Latin America. The Passion of Christ ended on Good Friday. No doubt the Risen and Triumphant Christ shares in the continuing struggle of the Church Militant and the martyrs. The deeper sense of this interpretation is that God himself is not impassible but is "afflicted with all our afflictions." But the secret of the suffering of the Christian according to the New Testament is that this suffering is indissolubly merged with joy: "suffering but always rejoicing," what Luther called *Kreuzseeligkeit*. To leave this out is to fall back into heathenism and into the "sorrow of the world" which "worketh death." "For as we share abundantly in Christ's sufferings, so through Christ we share abundantly in comfort too."

* The references are to Unamuno's essay "The Spanish Christ" in his volume, *Perplexities and Paradoxes*, 1945, and to his poem *"The Christ of Velasquez."*

One consideration is highly important here. The accounts of the passion of Christ in the Gospels themselves are devoid of any sentimental or morbid features. The evangelists do not present the episodes of Christ's last hours in such a way as to harrow or exacerbate the feelings of the reader. The scenes are presented with a great austerity. This is related to the fact that the Gospels are not biographies or martyrologies or even tragedies. Their purpose is not to set forth the death of a hero or a martyr. They portray a divine transaction whose import far transcends the feelings of the protagonist or the sensibilities of the observer. What is important for the evangelists is the revelation mediated —the operation of God in the event—not the poignancies of the occasion.

Modern sentiment loves to linger over the crown of thorns or the flagellation. But our best understanding of Koine Greek usage today makes it doubtful whether the plant in question, the *akantha*, had any sharp spines. The crown of acanthus was placed on the head of Jesus, just as the purple robe and mock scepter were used, for purposes of ridicule, not to inflict pain. This was the garb of royalty. As for the flagellation, it is mentioned only in a passing phrase. The interest of the evangelist here is in the fulfillment of prophecy and in the due preliminaries of Roman crucifixion.

Thus the primary Christian sources show the way. The Cross of Christ should be a fountain of health and not of morbidity. The representation of the passion of Christ in art should not encourage the gratification with pain which is so widely evident in certain forms of Latin American art forms. The blood of Christ should not be dwelt on in cult or hymn or sermon in such a way as to feed men's regressive impulses toward excitement and self-mortification, as in some forms of Protestant orgiastic practice.

There is indeed a deep mystery in the Cross, and the agony of Christ is related to the law of suffering which runs through the whole story of life, human and subhuman. Here is one aspect of the fascination that the Cross exerts upon all beholders. This is one meaning of the words: "I, if I be lifted up, will draw all men unto me." A God without wounds can never hold men long. Robinson Jeffers recognizes this scarlet thread of blood and agony that runs through all of life. For him it is the lot even of those who escape the net of life and attain the "tower beyond tragedy."

Properly understood, the death of Christ, and blood of Christ, cannot evoke what Yeats calls turbulence and intolerance in the sequel. The only shadow that the Cross casts over history is one of shelter and asylum. If the legacy of the crucifixion has been compounded with sanguinary delusions in the annals of mankind, the fault is not with the Gospel. And in rejecting such perverted versions of Christianity, modern skepticism may play a useful part.

REFERENCES

1. From *The Collected Poems of W. B. Yeats* (New York: The Macmillan Company, 1937), p. 246. Reprinted by permission of the publishers.
2. New York: The Macmillan Company, 1940, p. 57.
3. Paris: Grasset, 1919.
4. From *Dear Judas and Other Poems* by Robinson Jeffers. Copyright 1929 and renewed 1957 by Robinson Jeffers. Reprinted by permission of Random House, Inc.
5. *Cf.* my previous discussion of Jeffers: "The Nihilism of Robinson Jeffers," in *Spiritual Aspects of the New Poetry* (New York: Harper and Brothers, 1940), chap. XII.
6. Ann Arbor, Mich.: The University of Michigan Press, 1956. For Squires' discussion of *Dear Judas* see especially pp. 96-102, 123-25.
7. Reprinted by permission of Random House, Inc. from the introduction to *The Double Axe and Other Poems* by Robinson Jeffers. Copyright 1948 by Robinson Jeffers.
8. Reprinted by permission of Random House, Inc. from *The Selected Poetry of Robinson Jeffers*. Copyright 1938 by Robinson Jeffers.
9. Reprinted by permission of Random House, Inc. from *Roan Stallion, Tamar and Other Poems* by Robinson Jeffers. Copyright renewed 1951 by Robinson Jeffers.
10. Reprinted by permission of Random House, Inc. from *The Double Axe and Other Poems* by Robinson Jeffers. Copyright 1948 by Robinson Jeffers.
11. "The Theory of Truth." Reprinted by permission of Random House, Inc. from *The Selected Poetry of Robinson Jeffers*. Copyright 1938 by Robinson Jeffers.
12. From *The Collected Poems of W. B. Yeats*, p. 215. Reprinted by permission of the publishers.
13. *Ibid.*, p. 246.
14. New York: The Macmillan Company, 1940; Book VII, iv, p. 57. Reprinted by permission of the author.
15. New York: Dodd, Mead & Company, Inc., 1933. Reprinted by

arrangement with the Public Trustee and The Society of Authors, London, England.

16. John Mackay, "Miguel de Unamuno," in Carl Michalson (ed.), *Christianity and the Existentialists* (New York: Charles Scribner's Sons, 1956), pp. 51-53. Reprinted by permission of the publishers.

4. On the First Three Chapters of Genesis

KENNETH BURKE

IF WE *set up a cycle of terms that tautologically imply one another, there is no one proper "progression" among them. They forever turn back upon themselves in endless circularity. In contrast, the terms of a narrative follow one another in one fixed, irreversible, rectilinear sequence. This essay considers the relations between such "circular" and "rectilinear" kinds of terminology. To that end, the Creation Myth at the opening of Genesis is taken as the paradigm of a narrative, or "rectilinear" terminology. And it is compared with a "circular" list of terms implicit in the idea of "Order."*

This is the third of "Three Talks on 'Logology'" which the author is now developing into a book on the subject. The first, "On Words and The Word," deals with six major analogies between words conceived secularly and The Word conceived theologically. The second, on "Verbal Action in St. Augustine's Confessions," analyzes Augustine's development from a teacher of pagan rhetoric (What he calls a "word merchant," venditor verborum) to a preacher of The Word. And quite as the Confessions ends on the study of Genesis, so our third essay makes this same turn except that the distinction between "time" and "eternity" is here treated in its analogous form, as the distinction between the unfolding of a sentence through the materials of its parts, and the unitary, nonmaterial essence or meaning of the sentence (an analogy which Augustine himself draws).

We lay great stress upon the sacrificial principle in the idea of Order because the contemporary world must doubly fear the cyclical compulsions of Empire, as two mighty world orders, each homicidally armed to the point of suicide, confront each other. As with dominion always,

118

each is much beset with anxiety. And in keeping with the "curative" role of victimage, each is apparently in acute need of blaming all its many troubles on the other, wanting to feel certain that, if but the other were eliminated, all governmental discord (all the Disorder that goes with Order) would be ended.

The author would propose to replace the present political stress upon men in rival international situations by a "logological" reaffirmation of the foibles and quandaries that all men (in their role as "symbol-using animals") have in common.

INTRODUCTION: ON COVENANT AND ORDER

WE WANT so to relate the ideas of Creation, Covenant, and Fall that they can be seen to implicate one another inextricably, along with ideas of Sacrifice and Redemption.

Creation implies authority in the sense of originator, the designer or author of the things created.

Covenant implies authority in the sense of power, sovereignty—the highest or more radical sovereignty in case the Covenant is made by God.

The possibility of a "Fall" is implied in the idea of a Covenant insofar as the idea of a Covenant implies the possibility of its being violated. One does not make a covenant with stones or trees or fire—for such things cannot break agreements or defy commands, since they cannot even understand agreements or commands.

Also, the possibility of a "Fall" is implied in the idea of the Creation, insofar as the Creation was a kind of "divisiveness," since it set up different categories of things which could be variously at odds with one another and which accordingly lack the proto-Edenic simplicity of absolute unity. Thus Coleridge observes (*Table Talk*, May 1, 1830):

A Fall of some sort or other—the creation, as it were, of the non-absolute—is the fundamental postulate of the moral history of man. Without this hypothesis, man is unintelligible; with it, every phenomenon is explicable. The mystery itself is too profound for human insight.

Though this may be a mystery theologically, its logological analogue is not mysterious. Logologically, there is a "fall" from a prior state of unity whenever some one term is broken into two or more terms, so that we have the "divisiveness" of "classification" where we formerly had had a "vision of perfect oneness." If the title of a book could be said to sum up the nature of that book, then the breakdown of the book into parts, chapters, paragraphs, sentences, words would be technically a "fall" from the Edenic unity of the title, or epitomizing "god-term." The parts of the book reduce its "idea" to "matter." Or, as Coleridge said (*Table Talk*, October 15, 1833): "The Trinity is the Idea: the Incarnation, which implies the Fall, is the Fact: the redemption is the mesothesis of the two—that is—the Religion."

Presumably he is thinking of "religion" here in the sense of *religare* (to bind, connect, fasten)—and the logological analogue to his theory in this instance would concern our way of tying the particulars of a work together in accordance with the over-all spirit signalized by its unitary and unifying title.

Narratively, there was the Creation; then came the "Edenic" Covenant (which included the injunction against eating of the tree of the knowledge of good and evil); then the Fall; and then the "Adamic" Covenant (III, 14-19), which included punishments for Adam's first disobedience. But though this order is irreversible from the standpoint of narrative, there is a sense in which we can reverse the order. For instance, we could "begin" with the idea of a punishment; next we could note that the idea of punishment implies the idea of some infraction which makes the punishment relevant; and such infraction implies the need for a set of conditions that make the infraction possible; and insofar as we looked for a "first" set of such conditions, the idea of them would imply the idea of the kind of Creation that allowed for disobedience.

Again, in the idea of punishment we might discern another kind of implication. Punishment being a kind of "payment" for wrong, we can see flickering about the edges of the idea of punishment the idea of redemption. To "pay" for one's wrongdoing by suffering punishment is to "redeem" oneself, to cancel one's debt, to ransom, or "buy back."

Next, since the idea of an agent is implicit in the idea of an act, we can say that in the idea of redemption there is implicit the idea of a personal redeemer. Or, if you think of redemption as a condition or situation (a "scene"), then you may extract the same implication by thinking of a redeemer as an instrument, or agency, for bringing about the condition. And this step, you will note, automatically includes the idea of a substitution: the possibility that one character may be redeemed through the act or agency of another.

The idea of such substitution, or vicarage, neatly parallels at one end of the series an idea at the other: the notion that, as one character can redeem another by suffering in his stead, so one character can impute guilt to another by sinning in his stead. This would be true of the Pauline logic whereby Adam's disobedience represents a guiltiness in Everyman with regard to Covenants ("In Adam's fall / We sinned all") and there is introduced a principle of representation whereby a "second Adam" can serve as sacrificial substitute for mankind when the categorical guiltiness is being "paid for."

More specifically, the conditions for such a doctrine of "original sin" are set up when our "first" parent who commits the crucial sin has a name at once individual and generic, a name that can be translated either as "Adam" or as "man." Thus, in his sin as "Adam," he can personate mankind in general. We shall later consider other ways in which the purely narrative style operates here, but this shift between individual and generic should be enough for the moment.

The other six great Covenants mentioned in the Bible are the Noachian, Abrahamic, Mosaic, Palestinian, Davidic, and New (as in Hebrews VIII, 8). But the two mentioned in the first three chapters (the Edenic and the Adamic) are sufficient for our purposes, except that the step from punishment to redemption is tenuous. There are the ceremony of redemption by vicarious atonement in connection with the feast of the Passover (Exodus XII) and the sacrificial slaying of the goat set apart for Azazel (Leviticus XVI). Earlier, the principle of a personal redeemer was clearly present in Abraham's offering of Isaac (Genesis XXII). And as early as Genesis VIII, 20-21 (in connection with the third Covenant), Noah makes burnt offerings "of every clean fowl" (whereat the Lord "smelled a sweet savour" and "said in his heart, I will not again curse the ground any more for man's sake").

Though the idea of a redemptive sacrifice is clear enough as regards the Biblical idea of a Covenant in general, it is but inchoately there as regards the two Covenants in the first three chapters of Genesis. We have tried to argue for its implicit presence by showing that the idea of redemption is a further stage in the idea of punishment, and the idea of a redeemer (hence, of vicarious atonement) is implicit in the idea of redemption. And as regards our over-all concern (with the notion that the idea of a redeemer is implicit in the idea of a Covenant in general), the later developments of the Bible itself with relation to God's "peculiar people" make this relation clear enough.

But I might add, incidentally, that one Bible I happen to be consulting, *The Scofield Reference Bible*, professes to find "the first promise of a Redeemer" in Genesis III, 15, where the Lord God, in cursing the serpent for having tempted Eve, decrees: "And I will put enmity between thee and the woman, and between thy seed and her seed; and it shall bruise thy head, and thou shalt bruise his heel." The editor asserts that here begins "the highway of the Seed," which he traces through Abel, Seth, Noah (Genesis VI, 8-10), Shem (Genesis IX, 26-27), Abraham (Genesis XII, 1-4), Isaac (Genesis XVII, 19-21), Jacob (Genesis XXVIII, 10-14), Judah (Genesis XLIX, 10), David (2 Samuel VII, 5-17), Immanuel-Christ (Isaiah VII, 9-14; Matthew I, 1, 20-23; 1

John III, 8; John XII, 31). Thus, however strained the point may seem, it should apply insofar as there is a continuity between the idea of temptation and the idea of a redeemer when this continuity is expressed in terms of a continuity of "the Seed," from the locus of "original sin" to the locus of its cancellation by redemptive sacrifice. Or, otherwise put: the hereditary line here listed would represent at every stage a contact with the principle of a Covenant, and the principle of a Covenant contains within itself the principles of both temptation (on the part of one who might break the Covenant) and "repayment" (or "redemption") insofar as the aggrieved party is willing to impose and accept a fine or forfeit. (The thought, incidentally, suggests how the ideas of "justice" and "mercy" will also be found implicit in the idea of a Covenant—"justice" being but the idea of a proper repayment and "mercy" the "good" word for the idea of a willingness to accept a repayment that in some notable respect is disproportionate to the gravity of the offense.)

In Rashi's *Commentary on the Pentateuch,* with regard to the opening formula ("In the beginning") another commentator is quoted to this effect: The main object of the Law (or Torah) being to teach commandments *(mitzvoth),* if this were the only consideration involved the Bible could have begun with the second verse of Exodus XII ("This month shall be unto you the beginning of months: it shall be the first month of the year to you"). Notably for our purposes, the passage he mentions deals with the rite of the paschal lamb sacrificed at Passover, and thus contains the thought that in a notable respect this book of beginnings might have begun with the principle of sacrifice.

For our purposes, this is a most important consideration. For we are to deal above all with "firsts" (or "principles"). More specifically, we are to be concerned with the "firsts" or "principles" of Covenants. And we are to be on the lookout for the important role played by the sacrificial principle in the cycle of terms that cluster about the idea of a Covenant. So it is notable that the

most famous Jewish commentary on Genesis begins by considering a possible alternative first, one having to do with the insti-
tuting of a sacrifice as regards the Lord's governmental contract
with his chosen people.

However, we are told in the Rashi commentary that the Bible
begins as it does rather than with the establishing of a paschal
ceremony because the first words of Genesis, by showing all the
world to be the property of God, make clear Israel's rights to
seize the lands of the Canaanites, since God could dispose of his
property as he chose, and he chose to give the lands of Canaan
to the Israelites. (Incidentally, there is a sense in which the
beginning of Genesis as we now have it would be the proper
"pre-first," even for the commentator's claim: it sets up the conditions of division and dominion necessary for the idea of a
Covenant by which Canaan became a promised land.)

Rashi also cites a rabbinical interpretation to the effect that
God created the world for the sake of the Law (the Torah). And
in connection with this position (as against the notion that the
Bible is attempting to say what came first in time), he notes that
there were waters before the creating of heaven and earth. (Also,
the very word for "heavens" is a combination of words for "fire"
and "water.")

Rashi is interested in bringing out the notion that the world
was created by God not solely to the ends of justice, but first of
all to the ends of mercy combined with justice. As regards our
cycle of the terms implicit in the idea of a Covenant, we need
but note that the ideas of both justice and mercy are present in
the idea of repayment for the breaking of a contract (justice when
the penalty is proportionate to the offense, mercy when the penalty is favorably disproportionate, while injustice would involve
a penalty unfavorably disproportionate).

As regards Rashi's questioning of the notion that the Creation
story in Genesis is dealing strictly with firsts in time, we should
find his reservations logologically much to our purposes. Logo-

logically, Genesis would be interpreted as dealing with principles (with logical "firsts," rather than sheerly temporal ones). From the very start it is dealing with the principles of governance (firsts expressed in quasi-temporal terms, since they are the kind most natural to the narrative style). That is, the account of the Creation should be interpreted as saying in effect: This is, in principle, a statement of what the natural order must be like if it is to fit perfectly the conditions of human socio-political order (conditions that come to a focus in the idea of a basic Covenant backed by a perfect authority).

To get the point, turn now to Pope's line, "Order is Heaven's first law." In Pope's formula, the idea of a "first" is ambiguous. The reader is not quite sure (nor need he be) whether it means first in time, or first in importance, or first in the sense of a logical grounding for all other laws, a kind of "causal ancestor" from which all other "laws" could be deduced or derived as lineal descendants.

Once we have brought out the strategic importance of the part played by the Biblical stress upon the idea of Covenant, there are advantages to be gained by locating our cycle of dramatistic terms about the term "Order" rather than about the term "Covenant."

The most general starting point for the dramatistic cycle of terms would be in the term "act." Under this head would belong God's creative acts in the first chapter of Genesis, God's enactment of the first Covenant (largely permissive, but with one crucial negative command), Adam's act of disobedience, and God's enactment of a second Covenant imposing penalties upon all mankind.

Also, of course, there would be terms for the many kinds of "rationally" purposive motion, along with their corresponding "passions," which characterize human life in all its aspects. These would be without such stress upon "sin" or "guilt" as necessarily arises when we deal with the story of a first temptation. But for this very reason, such a general approach to a dramatistic cycle of terms would not serve our present purpose. Frankly, it would not be morbid enough. We need an approach that, like the Bible itself, leads us from a first Adam, in whom all vicariously "sinned," to a "second Adam" by whom all might vicariously make atonement. For we are trying to analyze the respects in which the ideas of both guilt and redemption by vicarious sacrifice are intrinsic to the idea of a Covenant (which in turn is intrinsic to the idea of governance).

Yet the term "Covenant" is not wholly convenient for our purposes. Having no opposite in standard usage, it seems as purely "positive" as words like "stone," "tree," or "table," which are not matched by companion words like "counter-stone," "anti-tree," or "un-table" (except sometimes in the dialectic of E. E. Cummings). And perhaps the notion of "positive law" secretly contributes to one's feeling that "Covenants" can be treated as "positive," despite the all-importance of the negative in defining the conditions of Adam's fall. The term "Order," on the other hand, clearly reveals its dialectical or "polar" nature on its face. "Order" implies "disorder" and vice versa. And that is the kind of term we need.

However, when putting it in place of the word "Covenant," we should try never to forget Hobbes's emphasis upon the severities of sovereignty as integral to the kind of Order we shall be studying. The idea of "Order" is ambiguous not only in the sense that it contains an idea of "Disorder." The term "Order" is ambiguous also because it can be applied to two quite different areas, either to such natural regularities as tides and seasons or to socio-political structures in which people can give or receive orders, in which orders can be obeyed or disobeyed, in which offices are said to pyramid in an orderly arrangement of powers and responsibilities. The double notion of God's authority (in his roles as both originator and sovereign) obviously combines both of these meanings. It joins the idea of the creative verbal fiats by which

God brought the natural order into existence and the idea of a divine ruler laying down the law by words, in keeping with Hobbes's stout statement: "He only is properly said to reign, that governs his subjects by his word, and by promise of rewards to those that obey it, and by threatening them with punishment that obey it not."

Our task, then, is to examine the term "Order" by asking what cluster of ideas is "tautologically" present in the idea of Order. Such a cycle of terms follows no one sequence. That is, we may say either that the idea of Disorder is implicit in the idea of Order or that the idea of Order is implicit in the idea of Disorder. Or we might say that the idea of Order implies the ideas of Obedience and Disobedience, or that either of them implies the other, or that either or both imply the idea of an Order, and so on.

However, when such terministic interrelationships are embodied in the narrative style (involving acts, images, and personalities) an irreversibility of the sequence can become of major importance. For instance, the implications of a story that proceeds from order to disorder (or from obedience to disobedience) differ greatly from those of a story that proceeds in the other direction. We may say that "success" and "failure" imply each other, without equating the step from success to failure with the step from failure to success. There are also paradoxical complications whereby, for instance, a step from success to failure in some respects is at the same time a step from failure to success in other respects. And there is the possibility of a story so self-consistent in structure that an analyst could, ideally, begin at the end and deductively "prophesy" what earlier developments must have taken place for things to culminate as they did. But such considerations merely subtilize the narrative or temporal principle of irreversibility; they do not eliminate it.

The plan, then, is first to evolve a cluster of interrelated key terms implicit in the idea of "Order." Then we shall ask how the narrative, or "rectilinear," style of Genesis compares with the "cycle of terms" we have found to revolve "endlessly" about the idea of "Order." And, finally, we shall draw some conclusions from the comparison of the two styles (the "timeless" terministic cluster and the kind of "temporal" sequence embodied in the Biblical myth). The distinction is one touched upon by Coleridge ("Idea of the Prometheus of Aeschylus," in Volume IV of the Shedd edition of his *Complete Works*), where he speaks of the Biblical method as "sacred narrative" and "Hebrew archæology," in contrast with Greek "philosopheme."

TAUTOLOGICAL CYCLE OF TERMS FOR "ORDER"*

First, consider the strategic ambiguity whereby the term "Order" may apply both to the realm of nature in general and to the special realm of human socio-political organizations (an ambiguity whereby, so far as sheerly empirical things are concerned, a natural order could be thought to go on existing even if all human beings, with their various socio-political orders, were obliterated). This is a kind of logical pun whereby our ideas of the natural order can become secretly infused by our ideas of the socio-political order.

One might ask: Is not the opposite possibility just as likely? Might not the terms for the socio-political order become infused by the genius of the terms for the natural order? They do, every time we metaphorically extend the literal meaning of a natural image to the realm of the socio-political. It is the point that Bentham made much of in his Theory of Fictions, his systematic procedure ("archetypation") for locating the natural images that may lurk undetected in our ideas and so may mislead us into attempting to deal too strictly in terms of the irrelevant image.

* When reading this chapter and later references to the same subject, the reader might find it helpful to consult the chart on page 131 outlining the terministic conditions for "Original Sin" and "Redemption" (intrinsic to the idea of "Order").

For instance, if Churchillian rhetoric gets us to thinking of international relations in such terms as "iron curtains" and "power vacuums," then we must guard lest we respond to the terms too literally—otherwise we shall not conceive of the political situation accurately enough. The Arab nations are no "vacuum." Theologians have made similar observations about the use of natural images to express the idea of godhead.

But it is much more important for our present purposes to spot the movement in the other direction. We need to stress how a vision of the natural order can become infused with the genius of the verbal and socio-political orders.

Thus, from the purely logological point of view we note how, inasmuch as the account of the Creation in Genesis involves on each "day" a kind of enactment done through the medium of God's "Word," the sheerly "natural" order contains a verbal element or principle that from the purely empirical point of view could belong only in the socio-political order. Empirically, the natural order of astrophysical motion depends upon no verbal principle for its existence. But theologically it does depend upon a verbal principle. And even though one might say that God's creative fiats and his words to Adam and Eve are to be conceived as but analogous to ordinary human verbal communication, our point remains the same. For from the empirical point of view, there would not even be an analogy between natural origins and responses to the power of words. The world of natural, nonverbal motions must be empirically the kind of world that could continue with its motions even if it contained no species, such as man, capable of verbal action: and it must be described without any reference to a Creation by verbal fiat, whether or not there had been such.

By a dramatistic ambiguity, standard usage bridges this distinction between the realms of verbal action and nonverbal motion when it speaks of sheerly natural objects or processes as "actualities." Here even in a purely secular usage we can discern a trace

of the theological view that sees nature as the sign of God's action
—and thus by another route we see the theological way of merg-
ing the principle of the natural order with the principle of verbal
contract or covenant intrinsic to legal enactment in the socio-
political order.

But to proceed with the "tautologies":

If, by "Order," we have in mind the idea of a command, then
obviously the corresponding word for the proper response would
be "Obey." Or there would be the alternative, "Disobey." Thus
we have the proportion: Order is to Disorder as Obedience is to
Disobedience. However, there is a logological sense in which the
things of nature could be called "innocent." They cannot disobey
commands, since they cannot understand commands. They do
not have a "sense of right and wrong" or, more generically, a
"sense of yes and no." They simply do as they do—and that's that.
Such would be the *non posse peccare* of natural things or even of
humans insofar as their "natural" state was not bound by moralistic negatives. All was permissive in Eden but the eating of the
one forbidden fruit, the single negative that set the conditions for
the Fall (since, as St. Paul pointed out, only the law can make sin,
as Bentham was later to point out that only the law can make
crime). The Biblical myth pictures natural things as coming
into being through the agency of God's Word; but they can
merely do as they are told, whereas with God's permission,
though not without his resentment, the seed of Adam can do
even what it has been explicitly told not to do. The word-using
animal not only understands a thou-shalt-not; it can carry the
principle of the negative a step further, and answer the thou-
shalt-not with a disobedient No. Logologically, the distinction
between natural innocence and fallen man hinges about this
problem of language and the negative. Eliminate language from
nature and there can be no moral disobedience. In this sense,
moral disobedience is "doctrinal." Like faith, it is grounded in
language.

God as Author & Authority

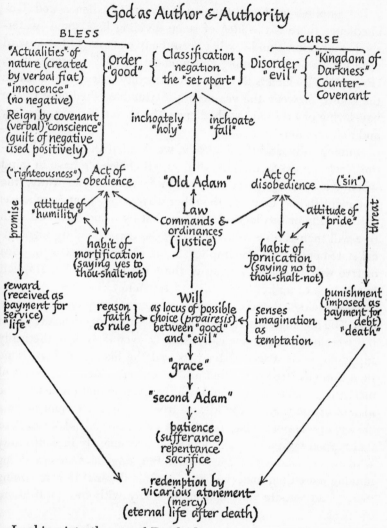

BLESS   CURSE

"Actualities" of nature (created by verbal fiat) "innocence" (no negative)

Reign by covenant (verbal) "conscience" (guilt of negative used positively)

Order "good" { Classification negation the "set apart" } Disorder "evil" { "Kingdom of Darkness" Counter-Covenant

inchoately "holy"   inchoate "fall"

("righteousness") Act of obedience   "Old Adam"   Act of disobedience ("sin")

promise   attitude of "humility"   Law Commands & ordinances (justice)   attitude of "pride"   threat

habit of mortification (saying yes to thou-shalt-not)   habit of fornication (saying no to thou-shalt-not)

reward (received as payment for service) "life"   reason faith as rule } Will as locus of possible choice (proairesis) between "good" and "evil" { senses imagination as temptation   punishment (imposed as payment for debt) "death"

"grace"

"second Adam"

patience (sufferance) repentance sacrifice

redemption by vicarious atonement (mercy) (eternal life after death)

Looking into the act of Disobedience, we come upon the need for some such term as "Pride" to name the corresponding attitude that precedes the act. And some such term as "Humility" names the idea of the attitude that leads into the act of Obedience.

But implicit in the distinction between Obedience and Disobedience there is the idea of some dividing line, some "watershed" that is itself midway between the two slopes. Often a word used for naming this ambiguous moment is "Will" or, more fully, "Free Will," which is thought of as a faculty that makes possible the choice between the yea-saying of Humble Obedience or the nay-saying of Prideful Disobedience (the choice between *serviam* and *non serviam*).

Ontologically, and theologically, we say that this locus of freedom makes possible the kind of personal choice we have in mind when we speak of "Action." But note that, logologically, the statement should be made the other way round. That is, whereas ontologically or theologically we say that by being endowed with free will man is able to act morally, the corresponding logological statement would be: Implicit in the idea of an act is the idea of free will. (Another version of the formula would be: Implicit in the idea of an act is the idea of freedom.)

The ontological and theological statements may or may not be true. The logological statement would be "true logologically" even if it were not true ontologically. That is, even if we hypothetically supposed, with strict behaviorists and the like, that there is no such thing as "free will," that all "action" is reducible to terms of mechanical "motion," it would still remain true that implicit in the idea of action there is the idea of freedom. If one cannot make a choice, one is not acting, one is but being moved, like a billiard ball tapped with a cue and behaving mechanically in conformity with the resistances it encounters. But even if men are doing nothing more than that, the word "act" implies that they are doing more—and we are now concerned solely with the implications of terms.

As regards the dramatistic tautology in general, an act is done by an agent in a scene. But such an act is usually preceded by a corresponding attitude, or "incipient act" (as when an act of friendliness follows a friendly attitude on the part of the agent).

The scene is the motivational locus of the act insofar as the act represents a scene-act ratio (as, for instance, when an "emergency situation" is said to justify an "'emergency measure"). But as the act derives from an attitude of the agent, the agent-act ratio can be narrowed to an attitude-act ratio, as when a friendly agent does a friendly act. The term "Will" is apparently designed to assign a "place" to the choice between different possibilities of attitude-act development. Here a verb is thought of as a noun; the idea of "the will" as willing is conceived after the analogy of rain raining, though we do not speak of fear as fearing. But the idea of such a locus for "the Will" brings up a further problem: What in turn influences "the Will"?

On the Disorder side, this role is assigned to the Imagination, insofar as the imagination's close connection with sensory images is thought both to make it highly responsive to the sensory appetites and to make sensory appetites more enticing. In brief, the combination of Imagination and the Senses, by affecting the Will from the side of Disorder, is said to predispose toward Temptation, except as Imagination in turn is corrected from the side of Order by the controls of Reason and Faith (which can also be thought of as having a controlling effect upon each other). Another refinement here is the notion that, once Imagination is on the side of Reason, it can contribute to Order, rather than to Disorder, by making reasonable things seem sensible and thus inducing the Wills of persons weak in Reason to none the less freely choose, as it were, reasonably and thus to act on the side of Order, eschewing Temptation.

The idea of Reason in such a system is obviously permeated with ideas of Dominion, owing to its identification with ideas of control and as indicated in the formula, "the Rule of Reason." So it brings us clearly back to the principle of sovereignty underlying the general idea of Order by Covenant. The relation between Reason and Faith becomes ambiguous because of the possible shift between the natural order and the socio-political order as grounds of Reason. For if the socio-political Order is conceived in "ultimate" terms (as it is in the idea of a Covenant derived from God), then Faith must be a kind of control higher than Reason, insofar as Reason is identified with "Natural Law" and with purely worldly rules of governance. (Incidentally, we might note the strongly verbal element in both, as indicated by the close relation between Rational and Logical and by St. Paul's statement that the doctrines of the Faith are learned "by hearing." However, there is said to be a further stage of supernatural awareness, called by St. Anselm *contemplatio* and by Spinoza *scientia intuitiva*, which would by definition transcend the verbal.)

There is also an act-agent ratio, as with the Aristotelian notion of *hexis, habitus*, the notion that a person may develop a virtuous Disposition by the practices of virtue or a vicious Disposition by repeated indulgence in vice. And this brings us to the subtlest term of all as regards the set of major dramatistic terms clustering about the idea of Order; namely, Mortification.

Of all theology-tinged terms that need logological reclamation and refurbishment, this is perhaps the most crucial. Here the motives of sacrifice and dominion come to a head in everyday living. The possibility is that most ailments now said to be of "psychogenic" origin are but secularized variants of what might be called "mortification in spite of itself." That is, if we are right in assuming that governance makes "naturally" for victimage, either of others (homicidally) or of ourselves (suicidally), then we may expect to encounter many situations in which a man, by attitudes of self-repression, often causes or aggravates his own bodily and mental ills.

The derived meaning (humiliation, vexation, chagrin) would figure here. But mainly we have in mind the Grand Meaning, "subjection of the passions and appetites, by penance, abstinence, or painful severities inflicted on the body," mortification as a kind of governance, an extreme form of "self-control," the deliberate, disciplinary "slaying" of any motive that, for "doctrinal" reasons, one thinks of as unruly. In an emphatic way, mortification is the exercising of oneself in "virtue"; it is a systematic way of saying no to Disorder, or obediently saying yes to Order. Its opposite is license, *luxuria*, "fornication," saying yes to Disorder, no to Order.

The principle of Mortification is particularly crucial to conditions of empire, which act simultaneously to awaken all sorts of odd and exacting appetites, while at the same time imposing equally odd and exacting obstacles to their fulfillment. For "mortification" does not occur when one is merely "frustrated" by some external interference. It must come from within. The mortified must, with one aspect of himself, be saying no to another aspect of himself—hence the urgent incentive to be "purified" by "projecting" his conflict upon a scapegoat, by seeking a sacrificial vessel upon which he can vent, as from without, a turmoil that is actually within. "Psychogenic illness" would occur in cases in which one was scrupulous enough to deny himself such easy outgoing relief and, instead, in all sorts of roundabout ways, scrupulously circled back upon himself, unintentionally making his own constitution the victim of his hierarchally goaded entanglements.

To complete the pattern: On the side of Order, where the natural actualities created by verbal fiat are completed in sovereignty and subjection by Covenant, with Obedience goes promise of reward (as payment for service), while on the other side goes Disobedience, with threat of punishment as enforced payment for disservice.

Then comes the Grand Rounding Out, where the principle of reward as payment (from the Order side) merges with the principle of punishment as payment (from the Disorder side), to promise of redemption by vicarious atonement. Sovereignty and subjection (the two poles of governance) are brought together in the same figure (Christ as King and Christ as Servant, respectively)—and the contradiction between these principles is logically resolved by a narrative device, the notion of two advents whereby Christ could appear once as servant and the second time as king. Here is the idea of a "perfect" victim to cancel (or "cover") what was in effect the "perfect" sin (its technical perfection residing in the fact that it was the first transgression of the first man against the first and foremost authority).

However, the symmetry of the design does not resolve the problem of the "watershed moment," the puzzle of the relation between "determinism" and "free will." The search for a cause is itself the search for a scapegoat, as Adam blames Eve, Eve blames the serpent, the serpent could have blamed Lucifer, and Lucifer could have blamed the temptations implicit in the idea of Order (the inchoate "fall" that, as we saw in the quotation from Coleridge, is intrinsic to the "creation of the non-absolute"). Adam himself has a hint of the Luciferian rejoinder when he says to the Lord God that he received the fruit from "the woman whom thou gavest to be with me." Also, from the purely imagistic point of view, there is a sense in which the Lord God has caused Adam to be tempted by an aspect of himself, in accordance with the original obstetrical paradox whereby woman was born of man.

Here would be a purely "grammatical" way of stating the case: If order, implying the possibility of disorder, implies a possible act of disobedience, then there must be an agent so endowed, or so minded, that such an act is possible to him—and the motives for such an act must eventually somehow be referred to the scene out of which he arose and which thus somehow contains the principles that in their way make a "bad" act possible.

Arrived at this point, we might shift the problem of the "watershed moment" to another plane, by recalling that the same conditions of divisiveness also make for the inchoately "holy," inasmuch as the Hebrew word for "holy," qodesh, means literally the "separate," the "set apart," as does the word qadesh, which means "Sodomite." This verbal tangle has often been commented on, and it applies also to the New Testament word *hagios,* which means both "holy" and "accursed," like its Latin counterpart, *sacer.* Here, we might say, is a purely terministic equivalent of the problem of choice, or motivational slope. The question of determinism narrows down to a kind of term that within itself contains two slopes (two different judgments or "crises").

As regards the matter of terms, we could move into the area of personality proper by equating human personality with the ability to use symbol-systems (centering in the feeling for the negative, since "reason," in its role as the "sense of right and wrong," is but a special case of the "sense of yes and no"). Thus, more broadly, we could say that the conception of the creative verbal fiat in Genesis is essentially the *personal principle.* But insofar as personal character is defined by choice (*cf.* Aristotle on *proairesis, Poetics,* VI, 24), the question becomes one of deciding how far back the grounds of choice must be traced. Since Genesis would depict us as arising from a scene that is the act of a super-person and redemption is thought to be got by voluntary enlistment on the side of Order, conceived sacrificially, the ultimate formula becomes that of Jeremiah XXXI, 18: "Turn thou me, and I shall be turned" *(converte me, et convertar).* Here the indeterminate watershed of "free" choice is reducible to a question of this sort: Though all men are given enough "grace" to be saved, how can anyone be saved but by being given enough grace to be sure of using it? Yet how could he have as much saving grace as that, without in effect being compelled to be saved (in which case he would not, in the last analysis, have "free will")?

Fortunately, it is not our duty, as logologers, to attempt solving this ultimate theological riddle, entangled in ideas of providence, predestination, and the possibilities of an elect, chosen from among the depraved, all of whom deserve eternal damnation, but some of whom are saved by God in his mysterious mercy and may attest to their future glory by becoming a kind of materially prosperous elite here and now.

Fortunately, as logologers, we need but consider the ways in which such ideas are interwoven with the conditions of dominion, as they prevail among human symbol-using animals. As seen in this light, the thought of all such issues leads us to revision of our initial dialectical pattern. That is, the Order-Disorder pair is not enough. And what we need now is another kind of antithesis, setting Order against Counter-Order.

Methodologically, we might say that we have now come upon the penalties resulting from our earlier decision to approach this problem in terms of "Order" rather than in terms of "Covenant." For the idea of a "Counter-Covenant" would have been somewhat different from the idea of such a mere disintegration as is usually suggested by the term "Disorder."

In sum, there is a notable qualitative difference between the idea of a mere "fall" from a position in which one still believes, but to which one is at times unequal, and the idea of a deliberate turn to an alternative allegiance. It would be a difference between being "weak in virtue" and being "strong in sin."

But perhaps we should try to sum up the line of reasoning we have been pursuing in these last paragraphs. We have been considering the problem of a possible ultimate ground for "Temptation." Logologically, "Temptation" is but a tautological aspect of the idea of "Order." It is grounded in the idea of a verbal command, which by its very nature contains possibilities of both obedience and disobedience. We do not "command" the non-verbalizing things of nature. To the best of our ability, we simply set up conditions which we think likely to bring about the kind of situation we desire. We reserve our commands (or requests!) for language-using entities that can, to varying degrees, resist. And the command is backed, explicitly or implicitly, by promises or threats.

However, ontologically, or theologically, such a purely "tauto-logical" point of view would not be enough. And we confront such problems as St. Augustine was concerned with in his battles with the Manichaeans. We may, like the Manichaeans, conceive of an ultimate Tempter, existing in his own right and with powers rivaling those of God. Or we may derive everything from a God who is by definition merciful, and good, the author of a wholly good Creation, yet who not only lets man sin but permits the existence and incessant schemings of a supernatural tempter en-dowed with diabolical ingenuity and persuasiveness. Hence arises the "problem of evil" (as with Augustine's urgent question, *"Unde malum?"*). We have considered in the previous talk how Augus-tine proposed to solve the problem theologically by his notion of evil as a "deficient cause," a kind of "eclipse."

But logologically, the question takes on a different form. Logo-logically, moral "evil" is a species of negative, a purely linguistic (or "rational") principle. And insofar as natural calamities are viewed in terms of moral retribution, we should say that the positive events of nature are being seen through the eyes of moral negativity (another instance of ways whereby the genius of the verbal and socio-political orders can come to permeate our ideas of the natural order). All told, "evil" is implicit in the idea of "Order" because "Order" is a polar, or dialectical term, imply-ing an idea of "Disorder."

But there can be two kinds of "Disorder": (1) a tendency toward failure to obey completely always; (2) disobedience due to an out-and-out enrollment in the ranks of a rival force. We might call this a distinction between mere Disorder and deliberate alle-giance to a Counter-Order. (There is an analogous situation in contemporary politics, since a person's disagreements with those in authority may be interpreted either as temperamental devia-tion from the prevailing orthodoxy or as sinister, secret adherence to an organized enemy alien power.)

Theologically, perhaps the analogous distinction would be between the kind of "Temptation" that is intrinsic to the possibility of choice and the kind that attains its ideal perfection in the notion of a Faustian pact with the Devil—the difference between ordinary "backsliding" and "heresy" or "black magic." Problems of "predestination" lie in the offing, inasmuch as different people are differently tempted or differently enlightened and such differences are not of their own choosing but arise in connection with the accidents of each man's unique, particular destiny. (In the *Confessions,* for instance, we see St. Augustine interpreting as God's will many decisions which he had made for quite different personal reasons. And no man could sell his soul to the Devil if God, who was necessarily present at the signing of the contract, but chose that moment to flood the victim's imagination with the full realization of his danger.)

At this point, we should look at Hobbes's *Leviathan,* since it illustrates so well the idea of Disorder in this more aggressive sense of a Covenant matched by a "Counter-Covenant." And in the course of doing so, it well illustrates the role of the sacrificial principle which we believe to be "logologically inseparable" from the idea of dominion.

COVENANT AND "COUNTER-COVENANT" IN HOBBES'S *LEVIATHAN*

Part I of the *Leviathan* is "Of Man." But this subtitle can easily mislead us. For Part I is not just "Of Man." It is *of man in the commonwealth.* That is, the principle of Part II, which explicitly concerns commonwealth, is already implicit as a germ in Part I. Thus there is no break in continuity as we turn from Part I to Part II. The quickest way to make it obvious that the motives of commonwealth are already operating in the first section, and coloring the philosopher's view of man qua man, is to cite such chapter headings as: "Of Power, Worth, Dignity, Honour, and Worthiness" and "Of Persons, Authors, and Things Personated."

Perhaps one cannot explicitly write just "of man" without implicitly writing of man in the commonwealth (or, at least, of man in the tribe), since man is, as Aristotle puts it in good Athenian fashion, a "political animal."

Similarly, in Genesis, though the first three Covenants have to do with man and woman, brothers, parents, and children, and though it is not until the fourth, or Abrahamic, Covenant that God deals with Israel as a nation, yet the generic and familial motives exemplified in these early Covenants are but the beginnings of such motives as come clear in terms of dominion, however theocratically conceived. This is to say that man's notion of his "pre-political" self will necessarily be seen in the light of a socio-political perspective. And all the more so because "pre-political" childhood is experienced in terms of family relationships that are themselves shaped by tribal or national conditions as a whole.

As regards Part II, "Of Commonwealth": If one reads this section along the lines of our notion that the first section is "in principle" saying the same thing, one gets the essence of Hobbes's politics. Here, near the end of Chapter XVII, occurs an almost gloriously resonant passage succinctly summing up the Hobbesian notion of a Covenant, made with a "common power" and designed to keep the covenanters "in awe and to direct their actions to the common benefit":

The only way to erect such a common power, as may be able to defend them from the invasion of foreigners, and the injuries of one another, and thereby to secure them in such sort, as that by their own industry, and by the fruits of the earth, they may nourish themselves and live contentedly; is, to confer all their power and strength upon one man, or upon one assembly of men, that may reduce all their wills, by plurality of voices, unto one will: which is as much as to say, to appoint one man, or assembly of men, to bear their person; and every one to own, and acknowledge himself to be author of whatsoever he that so beareth their person, shall act, or cause to be acted, in those things which concern the common peace and safety; and therein to submit their wills, every one to his will, and their judgments, to his judgment. This is more than consent, or concord; it is a real unity of them all, in one and the same person, made by covenant of every man with every man, in such manner, as if every man should say to every man, *I authorize and give up my right of governing myself, to this man, or to this assembly of men, on this condition, that thou give up thy right to him, and authorize all his actions in like manner.* This done, the multitude so united in one person, is called a COMMON-WEALTH, in Latin CIVITAS. This is the generation of that great LEVIATHAN, or rather, to speak more reverently, of that *mortal god,* to which we owe under the *immortal God,* our peace and defense. For by this authority, given him by every particular man in the common-wealth, he hath the use of so much power and strength conferred on him, that by terror thereof, he is enabled to form the wills of them all, to peace at home, and mutual aid against their enemies abroad. And in him consisteth the essence of the commonwealth; which, to define it, is *one person, of whose acts a great multitude, by mutual covenants one with another, have made themselves every one the author, to the end he may use the strength and means of them all, as he shall think expedient, for their peace and common defense.*

And he that carrieth this person, is called SOVEREIGN, and said to have *sovereign power;* and every one besides, his SUBJECT.

In Part III ("Of of Christian Commonwealth") Hobbes adds a dimension, by introducing from the Bible his terms for what he calls "Christian politics." Essentially, this section involves his devices for subjecting priest-rule to the powers of secular sovereignty. That is to say: In another way, by new ingenuities, he reaffirms the principles of the commonwealth that were adumbrated in Part I and explicitly expounded in Part II. Perhaps the most quotable passage for our purposes is the last paragraph of Chapter XXVIII:

Hitherto I have set forth the nature of man, whose pride and other passions have compelled him to submit himself to government: together with the great power of his governor, whom I compared to *Leviathan,* taking that comparison out of the two last verses of the one-and-fortieth of *Job;* where God having set forth the great power of

Leviathan, calleth him King of the Proud. *There is nothing,* saith he, *on earth, to be compared with him. He is made so as not to be afraid. He seeth every high thing below him; and is king of all the children of pride.* But because he is mortal, and subject to decay, as all other earthly creatures are; and because there is that in heaven, though not on earth, that he should stand in fear of, and whose laws he ought to obey; I shall in the next following chapters speak of his diseases, and the causes of his mortality; and of what laws of nature he is bound to obey.

The reference to Leviathan as "King of the Proud" is perfect for our purposes. However, we have said that where Governance is, there is the goad to scapegoats.

And that brings us to Part IV ("Of the Kingdom of Darkness"). The curative victim here is not Christ, but Popery, conceived as Anti-Christ.

At this point (praise Logology!) we most decidedly need not enter the fray on Hobbesian terms. But we most decidedly should be admonished by Hobbes, in accordance with our ways of translating. And his methodologically fundamental admonition gets down to the fact that, in the light of his title for Part IV, "Of the Kingdom of Darkness," we must shift from Order-thinking back to Covenant-thinking and thereby concern ourselves with the sheerly dialectical possibilities of a Counter-Covenant, though the word itself is not in Hobbes.

Viewed here not as doctrine, but as design, Hobbes helps us realize that implicit in the idea of a Covenant is the idea not just of obedience or disobedience to that Covenant, but also of obedience or disobedience to a rival Covenant. The choice thus becomes not just a difference between seeking the light and not seeking the light, but rather the difference between eagerly seeking the light and just as eagerly seeking darkness (a "Disorder" having an "Order" all its own, however insistent the orthodoxy must be that the Satanic counter-realm can exist only by the sufferance of the One Ultimate Authority).

About the edges of all such speculations lie variants of the Manichæan "heresy," according to which Evil is a power in its own right. As we have observed before, logology must side with Augustine's attacks upon this position. For logology looks upon "evil" as a species of the negative and looks upon the negative as a linguistic invention. This would be the logological analogue of Augustine's theological doctrine that *malum* is a *causa deficiens,* a mere deficiency, like an eclipse. And from the purely dialectical point of view, we take it that all admonishment against the temptations of a Counter-Covenant are a recognition of the moral certainty that the mere stating of a position is likely to call forth some opposition. Hobbes's strongly nationalist position made it inevitable that Roman Catholicism would be his scapegoat.

But whether the scapegoat principle be conceived after the analogy of a villain, or after the analogy of arbitrarily chosen vessel that gets its function purely by appointment, or after the analogy of divine paraclete combining exhortation and guidance with victimage, the principle of Mortification is basic to the pattern of governance, as summed up in Paul's paradox (2 Corinthians, XII, 10): "Therefore I take pleasure in infirmities, in reproaches, in necessities, in persecutions, in distresses for Christ's sake: for when I am weak, then I am strong."

The idea of the Sacrificial Redeemer, in bringing together ideas of patience, repentance, and obedience to the verbalities of the faith, reproduces in the large the same principle that prevails in the minute scruples of Mortification. Here also would belong the idea of the "remnant," those especially good Jews who maintained the continuity of a blessed relation to the deity despite the backsliding of the people as a whole. And the priesthood, too, would be an extension of the principle of sacrifice, in that it involves special persons set apart for the sacrificial services. The priests extend the sacrificial principle to themselves insofar as they practice special acts of mortification deemed to fit them for their special office.

The companion principle to such an idea of graceful, voluntary subjection being, of course, sovereignty, the other side of the sovereign-subject relation is presented in terms of the ultimate rewards in store for those of good will who subject themselves to the principle of governance. That is, as with the two advents of Christ, the logical contrast between sovereignty and subjection is resolved by translation into terms of narrative sequence whereby the principle of subjection, of mortification, first prevails, but is finally followed by the sovereign principle of boundless rejoicing. And in the meantime, the notion of "grace" itself (as a way of goading the sluggish Imagination to the proper fears) is extended to include the idea that natural calamities are "acts of God," designed to warn or chasten—whereupon the principle of Mortification is introduced under another guise.

Mortification is as true of Order as mortmain is of contract.

PRINCIPLES OF GOVERNANCE, STATED NARRATIVELY

Imagine that you wanted to say, "The world can be divided into six major classifications." That is, you wanted to deal with "the principles of Order," beginning with the natural order and placing man's socio-political order with reference to it. But you wanted to treat of these matters in narrative terms, which necessarily involve temporal sequence (in contrast with the cycle of terms for "Order," that merely cluster about one another, variously implying one another but in no one fixed sequence).

Stated narratively (in the style of Genesis, *Bereshith*, Beginning), such an idea of principles, or "firsts," would not be stated simply in terms of classification, as were we to say "The first of six primary classes would be such-and-such, the second such-and-such," and so on. Rather, a completely narrative style would properly translate the idea of six classes or categories into terms of time, as were we to assign each of the classes to a separate "day." Thus, instead of saying, "And that completes the first broad division, or classification, of our subject matter," we would say, "And the evening and the morning were the first day" (or, more accurately, the "One" Day). And so on, through the six broad classes, ending, "last but not least," on the category of man and his dominion.*

Further, a completely narrative style would personalize the principle of classification. This role is performed by the references to God's creative fiat, which from the very start infuses the sheerly natural order with the verbal principle (the makings of that "reason" which we take to be so essential an aspect of human personality).

Logologically, the statement that God made man in his image would be translated as: The principle of personality implicit in the idea of the first creative fiats, whereby all things are approached in terms of the word, applies also to the feeling for symbol-systems on the part of the human animal, who would come to read nature as if it were a book. Insofar as God's words infused the natural order with their genius, and insofar as God is represented as speaking words to the first man and woman, the principle of human personality (which is at the very start identified with dominion) has its analogue in the notion of God as a super-person and of nature as the act of such a super-agent. (That is, we take symbol-using to be a distinctive ingredient of "personality.")

---

* The clearest evidence that this principle of "divisiveness" is itself a kind of "proto-fall" is to be seen in the use made of it by the segregationists of the southern Bible belt. Members of the Ku Klux Klan refer to the classificatory system of Genesis as justification for their stress upon the separation of Negroes and whites. In an ironic sense, they are "right." For when nature is approached via the principle of differentiation embodied in the notion of Social Order, then "Creation" itself is found to contain implicity the guiltiness of "discrimination." Furthermore, the Word mediates between these two realms. And the Word is social in the sense that language is a collective means of expression, while its sociality is extended to the realm of wordless nature insofar as this nonverbal kind of order is treated in terms of such verbal order as goes with the element of command intrinsic to dominion.

Though technically there is a kind of "proto-fall" implicit in the principle of divisiveness that characterizes the Bible's view of the Creation, and though the principle of subjection is already present (in the general outlines of a government with God at its head and mankind as subject to his authority while in turn having dominion over all else in the natural realm), the Covenant (as first announced in the first chapter) is necessarily Edenic, in a state of "innocency," since no negative command has yet been pronounced. From the dialectical point of view (in line with the Order-Disorder pair) we may note that there is a possibility of "evil" implicit in the reference to all six primary classifications as "good." But in all three points (the divisiveness, the order of dominion, and the universal goodness) the explicit negative is lacking. In fact, the nearest approach to an outright negative (and that not of a moralistic hortatory sort) is in the reference to the "void" *(bohu)* which preceded God's classificatory acts. Rashi says that the word translated as "formless" *(tohu)* "has the meaning of astonishment and amazement." Incidentally, in connection with I, 29, the *Interpreter's Bible* suggests another implicit negative, in that the explicit permitting of a vegetarian diet implies that Adam may not eat flesh.

In the first chapter of Genesis, the stress is upon the creative fiat as a means of classification. It says in effect, "What hath God wrought (by his Word)?" The second chapter's revised account of the Creation shifts the emphasis to matters of dominion, saying in effect, "What hath God ordained (by his words)?" The seventh "day" (or category), which is placed at the beginning of the second chapter, has a special dialectical interest in its role as a transition between the two emphases.

In one sense, the idea of the Sabbath is implicitly a negative, being conceived as antithetical to all the six foregoing categories, which are classifiable together under the single head of "work," in contrast with this seventh category, of "rest." That is, work and rest are "polar" terms, dialectical opposites. (In his *Politics,*

Aristotle's terms bring out this negative relation explicitly, since his word for business activity is *ascholein,* that is, "not to be at leisure," though we should tend rather to use the negative the other way round, defining "rest" as "not to be at work.")

This seventh category (of rest after toil) obviously serves well as transition between Order (of God as principle of origination) and Order (of God as principle of sovereignty). Leisure arises as an "institution" only when conditions of dominion have regularized the patterns of work. And, fittingly, just after this transitional passage, the very name of God undergoes a change (the quality of which is well indicated in our translations by a shift from "God" to "Lord God."* Here, whereas in Chapter I, verse 29, God tells the man and woman that the fruit of "every tree" is permitted them, the Lord God (II, 17) notably revises thus: "But of the tree of the knowledge of good and evil, thou shalt not eat of it: for in the day that thou eatest thereof thou shalt surely die." Here, with the stress upon governance, enters the negative of command.

When, later, the serpent tempts "the woman" (III, 4), saying that "Ye shall not surely die," his statement is proved partially correct, to the extent that they did not die on the day on which they ate of the forbidden fruit. In any case, III, 19 pronounces the formula that has been theologically interpreted as deriving

---

* Grammatically, the word for God in the first chapter, "Elohim," is a plural. Philologists may interpret this as indicating a usage that survives from an earlier polytheistic period in the development of Jewish Monotheism. Or Christian theologians can interpret it as the first emergence of a Trinitarian position, thus early in the text, with the Creator as first person of the Trinity, the Spirit that hovered over the waters as third person, and the creative Word as second person. (Incidentally, the words translated as "Lord God" in Chapter II are *Jehovah-Elohim.* Later, in connection with the Abrahamic Covenant, the words translated as "Lord God" are *Adonai Jehovah. Adonai,* which means "master," applies to both God and man—and when applied to man it also includes the idea of husband as master.) The distinction between authority and authorship is approached from another angle in Augustine's *Confessions* I, X, where God is called the *ordinator* and *creator* of all natural things, but of sin he is said to be only the *ordinator.*

mankind's physical death from our first parents' first disobedience: "In the sweat of thy face shalt thou eat bread, till thou return unto the ground; for out of it wast thou taken: for dust thou
art, and unto dust shalt thou return."

The *Interpreter's Bible* (page 512) denies that there is any suggestion that man would have lived forever had he not eaten of
the forbidden fruit. Verse III, 20 is taken to imply simply that
man would have regarded death as his natural end, rather than
as "the last fearful frustration." Thus, the fear of death is said to
be "the consequence of the disorder in man's relationships" when
they are characterized "by domination" (along with the fear that
the subject will break free of their subjection). This seems to be
at odds with the position taken by the *Scofield Bible*, which, in
the light of Paul's statements in Romans V, 12-21 ("by one man
sin entered the world, and death by sin" and "by one man's
offence death reigned by one") interprets the passage as meaning
that "physical death" is due to a "universal sinful state, or nature," which is "our heritage from Adam."

It is within neither our present purpose nor our competency to
interpret this verse theologically. But here is how it would look
logologically:

First, we would note that in referring to "disorder" and "domination," the *Interpreter's Bible* is but referring to "Order" and
"Dominion" as seen from another angle. For a mode of domination is a mode of dominion, and a socio-political order is by
nature a ziggurat-like structure which, as the story of the Tower
makes obvious, can stand for the principle of Disorder.

If we are right in our notion that the idea of Mortification is
integral to the idea of Dominion (as the scrupulous subject must
seek to "slay" within himself what ever impulses run counter to
the authoritative demands of sovereignty), then all about a story
of the "first" dominion and the "first" disobedience there should
hover the theme of the "first" mortification.

But "mortification" is a weak term as compared with "death."

And thus, in the essentializing ways proper to the narrative style, this stronger, more dramatic term replaces the weaker, more "philosophic" one. "Death" would be the proper narrative-dramatic way of saying "Mortification." By this arrangement, the natural order is once again seen through the eyes of the socio-political order, as the idea of mortification in the toil and subjection of Governance is replaced by the image of death in nature.

From the standpoint sheerly of imagery (once the idea of mortification has been reduced to the idea of death, and the idea of death has been reduced to the image of a dead body rotting back into the ground), we now note a kind of "imagistic proto-fall," in the pun of II, 7, where the Lord God is shown creating man (adham) out of the ground (adhamah). Here would be an imagistic way of saying that man in his physical nature is essentially but earth, the sort of thing a body becomes when it decays; or that man is first of all but earth as regards his place in the sheerly natural order. You would define him in narrative or temporal terms by showing what he came from. But insofar as he is what he came from, such a definition would be completed in narrative terms by the image of his return to his origins. In this sense, the account of man's forming (in II, 7) ambiguously lays the conditions for his "return" to such origins, as the Lord God makes explicit in III, 19, when again the subject is the relation between adham and adhamah: "For dust thou art, and unto dust shalt thou return." Here would be a matter of sheer imagistic consistency, for making the stages of a narrative to be all of one piece.

But the death motif here is explicity related to another aspect of Order or Dominion: the sweat of toil. And looking back a bit further, we find that this severe second Covenant (the "Adamic") also subjected woman to the rule of the husband—another aspect of Dominion. And there is to be an eternal enmity between man and the serpent (the image, or narrative personification, of the principle of Temptation, which we have also found to be intrinsic to the motives clustering about the idea of Order).

Logologically, then, the narrative would seem to be saying something like this: Even if you begin by thinking of death as a merely natural phenomenon, once you come to approach it in terms of conscience-laden mortification you get a new slant on it. For death then becomes seen, in terms of the socio-political order, as a kind of capital punishment. But something of so eschatological a nature is essentially a "first" (since "ends," too, are principles—and here is a place at which firsts and lasts meet, so far as narrative terms for the defining of essences are concerned). Accordingly, death in the natural order becomes conceived as the fulfillment or completion of mortification in the socio-political order, but with the difference that, as with capital punishment in the sentencing of transgressions against sovereignty, it is not in itself deemed wholly "redemptive," since it needs further modifications along the lines of placement in an undying Heavenly Kingdom after death. And this completes the pattern of Order: the symmetry of the socio-political, the natural, and the supernatural.

5. The Pattern of Religious Organization in the United States

TALCOTT PARSONS

As IN a number of other fields the United States has, in formal constitutions and otherwise, from the beginning of its independent national history presented a rather new and striking pattern of the relation between organized religion and society. On the constitutional level the striking innovation was the repudiation of the ancient European institution of the Establishment, through the separation of Church and State on both the federal and the state level, in that the State Constitutions or subsequent enactments, as well as the First Amendment to the Federal Constitution, excluded an established church. On the informal level the striking innovation was acceptance of what may be called "denominational pluralism," namely the presence in the community, with equal formal rights, of an indefinite number of competing religious collectivities, or "churches," none of which, however, was allowed to enjoy positive governmental support, though they did have such privileges as tax-exemption.* Implied also, in the freedom of the individual to belong to and support any one of the plurality of denominational groups, was his freedom to dissociate himself from all of them. Citizenship did not imply either subscription to any religious creed or subjection

* A privilege which has been shared with educational and charitable organizations generally.

to the authority or pressure of any religious body. As far as the organization of political authority was concerned, religion ceased to be a subject of "public" concern and was relegated to the sphere of private affairs, except for political guardianship of religious freedom. In its broad outline this system has proved to be stable over the hundred and seventy years of our national existence, a fairly long period as such things go. There is no sign of a tendency for it to break down now.

This pattern stands in sharp contrast to the main European tradition. There it may be said that the chief background institution has been that of the Established Church where, though political and religious authorities were structurally differentiated from each other, it was understood that the one church should enjoy a legitimate monopoly of religious authority and benefits for the whole politically organized society and that it could legitimately call on political authority to enforce this monopoly by physical coercion, as well as to ensure the financial support of the Church. The prototype of this older pattern was of course the Catholic Church before the Reformation. But the same basic pattern in these essentials was taken over by the main Reformation churches, both Lutheran and Calvinistic, as distinguished from the sects, and in most European countries the further development has been characterized by large elements of this pattern.

The pattern has, of course, been greatly modified in the course of European history since the Reformation. The break in the religious unity of Western Christendom which that movement signalized was in fact coincident with the final break in its political unity—the unity of the Holy Roman Empire had already been very seriously compromised by the independence of the English and French monarchies, but after the Reformation the religious schism within its central structure made the "Empire" little more than a fiction. But the formula *cuius regio, eius religio* also proved to be unstable and, more and more, religious unity under an established church within the political unit broke down.* The Elizabethan policy of religious tolerance in England was perhaps the first main step in this process. Now every important European state (except Spain) has at least some important degree of religious toleration and in a few, like France, formal separation of Church and State has been put through.

On the other hand, there are still many residua of the old pattern. Most countries, while tolerating other churches, still permit the privileges of an established church to one, though it is Catholic in some and Lutheran in some, and England has its special Anglican and Scotland its Presbyterian Establishment. This is likely to be associated with special privileges in the field of tax-support, education, and other matters.

But apart from the legal privileges of religious bodies, there are other phenomena related to the incomplete resolution of problems stemming from the older pattern. One of the most notable, to Americans, is the persisting tendency to form religiously based political parties. This is least evident in Great Britain, though it may be argued that the ultimate break with Ireland had a good deal to do with this issue, and the religious separatism of Scotland is still a major focus of Scottish nationalism. On the Continent, however, it is prominent in various countries, France with the M.R.P., Holland, Belgium, and Italy.

Very much associated with this tendency has been the tendency for secularism, in the sense of opposition to organized religion in general, also to assume political forms transcending other particular issues. Thus for a century French politics was polarized to a considerable degree about the issue of anticlericalism. In general, political secularism has been a major component of the orientation of the parties of the left in Europe—again apart from Great Britain—and in the extreme case of Communism it may be

* There was a complicated series of developmental stages falling between this historic settlement and the American system of denominational pluralism which cannot be entered into here.

said that the aim has been to set up a counter-Establishment, making militant secularism itself a dogma to be rigidly enforced by a party backed by governmental authority. It may be suggested that the lack of appeal of this European secularist leftism, particularly Communism, in Anglo-Saxon countries, and most especially in the United States, has been associated with the uncongeniality there of any polarization of the body politic over religious issues.

It is understandable that the American institutional structure in this respect should, to many Europeans and to some Americans, appear to be the last stage in the general process of secularization relative to the European heritage, with its roots in Mediæval Catholic unity. How can it be maintained that religion has any vitality if, on the one hand, it has become so splintered that the religious unity of a society cannot be maintained, but an indefinite diversity of denominational groups must be tolerated, and, on the other hand, people's level of commitment to institutionalized religion has sunk so low that they are unwilling to fight for their churches through political means?

As over against this interpretation I would like to suggest that in the United States there has appeared, though probably not yet fully matured, a new mode of institutionalization of the relations between religion and society, which, however, is not secularization in the sense that its tendency is to eliminate organized religion from the social scene, but is rather to give it a redefined place in the social scene. The recent American "religious revival," which has occasioned a good deal of comment, is important evidence for this thesis. There are two primary possible interpretations of this phenomenon. The more popular one, even among American intellectuals, is that, from a religious point of view, it is not really "genuine," but must be explained on extraneous grounds as meeting the needs for neighborliness and security in group memberships of the highly mobile populations of American cities in the industrial age, particularly in the new suburbs. The other is that it is connected with a new equilibrium in the relation between the religious and the secular elements in the social system. I shall comment briefly on this problem later.

A FEW HISTORICAL ANTECEDENTS OF THE AMERICAN PATTERN

It may be argued that at the time of the American Revolution the principle of the separation of church and state was something of a tour de force and was precipitated by two main factors extraneous to the place of religion in the deeper social structure. One of those factors was political expediency deriving from the religious diversity of the thirteen colonies. Clearly the Puritans of New England, the Catholics of Maryland, the Quakers of Pennsylvania, the Anglicans of Virginia, and the Presbyterians of a good part of the South could not have agreed that any one of their denominations could be accorded the privileges of an Established Church, so it was relatively easy to agree that there should be none at all. The other factor was the prominence among the Founding Fathers of a group of intellectuals, typified by Thomas Jefferson, who were deeply influenced by the Deism of the French Enlightenment.

The process of institutionalization of the new pattern has been a long one and has been involved with a general process of social change, the major keynote of which has been structural differentiation. Religious issues have, of course, made their appearance in American politics from time to time, as for example in the various anti-Catholic movements from the "Know-Nothing Party" on. But structurally the separation of church and state has proved stable and there has been no really serious challenge to it.*

---

* It is conceivable that growing prominence and power of the Catholic Church might precipitate a major change. Though the seriousness of the tension over this problem should not be underestimated, for reasons which cannot be entered into here I think it unlikely that this will happen.

A good example of the process of structural differentiation involving religion has been the field of education. It must be realized that in the earlier days of the American Republic education at the lower levels was not treated as a public responsibility in any sense but was privately arranged by the privileged upper-class minority for their own children. The focus of formal educational arrangements was in higher education and it, in turn, was oriented religiously to the education of ministers of religion. Even at the time when various groups other than prospective ministers were attending the colleges, the latter were overwhelmingly governed under denominational auspices.

In early, colonial days, a partnership of local church and public authority in the provision for higher education was taken for granted, as in the case of the founding of Harvard College and of King's College in New York, which later became Columbia University. But after the advent of independence the responsibility fell almost entirely to religious denominations until the beginning of the wave of founding of state universities in the western territories toward the middle of the nineteenth century. This followed closely on the spread of public education at the primary and secondary levels. Though the wider spread of education in the United States occurred under governmental auspices, it should be noted that the local community assumed the responsibility. The pattern still holds in main outline, with state governments carrying a moderate share of responsibility and the Federal Government as yet scarcely any at all. Probably the United States is the only important government in the world which does not have a central department or ministry of education.

It can thus be seen that there is a sense in which in Europe the State took over the educational function from the Church. In the United States it remained in religious hands considerably longer, but then was secularized in the first instance to private bodies, secondarily to public authority, but even there above all to local authority. The colleges, and later universities, have in general evolved from denominational foundations to general private fiduciary agencies with only tenuous denominational affiliations. There has been a similar evolution in the case of hospitals. To an American the difference in the latter connection is striking, for in Europe the nurse, as a "sister," is still hardly distinguishable from the member of a religious order, indeed often is an actual member.

It is perhaps to be expected that in this setting the policies of the Catholic Church should exhibit a certain lag relative to the rest of American society. It has, particularly in the last generation or two, taking advantage of the framework of American religious toleration, set out to create a complete system of religious education whereby, in ideal, the Catholic child will from primary school through the university be educated exclusively in church-controlled organizations. This is only one of the variety of respects in which the Catholic Church occupies a special position in American society, but it may be a question how far it will be able to maintain this special policy in the face of powerful general forces pointing in another direction.

I have suggested that the keynote of the special position of religion in American society lies in structural differentiation. When a previously less differentiated structure becomes differentiated into more specialized subsystems, it is in the nature of the case that, if an earlier and later structural unit bear the same name, the later version will, by comparison with the earlier, be felt to have lost certain functions and hence, perhaps, from a certain point of view to have been weakened. This may be illustrated from a nonreligious case. Thus in peasant societies, where the bulk of the population have been engaged in agriculture, the family household has been at the same time both the main agency of economic production in the society and the main focus of early child-rearing and of the intimate personal life of its members. In modern industrial societies this function of economic production has been largely lost to the family household and transferred to factories, offices, etc. In these terms the family has lost functions and has become a more specialized agency in the society. The modern urban family is clearly different from the peasant family; whether it is better or worse may be a matter of opinion, but the difference of its place in the larger social structure surely cannot be ignored in forming that opinion, including the fact that the social and economic advantages of industrialism cannot be secured through a household organization of production.

In order to appraise this type of structural differentiation it is necessary to have in mind a standard for defining the primary functions of a part of the social structure, the nature of which can be conceived to set the limits beyond which the "reduction" of function is unlikely to go. "Secondary" functions on the other hand may, through the process of differentiation, be transferred to other agencies. In the case of the family, just discussed, I think it is clear that the primary functions for the social system as such (physical care of the body being thus excluded) are its contributions to the personality development of the child—what sociologists have come to call "socialization"—and its functions in the stabilization of the personality equilibrium of the adult members. The family as an agency of society is above all a set of mechanisms which manipulate the motivational structures of its individual members as these bear on the performance of social roles. Can anything parallel be said about the primary function of religion in society?

This is, in the present state of sociological knowledge, a more uncertain field than that of the family. I should, however, wish to emphasize as the "core" function of religion in the social system the regulation of the balance of the motivational commitment of the individual to the values of his society—and through these values to his roles in it as compared with alternative considerations concerning his ultimate "fate" as a knowing,

sentient being, and the bases on which this fate comes to have
meaning to him, in the sense in which Max Weber refers to
"problems of meaning."* Religion, thus conceived, is close in its
social functions to the family, though in terms of formal organization it has taken the form of the church.

I think it can be said that the main reference of the "motivational" regulation performed by the family is regressive; it relates
to the sources of motivational patterning in the early life experience of the individual, particularly in the family relations in
which he is currently growing up or did grow up as a child.
Religion, on the other hand, is primarily oriented to the adult
phases of life and the problems of meaning involved in its basic
limitations, thus including the finiteness of life's duration and the
meaning of death. It involves such questions as What, in the last
analysis, am I? Why do I exist? What is the meaning of my
relations to others? Why must I die and what happens to me at
and after death? The cognitive meaning of existence, the meaning of happiness and suffering, of goodness and evil, are the
central problems of religion.†

An essential cognitive, i. e. philosophical, element is always
involved in religion, but, as Durkheim held, the main emphasis
is not cognitive, but practical. It is the question of what, in view
of my understanding and its limits, are my basic commitments
in life. Of course the influences of others and involvements of
various kinds in relations of solidarity or antagonism with others
are of very great importance; yet I should contend that in the
last analysis religion is an individual matter, a concern of the
innermost core of the individual personality for his own identity
and commitments. In view of this fact, the nature of the social

* A concept used especially by Max Weber. See particularly "The Social
Psychology of the World Religions," Chapter XI in *From Max Weber: Essays
in Sociology,* translated and edited by Hans Gerth and C. Wright Mills, New
York, Oxford University Press, 1946.

† See Paul Tillich, *The Courage To Be,* (Yale, 1952) for an excellent
brief discussion of these central problems.

structuring of religion should be regarded as empirically prob-
lematical; it cannot be deduced from the most general characteristics of religion itself.

RELIGION AND THE PROCESS OF SOCIAL DIFFERENTIATION

My suggestion is thus that a process of differentiation similar
to that which has affected the family has been going on in the
case of religion and has reached a particularly advanced stage
in the United States, producing a state which may or may not
provide a model for other societies. It is well known that in
primitive societies and in many other civilizations than that of
the West, no clear-cut structural distinction could be made
between religious and secular aspects of the organization of
society; there has been no "church" as a differentiated organiza-
tional entity. From this point of view the differentiation (as
distinguished from "separation") of Church and State, which has
been fundamental to Western Christianity from its beginning,
may be regarded as a major step in differentiation for the society
as a whole.

Through this process of differentiation religion already had
become a more specialized agency than it had been in most
other societies. But since the Renaissance and the Reformation
a process has been going on which has tended to carry the differentiation further still. The steps by which this process has taken
place and the exact patterns which have resulted have been
different in different countries. This brief article cannot attempt
to trace and compare them all. Besides space, this task would
require a level of historical scholarship which I do not command.
I must confine myself to pointing out a few features of the
American case and of its consequences for the structure of
American society.

Perhaps the first major point is that though a solid structure
of Federal Government was established for the new republic it

was, probably more than any European government, built on a system of constitutional restraints on governmental power. The relative insulation of the United States from the politics of the European world—by sheer distance and by the Pax Britannica—then gave our institutions an opportunity to crystallize within the framework of the Constitution without sudden or unbearable pressures to break down these restraints. Then the fact that separation of Church and State was itself written into most of the State Constitutions and into the First Amendment to the Federal Constitution gave a basis for a general tradition that religious issues were not a proper subject for political action. One fundamental consequence of this patterning was that when the time arrived for governmental initiative in the field of education, predominantly, as I have said, at the local level, there was the strongest presumption that tax-supported schools could not serve the interests of, or be controlled by, any religious denomination.

In the background of all this, of course, lay the characteristics of American religious traditions themselves. Though exceedingly diverse, the main influences were derived from the "left wing" of European, especially English, Protestantism, where the traditions of the Established Church were weakest. To be sure there was a Congregational Establishment in early New England, but by the time of the Revolution it was greatly attenuated and religious toleration fairly firmly established. The fact that after the first generation royal governors were present in the colonies reinforced this, because of the fear that if there was to be a firm religious establishment, the Anglican Church would be imposed by British authority. Even as early as the late eighteenth century, the strength of such groups as the Quakers, various Congregational splinter groups, Baptists and, starting at a crucial time, the Methodists, was great. These were all groups which on religious bases had opposed the backing of religion by political authority; without their relative strength the American pattern probably could not have survived. Again, it is important that a large Catholic minority did not exist until the pattern was well crystallized.

Another important circumstance lies in the fact that the great movement of settlement of the newer parts of the country preserved the pattern of religious diversity which had begun in the thirteen colonies. The effect of this was that none of the central political issues which divided the country, above all economic and sectional issues, could be closely identified with a religious division. The main exception has been the concentration, since about the turn of the last century, of the Catholic population in the northern and eastern cities. But for a variety of reasons Catholics could not as such stably dominate the politics of a solid regional block, and in particular the peculiarities of the South were enough to prevent the emergence of a stable southern-western Protestant coalition against Catholic influence in the East. The upshot is that, though religious issues flared up from time to time, occasionally dominating local issues and alignments, the broad pattern of keeping religion out of politics has come to be stably institutionalized in American society.

Perhaps the second most important context of differentiation involving religion has involved its relation to education, and with it the institutionalization of the intellectual life and its constituent professions. In part, as noted, such differentiation goes back to the separation of Church and State and the fact that when government, even local government, became involved in educational responsibilities, it could not back religious denominationalism in this sphere.* The same principle of course had to apply to

* How a combination of regional, ethnic, and religious distributions in politically powerful blocks can work out to a different outcome is illustrated by the case of Canada, particularly the Province of Quebec. Here, though there is religious toleration, the educational system is publicly supported but control of the schools is given to Catholic and Protestant religious groups, respectively, with parents given their choice of religious school to which to send their children. That this was tolerated by the English majority (which has been a minority in Quebec) is partly explained by the far greater proportion of Anglicans there than in the United States, with their greater sympathy for the Establishment principle.

the state universities as to the locally controlled primary and secondary schools.

As I have noted, private higher education in the United States was originally mainly controlled by religious denominations. Why did its secularization occur? It seems to me probable that among the decisive factors were those involved in the transition from primary emphasis on the college to that on the university. This in turn was involved with the rise to immensely increased strategic importance of the secular professions, especially those based on scientific training. It is interesting that the models for this development were drawn largely from the Continental European governmentally controlled universities. But under American conditions, if the private institutions of higher education were to retain their position, some of them had to develop into universities. And again, if as universities they were to serve as primary agencies for the training of the whole national professional class of lawyers, physicians, engineers, scientists, civil servants, and the academic profession itself, as well as ministers of religion, in a religiously diversified society like the American, they could not do so successfully if they remained denominational organizations in a strict and traditional sense. Above all, particularly the universities aspiring to national rather than local importance could not use denominational loyalty as a main criterion for recruitment either of their faculties or of their student bodies. In any case, whatever the social mechanisms involved, the American system of higher education in both its publicly supported colleges and universities (state and municipal) and its private sector is now firmly secular in its major orientation. The sole major exception is the educational system controlled by the Catholic Church, though there are smaller-scale ones for Lutherans, Jews, etc. The Catholic is a large minority, but there seems to be no basis for believing that its pattern can serve as a model for the reversal of this fundamental trend, if indeed the Catholic educational pattern can itself survive for very long against the trend.

There is one particularly crucial consequence for religion of the secular character of the American educational system. This is that the main standards for the evaluation and inculcation of intellectual culture are not and cannot be controlled by organized religious bodies. Real control of the development of science has long since been lost by religious bodies everywhere—and the attempts of semireligious bodies like the Communist Party to restore that control do not seem likely to be successful in the long run. But the American situation goes farther than this in two vital respects. The first is the extension of scientific methods and theories into the fields of human behavior, a world-wide development which, however, has gone farther in the United States than anywhere else. This development inevitably introduces the relevance of scientific, non-religious canons into many spheres which have traditionally been considered to be spheres of religious prerogative, such as many aspects of "morals." The second is the secularization of philosophy and the humanities. However seriously the secular philosopher (who may be a practicing member of a religious denomination) may take cognizance of historic and contemporary religious positions on his problems, in the last analysis his professional responsibility cannot be defined as the defense of the official position of any religious body, but is a responsibility to "seek the truth" as he sees it in the light of the general traditions of rational knowledge. No responsible modern American university in the main tradition could appoint him to its faculty on any other assumption.

Finally, reference may again be made to the fact that rights of predominantly secular orientation are clearly institutionalized in the American system. There is no obligation either of the citizen in the strictly political sense or of the member of the community in good standing to accept participation in or control by any formally organized religious body. Besides the fields of politics and education, this is perhaps most important in matters affecting the family. In attempting to retain control over various spheres of social life other than a more narrowly defined religious sphere, one of the most tenacious tendencies of religious bodies has been to attempt to prescribe the conditions of marriage and divorce and the responsibilities of parents for children in various respects, particularly education. The American, like the citizen of other countries who violates his church's rules in these matters, may be in trouble with the authorities of that church. But the essential point is that neither his political rights as citizen nor his basic good standing in the American community is conditioned on his conforming with the rules of any particular religious body in these matters. The minimum standards are set by political authority—what constitutes legal marriage and legal divorce, for example. Beyond these, the matter is one of a community opinion which is composed of religiously diverse elements. In religious terms, it seems to be a sort of lowest common denominator which governs—if any one group attempts to impose standards at variance with this common attitude the person in question can, at the cost of trouble with his own group, retain a good general community standing if his conduct is not generally condemned by members of the other groups.*

THE AMERICAN RELIGIOUS PATTERN

Seen in these terms, it is clear that by the standard of older ideals of Western Christianity organized religion has lost much in America. First it has lost the basic legitimation of the claim to religious unification even within the politically organized society. The right both to religious pluralism and to secular orientation (though not necessarily to combat religion except within limits) is a fundamental institutionalized right in American society. Organized religion has lost the right to claim the support of the

* This lowest common denominator of institutionalized moral standards must be carefully distinguished from the deviant behavior which is bound to be fairly prominent in a complex society. It is defined by the consensus of responsible opinion and does not in general condone extreme moral laxity.

state by compulsory enforcement of uniformity or even by taxation either for a single established church or for any religious body. It has lost the right to control the main lines of the educational process, above all perhaps to prescribe the legitimate framework of secular intellectual culture, with special reference to philosophy. It also has lost the right to prescribe effectively certain vital matters of private morals, with special reference to marriage and family relationships. Has it anything left?

My own view is most definitely that it has a great deal. Ernest Troeltsch, in his classic work, *Social Teachings of the Christian Churches,* maintained that in the history of Western Christianity there had been only three versions of the conception of a Christian Society, one in which the values of Christian religion could be understood to provide the main framework for the value system of the society as a whole. These cases were Mediæval Catholicism, Lutheranism, and Calvinism. All of them involved the conception of a single Established Church as the agent of implementing and symbolizing this fundamental Christian orientation of the society as a whole. Troeltsch considered that the "sects" which did not recognize the religious validity of an Established Church had in effect abandoned the ideal of the Christian Society altogether.

Over against this view of Troeltsch I should like to suggest that in American society there has, in its main outline, evolved the conception of an institutionalized Christianity which is in line with the great tradition of the Christian Society but differs from its earlier version in the fundamental respects outlined above. First in order of evidence in favor of this view is the fact that the values of contemporary American society have fundamental religious roots, above all in the traditions which Max Weber, in *The Protestant Ethic and the Spirit of Capitalism,* called those of "ascetic Protestantism," and that these values have not been fundamentally changed in the course of our national history. The enormous changes which have occurred constitute funda-

mental changes not of values but of the structure of the society
in which those values are maintained and implemented.* Essentially by this system of values I mean the continued commitment
to values of "instrumental activism," the subordination of the
personal needs of the individual to an objective "task" to which
he is expected to devote his full energies, and the subjection of
the actions of all to universalistic standards of judgment. Associated with this is the importance of universalizing the essential
conditions of effective performance through equalization of civil
rights and of access to education and health. It should be particularly noted that the shift from a primarily transcendental
reference to one with mainly terrestrial focus did not occur as a
phase of secularization but, as Weber so strongly emphasizes,
within the highly active religious tradition of ascetic Protestantism. It was the conception of the service of the Glory of God,
first through helping to build the Kingdom of God on Earth,
which was the main focus of Calvinist ethics.

"Secularization" has, essentially, taken the form of differentiation, so that this Kingdom is no longer thought of as exclusively
governed by religious considerations, but there is an autonomous
secular sphere of the "good society" which need not reflect only
man's activities and obligations in his capacity as a member of
the church. But this good society may still be interpreted as
"God's work" in a sense similar to that in which physical nature
has always been so interpreted within that tradition.

The new sectarian or, better, "denominational," form taken by
the religious organization itself is broadly in line with the general
development which produced Protestantism and then evolved
further within it. The keynote of it is the personal intimacy and
privacy of the individual's faith and relation to his conception
of Divinity. The further this trend of development has gone the

* This statement implies use of the concept "values" in a technical sociological sense which may not be in accord with all versions of common usage.
In some usages any significant change in concrete behavior is by definition
indicative of a change in values.

more basically repugnant to it have two features of the older traditions tended to become: first, the invoking of secular authority to apply coercive, ultimately physical sanctions in matters of religious faith and, second, the claim of any human agency to hold a monopoly of all religiously legitimate access to religious goods. This position clearly challenges all claims to authorization by exclusively valid divine revelation, but in the main tradition this consequence has been clearly recognized and accepted. The implication is that the religious body must be a fully voluntary association and that coercion in these matters is contrary to the most essential spirit of religion itself.*

Denominational pluralism is almost a direct implication of the above two departures from older tradition. If no human agency has a right to claim a monopoly of religious legitimacy and enforce it by coercion, then there is no basis on which to deny the legitimacy of plural competing claims at least to the point that many groups may have enough access to the truth to justify their adherents in each "worshiping God in their own way."

If denominational pluralism of this sort is to be institutionalized as the religious system of a society, then certain conditions must be met. Two of the most fundamental are definition of the limits within which a group of religious associates may claim to be a

---

* A particularly good illustration of the differentiation of religious and non-religious components which have been fused in the past is the increasingly clear discrimination, conspicuous in the United States, between psychiatry and what here tends to be called "pastoral counseling." The most essential point is the emergence of a secular professional tradition for the treatment of disturbances of personality. The elements involved in these disturbances include many elements which in other societies have been handled in a religious or magical context. The line is by no means completely clear as yet, but it is notable that, a few years ago, a strong attack on psychoanalysis by Catholic Bishop Fulton Sheen was countered by a group of Catholic psychoanalysts and that the Bishop did not then persist in his attacks. Since the Catholic Church is, in this as in various other aspects, the largest conservative religious body, the fact that it is not sponsoring a general attack on psychiatry is significant. A careful statement of a limited sphere in which psychiatry was defined as legitimate has recently been made by the Pope.

legitimate "denomination" and, second, the rules of their competition with each other in terms of mutual respect and the like. A third basic problem area concerns the way in which the line is drawn between the legitimate sphere of religious concern and that of the primarily secular institutions which have been discussed.

With respect to the first question the American pattern is probably not fully crystallized, but its main outline seems to be clear. It draws the definition of a legitimate denomination rather broadly, leaving room for a good deal of free competition. All the main historical branches of Christianity are clearly included. But so also are now the main branches of Judaism. Also, a good many popular cults of more or less faddist character which do not enjoy the respect of the more highly educated elements are still tolerated so long as they do not become too great sources of disturbance. Similarly, groups which, like Jehovah's Witnesses, are sharply alienated from the normal loyalties of the ordinary society are tolerated though not widely approved. Indeed there is no bar to the toleration of groups altogether outside the main Western traditions, though they do not seem to have gained any serious foothold.

The main core of the tradition is clearly a theistic Judeo-Christian belief complex. The inclusion of Judaism is not strange in view of the fact that similar theological positions have evolved within the Protestant tradition in Unitarianism. Indeed, for reasons like these it may be said that Judaism presents, at least for the groups which have abandoned Orthodox Jewish separatism from the general community, less difficult problems of integration than is the case with the Catholic Church and the real Protestant "Fundamentalists." Clearly there are many degrees of integration and many fringe groups. But there is, as noted, a general Theism, which is even politically recognized—as in the inscription on coins "In God We Trust." Further, sessions of Congress are regularly opened by Protestant, Catholic, or Jewish clergymen offering prayer, and chaplains of all three faiths are provided by the Armed Services.

It is further essential to recognize again that secularism, in the sense of repudiating affiliation with any organized religious body, is clearly institutionalized as legitimate. The central significance of this fact lies, I think, in the relation of religion to the main traditions of the intellectual culture of the society. The institutionalization of rights to secular orientation means that in struggling with the basic problems of meaning which confront the members of any society individually and in their collective capacities, the individual is not rigidly bound within the framework of a particular tradition of beliefs. Individuals and groups are free to define their positions in ways which are explicitly at variance with any of the denominational carriers of the religious tradition.

It seems to me that this protected position of secular orientation is particularly important in determining the circumstances under which, in several areas with which religion has historically been intimately concerned, patterns with secular primacy have come to be institutionalized in positions of high strategic importance in the society. The deeper roots both of religion itself and of some of these secular institutions are so closely interwoven, both historically and in current psychological terms, that any one of the "interests" involved would, if given a monopoly of jurisdiction over them, be likely to bias the balance between the religious sphere and that of the secular "good society" to a deleterious degree. I have in mind here particularly the two spheres of intellectual culture leading up to philosophy and of the attitudes toward a whole range of questions of "morals."

From this point of view religious and secular orientations may, to an important degree, thus be seen as constituting different aspects of the same system of orientation to "problems of meaning." Indeed the legitimacy of secularism seems to follow almost directly on the abandonment of coercively enforced dogma. But

above all secularism is important in defining the boundary between the religious sphere and the secular good society. Just as
in a politically democratic society the definition of the boundaries
of legitimate governmental authority is not permitted to be a
monopoly of the officials of government, so in a "religiously
liberal" society the determination of the boundaries of the legitimate sphere of organized religion is not left to the proponents
of that position alone; they must compete with proponents of a
position which in some respects is hostile to theirs. It is my belief
that the secularization of education and of control of certain
spheres of morals, which I regard as essential to the structure of
the American type of good society, could not have been brought
about without the influence of elements willing to oppose the
whole weight of organized religion.

But if the religious-secular balance is to work out in a well-
integrated social system, the opposition of secularists to religious
influence must not be unlimited. And I think it is correct to say
that in the United States (and Britain) on the whole, a regulated
competition rather than a "state of war" has prevailed. There
must be, and are, "rules of the game." From the secularist's point
of view his religiously committed fellow citizens are defined not
as beyond the pale but as "good people" who differ from him on
these points—and, of course, vice versa. Secularism may thus be
defined as a kind of "loyal opposition" to the religious point of
view. Each side has interests to protect which are vital, not only
to the proponents themselves but to the society as a whole.
Neither, alone, can legitimately hope to be exclusively influential
in the determination of the course of events. The fact that the
other "party" is there can serve as an important curb on the extremists on either side. Thus if a particular denomination tries
to put through extreme claims, for example in the direction of
denominational control of public education, the more moderate
denominations can be relied on to point out that such extremism
plays into the hands of the secularists—such claims may come

to be identified with "religion" as such. On the other side, extreme secularists who want too aggressively to combat all religion will tend to find themselves restrained by the influence of more moderate secularists who point out that their extreme position—for example, the requiring of civil marriage ceremonies on the presumption that a religious marriage is not "legally" valid—if insisted upon will tend to discredit all secularism and give the "religionists" an undue advantage.

Seen in these terms, the religious-secular balance in American society is analogous to the balance of political parties in a two-party system. The preponderance shifts from time to time—most recently apparently in a religious direction—but the system tends to insure that neither side will gain the kind of ascendancy which would enable it to suppress the other, and basically on the value level most good citizens on the one side do not want to suppress the other. Religion, that is to say, has come to be defined institutionally as quite definitely "a good thing" but equally definitely as not the only good thing, and as confined in its goodness to a fairly clearly defined sphere.*

Near the beginning of this paper the problem of the interpretation of the so-called American "religious revival" was mentioned. A very brief word may be said about it against the background of the above discussion. First I may point out that a prevailing interpretation stresses the extra-religious phenomena which have appeared in connection with church membership and attendance, above all the ways in which the church has become a center of community social activities and associations. From this observation it is an easy step to suggest that such interests as those in "sociability," to say nothing of opportunities to "meet the right people," account for the observed facts. A somewhat more sophisticated version of a similar view is the

---

* In the understanding of the nature and importance of this balance between religion and secularism and its analogy to the two-party system, I am particularly indebted to suggestions from Dr. Robert N. Bellah, of Harvard University.

suggestion that the "security needs" of isolated people in a mobile "mass society" constitute the focus of this new tendency.

There seems to be relatively little question about the broad facts. Church membership is currently the highest in American history, not only absolutely but in terms of proportions of the population. The same is true of attendance at church services, money spent in building of new churches, and a variety of other indices. Moreover, relative to general population growth there has been a marked increase in these phenomena in a short generation.

I would suggest that the phenomena of sociability, of desirable associations, and even of the relation to psychological security in interpersonal relations are quite real, but that they are secondary and do not impugn the religious genuineness of the revival. The central phenomenon seems to be the increased concern with values and hence the relation of the individual to his problems of "ultimate concern," to use Tillich's phrase. It is related to a new phase of emphasis on personal "inwardness" in American society, but it is not the first time in our history that this kind of thing has happened.*

A good many writers about the contemporary American scene have noted the prominence of a general "search for values" at a high level of generality.† Another phenomenon to which the religious revival seems to be closely related is the prominent increase in concern for the psychological problems of personality, especially with reference to such fields as mental health and child training. Religion generally is very closely associated with the equilibrium of the individual person, and that these two concerns should increase concomitantly makes sense, especially

---

* Probably the clearest historical case, which was in some but by no means all respects comparable, was the "Great Revival" in New England in the time of Jonathan Edwards.

† See especially Clyde Kluckhohn, "The Evolution of Contemporary American Values," published in an abridged version, *Daedalus*, Vol. 87, No. 2 (Spring, 1958).

when religion is considered to be so "personal" as in the American case.

It is often suggested that a relative lack of concern with theological problems is an argument against imputing religious "genuineness" to the movement. I question whether this is so. On sociological grounds it is quite reasonable to suppose that such a concern should focus on values rather than beliefs, particularly in the American milieu, where we have a general hesitancy against using too abstract thinking, above all on philosophical levels, and where, in the sense referred to above, the general cultural atmosphere has been highly "secular."

The broader sociological context lies in the fact that American society, in its values and its institutional structure, is organized about a kind of polarization between the external field of instrumental activity, the field of opportunity in economic production and in other occupational areas, and the capacities and other "internal" states of the acting units, notably the individual person.

We have recently been through a tremendous process of economic growth which has involved not only quantitative expansion but a major structural reorganization of the society, which in turn has very important repercussions on people. They are under pressure to perform such new and different roles that their personal values become involved. I should regard this restructuring of role-values, which is concomitant with the process of structural change in the society, as the main source of the increased concern with religion.* It is associated not only with concern with psychological problems but also with the increasing sense of urgency of problems of education and a variety of others.

It is reasonable to expect that the salience of religious concern should vary in something of a cyclical pattern, in shape somewhat similar to economic and political shifts, though involving

---

* It is most important not to confuse this role-value change with change in the *general* value-orientation of the society as a whole on the highest levels. In my opinion this has in the American case remained essentially stable. I am, of course, aware that many others have a different view.

considerably longer periods. It should be interpreted as part of a more general pattern of periodicities which one expects to find in a rapidly developing social system, of what Bales calls a "phase pattern."*

I therefore think that the religious revival fits into the interpretation of the place of religion in the structure of the society which has been presented in this paper. If this revival is religiously genuine, as I think it is, the fact that it should occur at all is one more bit of evidence that ours is a religiously oriented society, not a case of "secularization" in the usual sense. Further, the fact that it seems to fit into a cyclical pattern is in line with what we know about the more general significance of such periodicities in this type of society. Finally, the form it takes seems to fit the emphasis on the private and personal character of religion, which is one of the principal features of the American religious pattern and differentiates it from its antecedents in the traditions connected with established churches.

My main thesis in this paper has been that the religious constitution of American society is fundamentally in line with the great Western tradition of a society organized about Christian values, a Christian society in a sense not wholly out of line with that of Troeltsch. Looked at by comparison with earlier forms, religion seems to have lost much. But it seems to me that the losses are mainly the consequence of processes of structural differentiation in the society, which correspond to changes in the character of the religious orientation but do not necessarily constitute loss of strength of the religious values themselves.

The most essential "concession" was made by the Mediæval Catholic Church itself, namely through the view that society should not be a simple "theocracy" but that the secular arm was genuinely independent, responsible directly to God, not simply

* Cf. Robert F. Bales, *Interaction Process Analysis* (Cambridge, Mass.: Addison-Wesley Press, 1950).

through the organized Church. From this point on the basic question has been that of the limits of jurisdiction over the individual of the secular "good society." In the American case these limits have proved to be very different from, and much broader than, those envisaged by the Mediæval theorists; but they did not envisage modern society any more than the modern churches.

The American system is far from being fully integrated. It must contend with important elements which are anchored in earlier patterns of religious organization, notably fundamentalist Protestantism and the Catholic Church, both of which make claims which are anomalous within the main American framework. It must contend with the proliferation of exotic religious movements of dubious longer-run religious soundness, from the "Holy Rollers" to such "inspirationists" as Norman Vincent Peale. It must finally contend with the various aspects of secularism which to many religious people seem to have no place in a religiously committed society. On balance, however, I think that the main trend is toward greater integration of these various elements in a viable system which can be a vital part of a larger society. In this, as in other vital respects, American society is fundamentally an outgrowth of its European heritage, not an exotic "sport."

6. *The Broken Center: A Definition of the Crisis of Values in Modern Literature*

NATHAN A. SCOTT, JR.

> Things fall apart; the center cannot hold;
> Mere anarchy is loosed upon the world;
> ·
> The best lack all conviction, while the worst
> Are full of passionate intensity.
>
> —WILLIAM BUTLER YEATS, "The Second Coming." [1]

> We need a theme? then let that be our theme:
> that we, poor grovellers between faith and doubt,
> the sun and north star lost, and compass out,
> the heart's weak engine all but stopped, the time
> timeless in this chaos of our wills—
> that we must ask a theme, something to think,
> something to say, between dawn and dark,
> something to hold to, something to love.
>
> —CONRAD AIKEN, *Time in the Rock.*[2]

ONE OF the characters in the dialogue on which Richard Chase has based his recent brilliant book *The Democratic Vista* gives me a kind of text for this essay when he remarks: "... it seems that the greatest writers of the first half of the twentieth century lived in a high, tense world of strenuous and difficult metaphysics, moral doctrine, political ideology, and religious feeling."[3] The young man who says this is a graduate student of literature who, together with his wife and two children, is spending a late summer weekend on the Massachusetts coast in the home of a professor at his university, and it is to his senior friend that he offers this observation. He is perhaps being characteristic of his generation when he argues that "it is no longer possible to share" the intellectual and spiritual preoccupations of the great heroes of the modern tradition, of people like Eliot and Joyce and Pound. But though this may be a foreclosure that is too narrow and too premature, he does, nevertheless, identify accurately what is the most important distinguishing feature of the great classic tradition of modern letters, for that is most certainly a tradition that posits "a high, tense world of strenuous and difficult metaphysics . . . and religious feeling."

When we think, for example, of Mann and Lawrence and Kafka and Faulkner, it becomes immediately apparent that these are writers not all of whom are easily to be sheltered under the same umbrella; their methods of practicing the arts of fiction and the various gestures they make toward reality all represent the amazing differentiation of attitude and language that is a chief hallmark of literary art in our period. But, despite this multifariousness of creative technique and of fundamental point of view, they are writers whom we feel impelled to regard as constituting in some sense a genuine community and a unitary tradition. And this is a view that we take because these are writers whose own most emphatic insistence has been upon the fact of their being unsustained by any vital and helpful traditions; the community they form has been rooted, in other words, in their common awareness of their isolation. Nor has their isolation been primarily an affair of the artist's tenuous position in the polity of modern society. That position, to be sure, has been something uncertain and problematic, and the artist's social mar-

ginality has at times undoubtedly greatly added to his unease.
But what for him has most fundamentally given to life the aspect
of crisis has been that recession of faith and that erosion of the
religious terrain announced by Nietzsche in the nineteenth century, and, in our own time, by Sartre.

In such an age, when all is in doubt and when, as Yeats says,
"Things fall apart" and "the center cannot hold"—in such an age,
the philosopher may not be utterly crippled, if he is willing to
have his vocation confined to the analysis of nothing more than
the structure of sentences; and the social critic can always be kept
busy in notating the tics and the spasms that are the signs of our
distress. And in similar reduced ways the other custodians of the
cultural life may in some manner continue to function when
overtaken by a late bad time. But when the traditional premises
regarding the radical significance of things have collapsed and
when there is no longer any robust common faith to orient the
imaginative faculties of men with respect to the ultimate mys-
teries of existence—when, in other words, the basic presuppositions of a culture have become just yawning question marks, then
the literary artist is thrust upon a most desolate frontier indeed.
For, though he is sometimes spoken of as presiding over an act
of *communication*, this is a vulgar version of his role that could
pass muster only in an age of television and of what is called
"the mass-audience." The writer may, to be sure, take his stand
before a microphone and speak to a crowd in whose fate he is
not at all implicated; and, when he does this, it may be that he
plays a part in something that might be called a process of
communication. Yet, when this is his position, surely it is impossible for anything to be "shared, in a new and illuminating intensity of awareness."[4] Indeed, as Allen Tate has reminded us, the
very concept of literature as *Communication* may well, in its
current connotation, betoken a tragic victory of modern secularism over the human spirit. "Our unexamined theory of literature
as communication," he says, "could not have appeared in an age

in which communion was still possible for any appreciable majority of persons. The word communication presupposes the victory of the secularized society of means without ends. The poet, on the one hand, shouts to the public, on the other (some distance away), not the rediscovery of the common experience, but a certain pitch of sound to which the well-conditioned adrenals of humanity obligingly respond."[5]

No, Tate says, the language of *communication* may be the language of radio and television, but it is not the language which the artist seeks sensitively to supervise, for that is the language not of communication but of *communion:* it is a language into which an effort has been made to put a deep and authentic knowledge of what is involved in the life together of free men; so it is a language that invites us to re-enter what Martin Buber calls "the world of *I* and *Thou.*"

Which is, of course, to say that the language of imaginative literature is not the ethically and spiritually neutral jargon of any science: it is, rather, a language which, if it is to do its proper work, needs to be heavily weighted with the beliefs, the sentiments and valuations that are the deep source in the culture of its "hum and buzz of implication"[6] and that bind the people together with ties that separate them from the peoples of other cultures. Only when the artist's language bears this kind of freight can it be something more than a vehicle of communication: only then can it become an instrument of communion and what all art is ultimately intended to be—namely, a servant of love.

But now we are brought back to that desolate frontier on which I have said the modern writer has found himself, for what has made his position as an artist so insecure has been precisely the very great difficulty he has had in making contact with any significant body of belief that, having vital authority in our period, might furnish his imagination with the premises of its functioning and facilitate the transaction between himself and his reader.

"In the profoundest human sense," said Kenneth Burke in one of his early books, "one communicates in a *weighted* vocabulary in which the weightings are shared by [one's] group as a whole."[7] But it is just at this point that modern culture has represented great privation. There is, in fact, little of anything at all of profound significance that is widely shared by modern men. The dominant dispensation has been of a scientific character, but Max Planck tells us that "there is scarcely [even] a scientific axiom that is not now-a-days denied by somebody."[8] And, outside the realm of our scientific culture, the resistant pressure offered to the relativizing tendencies of our time has been negligible indeed.

In his important book *Diagnosis of Our Time,* Karl Mannheim proposes the interesting and cogent hypothesis that the despiritualization of modern life is best understood in terms of the gradual evaporation in our period of authentic "paradigmatic experience" and of those great "primordial images or archetypes" which, being formed out of this kind of experience, have directed the human enterprise in the most genuinely creative moments of cultural history. By "paradigmatic experience" Dr. Mannheim means those "basic experiences which carry more weight than others, and which are unforgettable in comparison with others that are merely passing sensations."[9] Without experiences of this kind, he says, "no consistent conduct, no character formation and no real human coexistence and co-operation are possible. Without them our universe of discourse loses its articulation, conduct falls to pieces, and only disconnected bits of successful behaviour patterns and fragments of adjustment to an ever-changing environment remain."[9] And his contention is that "paradigmatic experience," in so far as it yields some conviction as to what is radically significant, does also, in effect, create a kind of "ontological hierarchy," in accordance with which we say, " 'This is bad, this is good, this is better.' " But, of course, the whole drive of the positivistically oriented secularism of modern culture has been towards such "a neutralization of that ontological hierarchy in the world of experience" as encourages the belief that "one experience is as important as any other"[9] and that the question of right or wrong merely concerns the most efficient environmental adjustments. So the result has been the evaporation of those "primordial images" which objectify a people's faith and provide the moral imagination with its basic premises. And when there are no "paradigmatic experiences," then nothing is any longer revealed as having decisive importance, and men are ruled by a kind of "kaleidoscopic concept of life"[9] which, in giving an equal significance to everything, does, in effect, attribute radical significance to nothing at all. In such an age, the individual is condemned to the awful prison of his own individuality, since nothing means the same thing to any broad segment of people—and the primary fact about the human community is disclosed as being the complete collapse of anything resembling genuine community.

This is a fact which has been dramatized by much recent social criticism in its notation of the astonishing lack of drama in modern society. The life of the average megalopolitan today is ungraced by any rituals which strengthen the ties of sympathy and fellow-feeling. Nor is the civic scene complicated and enlivened by any round of celebrations and festivities comparable to the religious liturgies or the secular rites that figured so largely in the common life of earlier times. In the great cities of our day we are cave dwellers, scurrying about the urban wilderness from one vast compound to another, like "bits of paper, whirled by the cold wind"[10]; and, like the members of Captain Ahab's crew, we are, as Melville says, "nearly all Islanders," none "acknowledging the common continent of men, but each *Isolato* living on a separate continent of his own."

This, then, is the intractable and unpromising reality that confronts the modern writer. Burke says that it is the artist's task to supervise a *weighted* language whose weightings are shared by the commonalty. But it has been the fate of the modern artist to live in a time when the commonalty, as anything more than a statistical assemblage of unrelated atoms, is something to be remembered only by the historical imagination. And this is why the problem of understanding modern literature so largely involves the problem of understanding the stratagems that become inevitable for the artist when history commits him to the practice of his vocation in such a vacuum.

What the modern artist has needed to find are "systems of reference, acceptable to the experience of our time, by means of which he [could] give order and unity to his work."[11] This is, indeed, what the artist has always needed, and, when the circumstances of his culture have afforded a good soil for art to grow in, the ethos of his community has provided him with coordinating analogies and key metaphors and with myths and symbols which, in flowing out of the funded memories and experience of his people, could well serve him as instruments for the full evocation of the human communion. Surely it is no merely willful or sentimental nostalgia that leads us, when we roam back through the tradition, to account in these terms for the greatness of the achievement of Sophocles and Dante, of Shakespeare and Racine, or, on a far less exalted level, of, say, Madame de Lafayette or Jane Austen. In these older writers we feel a kind of freedom and a kind of security of reference that strike us as being a consequence of their having had the good fortune to live in cultures which, having a vital unity, could liberally provide those "primordial images" and "archetypes" which centralize and order the poetic imagination. These older writers were the lucky ones, for they did not have to invent ways of construing experience; they were lucky because the writer who has to expend energy on philosophical and theological enterprises before he can get his literary project under way will have squandered reserves of imaginative power that, in more favorable circumstances, would be used up in the practice of his art. And when one thinks, say, of Jane Austen in relation to the woman of our own time who wrote such a book as *Nightwood*, we cannot help but feel that the older writer was also lucky because, in receiving her ultimate terms of reference from her culture, she was relieved of any uncertainty about how to establish contact with her readers and was, therefore, enabled to make the kinds of assumptions that facilitate the poetic transaction.

This is precisely the kind of luck, however, that the writer in the modern period has not enjoyed. Inheriting no traditional and widely accepted frame of values from his culture, before his art could be steadied by some executive principle of valuation, it has been necessary for the artist to try to construct some viable system of belief for himself, by means of an effort of personal vision. He has had to be, in a sense, his own priest, his own guide, his own Virgil. He has been condemned by the cultural circumstances of his time to draw from within himself everything that forms and orders his art. The deep waters in which he has swum have been those of his own individual mind, and he has had to plunge deep in his search for the principles by which the anarchy of experience might be controlled and given a shape and a significance. Thus we might say that the reigning law of the modern movement in the arts has been that of the *principium individuationis*.

Indeed, all the great literature of the modern period might be said to be a literature of metaphysical isolation, for the modern artist—and this is perhaps the fundamental truth about him—has experienced a great loneliness, the kind of loneliness that is known by the soul when it has to undertake, unaided by ministries either of Church or of culture, the adventure of discovering the fundamental principles of meaning. Unquestionably, this accounts for the obscurity of so many great modern texts—of Rimbaud's *Une Saison en Enfer*, of Rilke's *Duino Elegies*, Joyce's *Finnegans Wake*, or Malcolm Lowry's *Under the Volcano*. Amidst the confusion in values of his age, the artist is attempting to invent for himself a system of attitudes and beliefs that will give meaning to his world. And it is this idiosyncrasy, this extreme individuality, of modern poetic vision that has often made our finest literature so difficult to penetrate. What has been most distinctive of the great heroes of the modern tradition is, as Stephen Spender says, that they assumed the task "of re-experiencing everything as though it had never been experienced before, and then expressing it not in terms with which traditions and education have made us familiar but in new ones minted out"[12] of their separate sensibilities. In a time when

> So various
> And multifoliate are our breeds of faith
> That we could furnish a herbarium
> With the American specimens alone[13]

the writer felt himself to be without a common background of reference which could orient and bring into a profound rapport his own imaginative faculties and those of his readers. So he has turned inward, pursuing a system of values or beliefs in the world of his own subjectivity. Thus, as Spender says, "it becomes increasingly more difficult for the reader to understand the significance of the writer's symbols and language, without his having experienced the process of the writer's experiencing. . . . Hence a vast literature explaining texts and the circumstances of each writer's life has grown up around the modern movement."[12] And this is a development that has tended to institutionalize the originally unique experimentations of the great pioneers and to make them, indeed, a staple of the new academic tradition—as is indicated, for example, by the notification we are given on the jacket of William York Tindall's book on Joyce that, as the publisher says, Tindall "is a member of the James Joyce Society, and has made the pilgrimage to Dublin."[14] Yet this is precisely what Joyce's work demands—membership in scholarly societies devoted to its study and foundation-sponsored tours to Dublin in search of scraps of information that may assist us in unraveling the bafflements of his incredibly complex art. For this writer "is in himself a culture and a country with myths and dialects derived from other ones."[12] And the necessity we confront, when we tackle a book like *Finnegans Wake,* is one of trying to make some sense of a vast chaotic array of notes toward what its author heroically strove to make the great modern novel.

Indeed, the Joycean experiment, however stillborn it may in part have been, does at least, in a way, succeed in stating the significant questions and in drawing attention to a fundamental dilemma of the artist in our period. For the lesson of Joyce's career teaches us that, though the artist cannot by fiat produce adequate surrogates for traditions of faith and culture no longer available to him, he can, in attempting to do so, dramatize with especial vividness the fact of the mythical vacuum in the modern period. And that is what Joyce succeeded in doing. As T. S. Eliot put the issue in his famous review of *Ulysses* in 1923: "In using the myth, in manipulating a continuous parallel between contemporaneity and antiquity, Joyce is pursuing a method which others must pursue after him. . . . It is simply a way of controlling or ordering, of giving a shape and a significance to the immense panorama of futility and anarchy which is contemporary history."[15] And it is the radicalism of his effort to find this shape and this significance that makes him the great exemplar of the literary artist in the modern age; he gives the age away, by which I mean that he puts us in mind of how much "the greatest writers of the first half of the twentieth century lived in a high, tense world of strenuous and difficult metaphysics . . . and religious feeling." And though they may seem to be "the more austerely religious in that [they have not often been] prejudiced by religious belief"[16] of an orthodox sort, we should not, even so, allow their heterodoxy to obscure the authenticity of their researches into the human condition and the immense courage with which they have steered their lonely, separate courses through the spiritual void of our time.

Now it is precisely the kind of extreme self-reliance in the quest for "first principles" that I have been positing as the inescapable necessity facing the modern writer; it is precisely this that makes evident his descendance from the great Romantics of the last century. And it also makes evident the fact that the literature of the age of Joyce and Kafka is essentially a late development of the Romantic movement. Here, we must not be misled by the vigorous anti-Romanticism that informs so much of twentieth-century literature. It is true, of course, that men like Valéry, Eliot and Pound in poetry, and Joyce and Proust in the novel, have sponsored programs of one sort or another whose aim has been to encourage a rejection of the legacy of Romanticism, with its inspirationist aesthetic, its cult of sincerity, its artlessness, and its confusions of art and religion. But, steady as this quarrel with the Romantic movement has been in our time, it is a family quarrel, and the fact remains that the great tradition of twentieth-century literature is, fundamentally, a product of the Romantic dispensation. As Robert Langbaum has recently observed,

Whatever the difference between the literary movements of the nineteenth and twentieth centuries, they are connected . . . by their response to the same wilderness. That wilderness is the legacy of the Enlightenment, of the scientific and critical effort of the Enlightenment which, in its desire to separate fact from the values of a crumbling tradition, separated fact from all values—bequeathing a world in which fact is measurable quantity while value is man-made and illusory. Such a world offers no objective verification for just the perceptions by which men live, perceptions of beauty, goodness and spirit. It was as literature began in the latter eighteenth century to realize the dangerous implications of the scientific world-view that romanticism was born. It was born anew in at least three generations thereafter as men of genius arrived intellectually at the dead-end of the eighteenth century and then, often through a total crisis of personality, broke intellectually into the nineteenth. As literature's reaction to the eighteenth century's scientific world-view, romanticism connects the literary movement of the nineteenth and twentieth centuries.[17]

This recognition of the havoc wrought by Enlightenment iconoclasm did not lead the great English Romantics to an exacerbation of spirit so extreme as that which is often noticeable in their French and German contemporaries. We can, however, detect the signs of this unrest in Coleridge and in Wordsworth, and in Keats and Shelley. They all make us feel that for them the traditional archetypes and systems of faith had ceased to be effective any longer and that, as a result, in their dealings with the world, they were thrown back upon their own private resources. They had all felt what Keats called in *Lamia* "the touch of cold philosophy," and, as a consequence, they knew themselves to be deprived of that mythical machinery for the ordering of experience which writers in earlier periods of the tradition had been blessed in having; they knew themselves to be fated by the logic of their culture to bear, alone and unassisted, what Wordsworth called "the weight of all this unintelligible world." Thus, in works like "Tintern Abbey," the "Ode on Intimations of Immortality," "The Rime of the Ancient Mariner," "Adonais," the "Ode to the West Wind," and the "Ode to a Nightingale," these men attempted what Coleridge believed to be the poet's task, "of spreading the tone, the *atmosphere*, and with it the depth and height of the ideal world around forms, incidents, and situations, of which, for the common view, custom had bedimmed all the lustre, had dried up the sparkle and the dew drops."[18]

When we turn, however, to Continental Romanticism, particularly in France, and here not to such relatively early figures as Rousseau and Chateaubriand and Lamartine but to such later writers as Baudelaire and Rimbaud and Lautréamont—when we turn to this French Romantic tradition, we leave the elegiac temper of the English school and come to a new kind of intensity and a new kind of violence that point directly toward the *Angst-*

ridden literature of the twentieth century. It was with this tradition in mind that the distinguished French critic Jacques Rivière
remarked in his essay on "La Crise du concept de littérature"
that "with Romanticism . . . the literary act began to be conceived as a kind of assault on the absolute, and its result as a
revelation," the writer becoming a kind of "priest." Indeed, said
Rivière, this whole literature is "a vast incantation toward the
miracle."[19]

But not only does the artist working under the dispensation of
Baudelaire and Lautréamont become a priest; he also becomes a
kind of scientist, for, wanting to rescue himself from the metaphysical void of his culture, he is so much in the grip of a
passion for knowledge that the poetic process itself becomes not
primarily a process of the artist's *making*, but rather a process
of the artist's *discovering* the ultimate frontiers of human existence and of there staking out his claim to dominion. Rimbaud,
for example, in writing to his friend Paul Demeny, says:

> The first study for a man who wants to be a poet is the knowledge
> of himself, entire. He looks for his soul, inspects it, learns it. As soon
> as he knows it, he cultivates it: it seems simple. . . . But the soul has
> to be made monstrous, that's the point. . . .
> One must, I say, be a *seer*, make oneself a *seer*.
> The poet makes himself a seer through a long, a prodigious and
> rational disordering of *all* the senses. Every form of love, of suffering,
> of madness; he searches himself, he consumes all the poisons in him,
> keeping only their quintessences. Ineffable torture in which he will
> need all his faith and superhuman strength, the great criminal, the
> great sickman, the utterly damned, and the supreme Savant! For he
> arrives at the unknown! Since he has cultivated his soul—richer to
> begin with than any other! He arrives at the unknown: and even if,
> half crazed, in the end, he loses the understanding of his visions, he
> has seen them! Let him croak in his leap into those unutterable and
> innumerable things: there will come other horrible workers: they will
> begin at the horizons where he has succumbed.[20]

Now here we have an inner dislocation which this particular
poet called a sacred disorder, but what is really signified is his

having yielded to "an invasion of vertigo"[21] and lost his footing. So it is not surprising that he abandoned poetry in 1873 at the age of nineteen to spend the rest of his brief life in exotic adventure and in angry defiance of bourgeois Philistinism. Yet, despite Rimbaud's abdication from literature, his prophecy was borne out, and other laborers did come after him, "who began at the horizons where he had collapsed."[21] The particular horizon where he collapsed was the point at which his own desperate need, as an artist and as a man, for metaphysical and religious order collided with the spiritual void of the nineteenth century. And this is the precise horizon on which we may locate that great modern procession that includes, in addition to Baudelaire and Rimbaud and Lautréamont, such earlier writers as Hölderlin, Leopardi and Vigny, and such later writers as Mallarmé, Valéry, Joyce and Hart Crane, André Gide, André Malraux, St. John Perse, and many others. For all these, in the sense that I am claiming for the term, are Romantics: they are writers bent upon *improvising* perspectives and principles in terms of which a shape and a significance may be given to "the immense panorama" of modern experience, thus making it accessible to art. This is their passion and their chosen task, and it is their dedication to this that makes them candidates for the special kind of sainthood that the *avant-garde* has tended to produce in the modern period. In a way, they have been martyrized by the dislocations of the time, and, when we think of artists like Kafka and Hart Crane and Dylan Thomas and Malcolm Lowry, it does seem, indeed, that they have borne upon their own souls the stigmata of the bent and broken world to which they were committed by modern history.

This, therefore, is the first major observation to be made about the great classic tradition of contemporary letters: we must say that, in its tone and style and outlook, it is an incorrigibly Romantic tradition. We see this even in apparently so un-Romantic a figure as T. S. Eliot, who, to be sure, has made his way back to a classical tradition of religious faith and has found in Christian history the deepest inspiration for his work of the past twenty-five years. Yet the particular tradition of Christian faith in which Eliot has chosen to live—the tradition, say, of Origen and Dame Julian of Norwich and Jacob Boehme and St. John of the Cross—hardly strikes us as belonging to the great central tradition of Christian culture: it is very special and irregular, and its very reclamation by a contemporary Christian poet suggests that even his orthodoxy will, in its attainment, represent something of the same kind of improvisation that has tended generally to characterize the philosophic and religious strategems of the modern artist.

But, now, a second major observation must be made of the modern tradition in literature, for we shall not fully comprehend it until we recognize it as a tradition which represents that particular late development of the Romantic movement which is an outgrowth of what Erich Kahler calls "the existentialist experience."[22] Not only, in other words, must we say that this is a Romantic literature; we must also say that it is an Existentialist literature as well. But when I denominate the central tradition in our literature as Existentialist, I do not intend to refer merely to certain recent writers, particularly in France, who have found a theoretical sanction for their vision in the doctrines of Existentialist philosophy. I use the term, rather, in a very much broader sense and intend it to define the literature of the last hundred years in which we find reflected an experience of existence as fundamentally and, perhaps even, essentially problematic.

This is an experience which it will doubtless be our first impulse to regard as having been occasioned by those ultimate exigencies in the history of the modern spirit to which Nietzsche called our attention in his announcement of "the death of God." But "the death of God," as a cultural fact of the modern age, is itself something whose fundamental cause, I believe, is to be sought in the "death of man" in our time, for this is the really primary fact in modern experience. What we confront, throughout the whole polity of modern society, is a tragic devitalization of the very concept of the person. The kind of life *en masse*, for example, that has been so distinctive of our period has been made possible by a system whose inner logic has necessitated a high degree of specialization in all fields of man's labor. And this, in turn, by a dreadful kind of inexorability, has accomplished what might even be said to be a mutation in human nature itself, in so far as the habit of requiring a man to justify himself by his ability to perform a special task has weakened in us the capacity to make the crucial distinction between the function and the human being who performs it. But not only has the distinction become a difficult one to make; the human act by which a man transcends his various social and economic functions has also, under the pressures of a commercialized culture, become an act that it is increasingly more difficult to perform. Many of the most thoughtful observers of modern life have noticed how the logic of a technocratic culture tends to reduce the concrete particularity of the unique human individual to a purely abstract and functional identity; and they have also noticed the gray anonymity of life that this reduction accomplishes. What every reporter on the present human condition has, indeed, to take into account is the sense men have today of being thrust into the nudity of their own isolated individual existence. Though "huddled together" in the great metropolises of the contemporary world "like dust in a heap," that which figures most prominently in their awareness is a sense of the world's vacancy, and the loss of which they are most acutely conscious is the loss of the real proximity of friends and neighbors. Life seems, as Karl Jaspers says, to have grown "indefinitely vast": it no longer has that "interlinkage" which holds it together, "so that it is not frittered away" and disintegrated into "the brief perspective of the [immediate] present."[23] A man has the function he performs for eight hours a day, and he has his bit of breathing-space somewhere in the urban or the suburban wilderness. But, as we are told in Mr. Eliot's "Choruses from 'the Rock' ":

> The desert is squeezed in the tube-train next to you,
> The desert is in the heart of your brother.[24]

So, though all the time we live closer and closer together in our great urban compounds, we find it more and more difficult to recognize one another or even to retain a sense of our own identities. And amidst this gray, dreary anonymity we know that we live in a world from which all the gracious marks of "presence" have been banished.

"Just as primitive man believed himself to stand face to face with demons and believed that could he but know their names he would become their master, so," says Karl Jaspers, "contemporary man [is] faced by . . . [something that is] incomprehensible, which disorders his calculations. . . . The nameless powers of Nothingness," he says, "are, in our world whence the gods have been driven forth, the analogy of the demons that confronted primitive man."[25] And this, I believe, is why men in the modern period have believed God to be silent and absent and even dead. This has been their conclusion because they have not lived out their days in real nearness to one another, and, not having known the gracious reality of "presence" in their relations with their neighbors, their imaginations have been unable to grasp the possibility of the world itself being grounded in a transcendent "Presence."

In such a world, where the human communion has been destroyed and man's condemnation is to an empty and unfertile solitude, what Gabriel Marcel calls *Presence*[26] appears to be an obsolescent relic of the past; not only does it appear that God is dead, but so too does it appear that an obituary notice is to be written memorializing the disappearance of man as well. In this "place of disaffection," as Mr. Eliot calls it, the only available dispensation seems to be that of loneliness and exile, and it is the sober acceptance of this icy alienation as the inescapable ground of human existence that constitutes that special modern sensibility which I am calling (after Erich Kahler) "the existentialist experience."

This is not an experience that is the sole property of those contemporary theorists of it whose program goes under the name of Existentialism. Their nineteenth-century predecessors were, to be sure, among the first to give it emphatic definition, and it first became a public fact in the Berlin lectures of Schelling *(Die Philosophie der Mythologie und der Offenbarung)* during the winter of 1841-1842 and in the later writings of men like Kierkegaard and Marx and Feuerbach and Nietzsche and Max Weber. But this is also an experience whose beginning is to be dated from the morning Baudelaire looked out upon the billboards of Paris—"that vast cemetery that is called a great city"—and felt an immense disgust. And not only do we find it in writers like Baudelaire and Rimbaud and Dostoievski and Strindberg, but we also find it in artists like Cézanne and Van Gogh, and the American Albert Pinkham Ryder. These were all men who belonged to that nineteenth-century vanguard of revolutionaries distinguished for the clarity and courage with which they acknowledged the bitter facts of alienation and estrangement as the central facts of modern existence. And when, as Paul Tillich says, "the nineteenth century came to an end" on 31 July 1914,[27] the existentialist experience ceased to be the experience of a sensitive minority and became the dominant experience of the age. In this century it has furnished the perspectives of the philosophic tradition established by such thinkers as Berdyaev and Shestov and Heidegger and Jaspers and Sartre and Marcel; it is the experience one feels in Stravinsky's *Pétrouchka*, in Schoenberg's *Pierrot Lunaire*, in Alban Berg's *Wozzeck*, in Bartok's *Second Quartet,* and in much of the great music of our time; and it is also the experience that has been painted into many of the canvases of such classic moderns as Picasso and

Rouault and the early de Chirico, or of such recent artists as
Willem de Kooning and Jackson Pollock and Hans Hofmann.

Now it is this strain of sensibility that is central in much of
twentieth-century literature: it is what we recognize in such
poets of verse as Rainer Maria Rilke and Hart Crane and Robert
Penn Warren and Gottfried Benn and in such poets of the novel
as Conrad and Kafka and Faulkner and Malraux. Indeed, as
Lionel Trilling has remarked, "There is scarcely a great writer of
our own day who has not addressed himself to the ontological
crisis, who has not conceived of life as a struggle to be—not to
live, but to be."[28] And what one feels to be formative in much
of the representative literature of our period is a deep need for
a deep restoration of confidence in the stoutness and reliability
and essential healthiness of the things of earth. The trauma that
has been suffered is the trauma that is inflicted upon the imagination when it appears that both God and man are dead.

So the narrative that is at the center of our literature is a
narrative of estrangement and alienation: the story that is told
is a story of our abandonment "in some blind lobby . . . or corridor
of Time. . . . And in the dark," says Penn Warren, "no thread."[29]
No thread. And we are given some measure of how emphatic is
the insistence upon our lostness by the apocalypticism and the
hyperaesthesia of the literary imagination in our day, "its feeling,"
as Richard Chase says, "that no thought is permissible except an
extreme thought: that every idea must be directly emblematic of
concentration camps, alienation, madness, hell . . .; that every
word must bristle and explode with the magic potency of our
plight."[30]

In our own American tradition, the figure of William Dean
Howells as a novelist has fallen into what is well-nigh a complete
eclipse, and we may partly understand the reason for this by
remembering the observation of Howells that was made many
years ago by Henry James, when he said: "He is animated by a
love of the common, the immediate, the familiar, and the vulgar

elements of life, and holds that in proportion as we move into the rare and strange we become vague and arbitrary. . . ."[31] When we re-read today books like *The Rise and Fall of Silas Lapham,* or *A Hazard of New Fortunes,* or *A Modern Instance,* we realize that, with his customary acuteness, James put his finger exactly on what is one of Howells's primary qualities. So it is no wonder that the contemporary reader finds it so difficult to enter into a happy and reciprocal relation with his work, for, as Professor Trilling has reminded us, "we consent to the commonplace [only] as it verges upon and becomes the rare and the strange": we "want something that has affinity with the common, the immediate, the familiar . . . [but] we like them represented in their extremity to serve as a sort of outer limit of the possibility of our daily lives, as a kind of mundane hell."[28]

All the great charismatic seers of modern literature from Baudelaire to Kafka and from Pirandello to Faulkner have, in one way or another, wanted us to understand that we are lost in a dark wood and that, in this maze, what is least trustworthy is the common, the immediate, the familiar. Thus the motion the modern artist has often performed before the revolving universe has been a motion of recoil. Sometimes, like Rimbaud, he has fallen in love with what Jacques Maritain calls "the blind glitter of nothingness"[21] and made of his art a kind of incantatory magic. Or, like the author of *Finnegans Wake,* sometimes he has decided himself to be God and to create *ex nihilo* a universe of his own. On occasion, his retreat, like Mallarmé's, has been into *la poésie pure,* or, like the early Hemingway or the Dos Passos of the *U.S.A.* trilogy, it has been into the neutral factuality of naturalistic documentation. The recoil may have been into the subjectivistic perspectives of a Proust or a Virginia Woolf, or into that distress which provokes the belch of disgust expressed, say, in Jean-Paul Sartre's *La Nausée.* But, various as the configurations are, it can, nevertheless, be said that many of the major literary artists of our time, whether they knew it or not, have had as their patron saint not St. Athanasius, but Dionysius the Areopagite, for, in their dealings with the body of this world, their Way has been not the Way of Affirmation but the Way of Rejection. They have not known, in other words, the kind of confidence in the world and in temporal reality that was managed in happier moments in the literary tradition.

Those Roman Catholic apologists who explain this attrition in terms of the anti-sacramentalism of a Protestant ethos are doubtless right in part—but they are right only in part, for the authentic sacramentalism of the Christian faith has also been obscured by what has often been the theological and cultural obscurantism of post-Tridentine Romanism. Nor can we also forget the role played in this development by the deep fears generated by the continual expansion of the universe mapped out by modern science and modern cosmology. Back in the seventeenth century, Pascal was already conscious of the anxiety caused by contemplating "the infinite immensity of spaces" revealed by the new science, and, in what is one of the great expressions of the modern consciousness, he said: "The eternal silence of these infinite spaces frightens me." And, of course, far more frightening than the universes of modern physics have been the perils of historical existence itself, which has tended increasingly in the modern period to involve a kind of global insecurity hitherto unexperienced. But by far the deepest cause of the despondency and sense of alienation in modern literature is to be found in the collapse of any real certainty that what is Radically and Ultimately Significant is not absolutely secluded from that which is only provisionally significant in nature and in history. To the men of our age God seems, as Heidegger says, to be "withholding" Himself: He seems to be absent and perhaps even dead. And, as a consequence, our journey through the world does itself seem to be a terribly uncertain and perilous journey: as Stanley Hopper puts it, "the familiar trails to reality are swallowed up in thickets of confusion: the spoors are thickly overlaid."[32] And the artist's motion of recoil before this dark and threatening wood is but type and example of the deep mistrust with which modern man faces the indigence and privation of the world of finite, historical existence.

W. H. Auden tells us that Kafka bears to our own age the kind of relation Dante bore to his, and a part of his meaning is, I am certain, that, whereas the hero of Dante's poem is a pilgrim and the movement of the poem is "from low to high . . . [or] from dark to light,"[33] the hero of the Kafkan fable is a man who, at the end of his journeying, is no nearer the Castle than he was at the beginning and who remains forever quavering in the dungeon of his dereliction. In the one case, we have the Christian drama of rebirth and redemption, and, in the other, we have a story of the soul's exclusion from the Courts of the Most High and of the despair by which it is overtaken in its abandonment and isolation—the story, in other words, that forms the characteristic judgment of the human condition rendered by the existentialist imagination in modern literature.

Ours is, then, an "extreme" literature which plunges us into "extreme" situations. Conrad's Decoud, Kafka's K., Gide's Lafcadio, Malraux's Kyo, Faulkner's Joe Christmas, and Penn Warren's Jeremiah Beaumont are all men who have been "thrown into a world without [their] willing it and with no place prepared for [them]."[31] Their life has to be lived at a great distance from whatever are the sources of ultimate meaning, and, as a consequence, the salient stigmata of the modern hero are to be seen in his scepticism and in his despondency and alienation. But the miracle that occurs in the existentialist universe of a Conrad or a Kafka or a Malraux or a Faulkner is that, through the grace of some power that is unnamed and perhaps unknown, this scepticism and this despondency are prevented from so completely encircling the hero as to undo his humanity. Which is to say that the modern hero, in his great moments, has had what Paul Tillich calls "the courage of despair"—the courage, that is, despite everything that is problematic and uncertain in his world, to affirm his humanity. And since, despite all the nihilism that is in modern literature, this is a courage which is an expression of a kind of faith—faith itself, as Tillich says, being simply "the state of being grasped by the power of being-itself"[24]—it is not surprising, therefore, that the redefinition in our time of classical traditions of faith has often been deeply informed by this whole body of testimony. The Orthodox thinker Nicolas Berdyaev, the Roman Catholics Romano Guardini and Jacques Maritain, and the Protestant theologian Paul Tillich are representative of many other leading strategists of contemporary religious thought who have been alert to the fact that, if the high forms of faith are once again to be made to appear at least *possible* for us, their interpretation must itself be informed by the kind of awareness that comes from facing the distresses of life without any of the supports and consolations of religious faith. And so, in the attentiveness with which the religious community today is often listening to our poets and novelists and dramatists, we may discern some earnest of the reconstructive role that may yet be played by modern negation and denial.

REFERENCES

1. YEATS, William Butler, "The Second Coming," *The Collected Poems of W. B. Yeats* (New York: The Macmillan Company, 1951), pp. 184-185.
2. AIKEN, Conrad, *Time in the Rock* (New York: Charles Scribner's Sons, 1936), p. 2.
3. CHASE, Richard, *The Democratic Vista: A Dialogue on Life and Letters in Contemporary America* (Garden City, New York: Doubleday, 1958), p. 16.
4. TATE, Allen, *The Forlorn Demon* (Chicago: Henry Regnery Co., 1953), p. 13.
5. *Ibid.*, p. 12.
6. TRILLING, Lionel, *The Liberal Imagination* (New York: The Viking Press, 1950), p. 206.
7. MULLER, Herbert, *Modern Fiction* (New York: Funk and Wagnalls, 1937), p. 10.
8. SLOCHOWER, Harry, *No Voice Is Wholly Lost* (New York: Creative Age Press, Inc., 1945), p. vii.
9. MANNHEIM, Karl, *Diagnosis of Our Time* (New York: Oxford University Press, 1944), p. 146-148.
10. ELIOT, T. S., "Burnt Norton," *Four Quartets* (New York: Harcourt Brace, 1943), p. 6.
11. HOPPER, Stanley R., "The Problem of Moral Isolation in Contemporary Literature." In *Spiritual Problems in Contemporary Literature*, ed. Stanley R. Hopper (New York: Harper & Brothers, 1952), p. 153.
12. SPENDER, Stephan, *The Creative Element* (London: Hamish Hamilton, 1953), p. 176-177.
13. SHAPIRO, Karl, *Essay on Rime* (New York: Reynal and Hitchcock, 1945), p. 63.
14. TINDALL, William York, *James Joyce* (New York: Charles Scribner's Sons, 1950).
15. ELIOT, T. S., "Ulysses, Order and Myth." In *Critiques and Essays on Modern Fiction*, ed. John W. Aldridge (New York: Ronald Press, 1952), p. 426.
16. HOPPER, Stanley R., *op. cit.*, p. 155.
17. LANGBAUM, Robert, *The Poetry of Experience* (New York: Random House, 1957), p. 11-12.

18. COLERIDGE, S. T., *Biographia Literaria,* ed. J. Shawcross (London: Oxford University Press, 1907).

19. RIVIERE, Jacques, "La Crise du concept de Littérature,"*Nouvelle Revue Française,* 1 February, 1924.

20. RIMBAUD, Arthur, "Letters to Paul Demeny: 1871," *Prose Poems from the Illuminations,* trans. by Louise Varese (New York: New Directions, 1946), pp. xxvi-xxvii.

21. MARITAIN, Jacques, *Creative Intuition in Art and Poetry* (New York: Pantheon Books, 1953), p. 186, 189.

22. KAHLER, Erich, *The Tower and the Abyss* (New York: George Braziller, Inc., 1957), pp. 168-175.

23. JASPERS, Karl, *Man in the Modern Age,* trans. by Eden and Cedar Paul (Garden City: Doubleday Anchor Books, 1957), p. 202.

24. ELIOT, T. S., "Choruses from 'The Rock'," *Collected Poems: 1909-1935* (New York: Harcourt, Brace and Co., 1936), p. 182.

25. JASPERS, Karl, *op. cit.,* p. 191.

26. MARCEL, Gabriel, *The Mystery of Being* (Chicago: Henry Regnery Co., 1951), vol. I, chapters IX and X; vol. II, chapter I.

27. TILLICH, Paul, *The Courage to Be* (New Haven: Yale University Press, 1952), p. 137, 172.

28. TRILLING, Lionel, *The Opposing Self* (New York: The Viking Press, 1955), p. 140, 88.

29. WARREN, Robert Penn, *Brother to Dragons* (London: Eyre and Spottiswoode, 1953), p. 7.

30. CHASE, Richard, "Christian Ideologue" (a review of Basil Willey's *Nineteenth Century Studies), The Nation* (8 April 1950), p. 330.

31. JAMES, Henry, "William Dean Howells," *The American Essays* (New York: Vintage Books, 1956), p. 152.

32. HOPPER, Stanley R., "On the Naming of the Gods in Hölderlin and Rilke," in *Christianity and the Existentialists,* ed. Carl Michalson (New York: Charles Scribner's Sons, 1956), p. 156.

33. VAN DOREN, Mark, "The Divine Comedy," *The Noble Voice* (New York: Henry Holt and Co., 1946), p. 213.

34. VOTAW, Albert, "The Literature of Extreme Situations," *Horizon,* Vol. XX, no. 117 (September, 1949), p. 155.

7. The Sense of Poetry: Shakespeare's "The Phoenix and the Turtle"*

I. A. RICHARDS

Is IT NOT fitting that the greatest English poet should have written the most mysterious poem in English? "The Phoenix and the Turtle" is so strange a poem—even so unlike anything else in Shakespeare, as to have caused doubts that he wrote it. And yet, no one else seems in the least likely as author.

One of the odd things about the poem is that it has engendered curiosity and praise only in relatively recent times. Emerson was among the first: "To unassisted readers," he says, "it would appear to be a lament on the death of a poet, and of his poetic mistress." "This poem," he adds, "if published for the first time, and without a known author's name, would find no general reception. Only the poets would save it."

Since then many notable efforts have been made to assist "unassisted readers" without taking us perhaps very much further than Emerson himself went: "a lament of the death of a poet"—or is it the poetic endeavor?—"and his poetic mistress"—or could it be that whereto the poetic endeavor devotes itself: poetry?

Let us see. Let us read the poem through twice, once for detail and structure and pondering, and then again for life and motion.

---

* Based on a talk in a series given during the winter 1957-1958 over WGBH-TV in Boston, and distributed nationally by the Educational Television and Radio Center.

The Phoenix and the Turtle

Let the bird of lowdest lay,
On the sole *Arabian* tree,
Herauld sad and trumpet be:
To whose sound chaste wings obay.

But thou shriking harbinger,
Foule precurrer of the fiend,
Augour of the feuers end,
To this troupe come thou not neere.

From this Session interdict
Euery foule of tyrant wing,
Saue the Eagle feath'red King,
Keepe the obsequie so strict.

Let the Priest in Surples white,
That defunctive Musicke can,
Be the death-deuining Swan,
Lest the *Requiem* lacke his right.

And thou treble dated Crow,
That thy sable gender mak'st,
With the breath thou giu'st and tak'st,
'Mongst our mourners shalt thou go.

Here the Antheme doth commence,
Loue and Constancie is dead,
Phoenix and the *Turtle* fled,
In a mutuall flame from hence.

So they loued as loue in twaine,
Had the essence but in one,
Two distincts, Diuision none,
Number there in loue was slaine.

Hearts remote, yet not asunder;
Distance and no space was seene,
Twixt this *Turtle* and his *Queene*;
But in them it were a wonder.

So betweene them loue did shine,
That the *Turtle* saw his right,

Flaming in the *Phoenix* sight;
Either was the others mine.

Propertie was thus appalled,
That the selfe was not the same:
Single Natures double name,
Neither two nor one was called.

Reason in it selfe confounded,
Saw Diuision grow together,
To themselves yet either neither,
Simple were so well compounded.

That it cried, how true a twaine,
Seemeth this concordant one,
Loue hath Reason, Reason none,
If what parts, can so remaine.

Whereupon it made this *Threne*
To the *Phoenix* and the *Doue*,
Co-supremes and starres of Loue,
As *Chorus* to their Tragique Scene.

THRENOS

Beautie, Truth, and Raritie,
Grace in all simplicitie,
Here enclosde, in cinders lie.

Death is now the *Phoenix* nest,
And the *Turtles* loyall brest,
To eternitie doth rest,

Leauing no posteritie,
Twas not their infirmitie,
It was married Chastitie.

Truth may seeme, but cannot be,
Beautie bragge, but tis not she,
Truth and Beautie buried be.

To this vrne let those repaire,

> That are either true or faire,
> For these dead Birds, sigh a prayer.

The Phoenix here is a unique bird, singular indeed—there can be but the one Phoenix. And the Turtle Dove is so devoted a lover of his Queen—so entirely hers, as she is his—that, like an Indian suttee, he is consumed, burnt up on the pyre, in the flames of her regeneration.

> Let the bird of lowdest lay,
> On the sole *Arabian* tree,
> Herauld sad and trumpet be:
> To whose sound chaste wings obay.

Who is speaking? Who is this "bird of lowdest lay" who summons this company of birds and has this authority over "chaste wings"? (You will note, near the end, a very strong use indeed of the word "Chastitie.")

I like best the suggestion that the reborn Phoenix herself is here summoning the birds to the celebration of her own (and the Turtle's) obsequies. If so, this Phoenix, this Queen, is perched on her own throne. In *The Tempest* (III, iii, 22-24) Sebastian cries:

> Now I will believe that . . . in Arabia
> There is one tree, the phoenix' throne; one
>   phoenix
> At this hour reigning there.
> [On the sole *Arabian* tree]

If so, she herself is *Herauld sad and trumpet;* and the sadness is for the Turtle—lost in the fiery rite required for the Phoenix' rebirth.

Various birds are excluded: the ill-omened, the screech-owl, say, because this is a beginning anew, another cycle of the Phoenix' life.

> But thou shriking harbinger,
> Foule precurrer of the fiend,
> Augour of the feuers end,
> To this troupe come thou not neere.

Birds of prey are to be kept out too—except the symbol of authority, the Kingly Eagle, which can overawe violence as Henry VII put an end to the Wars of the Roses. Nothing arbitrary or unjust has a place here:

> From this Session interdict
> Euery foule of tyrant wing,
> Saue the Eagle feath'red King,
> Keepe the obsequie so strict.

Obsequie is a deep word here: a following after and a due compliance. These birds are to take part in a commemorative procession chanting the anthem, a song with the power of a spell.

> Let the Priest in Surples white,
> That defunctive Musicke can,
> Be the death-deuining Swan,
> Lest the *Requiem* lacke his right.

Defunctive Musicke: music which has to do with death; the Swan knows how to sing its swan song before its death and knows beforehand when it is to die.

Lacke his right: lack a rightness his participation can give. Some dictionaries say *right* is just Shakespeare's misspelling of *rite* (ritual). More modern critics will call it a pun. It is better perhaps to reflect and recognize how closely interwoven the meanings of the two words can be. A rite may be the observance it is right to give, to accord.

This choral service contains an anthem, a song of praise and gladness; a requiem, a solemn dirge for the repose of the dead; and a *threne* or *threnos,* a lamentation or dirge of honor. Note, too, a curious thing about the structure of the poem: the mourning birds, when assembled and ordered, chant an anthem in which Reason (something being described, talked about, conjured up, released, in the anthem) after going through a strange change, cries out suddenly and then composes the threne, sung at the close, and this threne, so composed

> To the *Phoenix* and the *Doue*,
> Co-supremes and starres of Loue,
> As *Chorus* to their Tragique Scene

ends with directions for a pilgrimage and a prayer.

This singular involvement—each part of the poem being included in and produced by, put into a mouth created in the part before it—has a lot to do with the power and spring of this most concentered and compacted poem.

The next bird, the last of the birds, the only one to be mentioned after the Swan-Priest, may have an importance suited to this special position. The *treble dated* Crow lives, so the legend says, three times, any number of times, longer than man. A "lived happily ever after" flavor hangs about him. Moreover, he engenders his offspring by breathing: a very ethereal mode of propagation, the mode by which poems and poetic ideas interinanimate and beget their successors. He is as black as ink, dressed in proper funeral attire, and yet is directed, somewhat as though he did not belong and could not expect to be invited, to join the mourners. Perhaps, being a carrion crow, he is a kind of contaminated character. Here he is:

> And thou treble dated Crow,
> That thy sable gender mak'st,
> With the breath thou giu'st and tak'st,
> 'Mongst our mourners shalt thou go.
>
> Here the Antheme doth commence,
> Loue and Constancie is dead,

> *Phoenix* and the *Turtle* fled,
> In a mutuall flame from hence.

Loue and Constancie: the attraction to beauty and the attachment in truth.

Notice *is dead:* the two are so much one that even from the
first mention the verb is singular: "is" dead, not "are" dead.
This confounds grammar, as Reason, itself, is going to be confounded in what follows.

> So they loued as loue in twaine,
> Had the essence but in one,
> Two distincts, Diuision none,
> Number there in loue was slaine.

They loved as do two people who love one another, and yet
they were not two but one, and one is not a number. For this
duality the same questions arise as in the Doctrine of the Trinity.

> Hearts remote, yet not asunder;
> Distance and no space was seene,
> Twixt this *Turtle* and his *Queene:*
> But in them it were a wonder.

But in them it were a wonder: in any others than "this concordant one" all this would be "a wonder"; not so here.

> So betweene them loue did shine,
> That the *Turtle* saw his right,
> Flaming in the *Phoenix* sight;
> Either was the others mine.

The Phoenix' eyes are traditionally of fire; they flame like the
sun. But, more than that, the Turtle sees *his right* flaming in
them.

His right: all he can ask or be entitled to; all that is due and
just; all that he truly is, his true being.

Let me quote a few lines here from *The Birds Parliament* by Attar, the twelfth century Persian saint and mystic, also about the Phoenix, which in Attar's poem is the leader in the soul's return to God. The poem is translated by Edward Fitzgerald, who translated Omar Khayyám.

> Once more they ventured from the Dust to raise
> Their eyes up to the Throne, into the Blaze;
> And in the Centre of the Glory there
> Beheld the Figure of THEMSELVES, as 'twere
> Transfigured—looking to Themselves, beheld
> The Figure on the Throne enmiracled,
> Until their Eyes themselves and that between
> Did hesitate which SEER was, which SEEN.

Or as in Shelley's lines from his "Hymn of Apollo":

> I am the Eye with which the universe
> Beholds itself and knows itself divine.

Either was the others mine: diamond mine, ruby mine, yes, perhaps; but, more important, each entirely possessed and was possessed by the other.

> Propertie was thus appalled,
> That the selfe was not the same:
> Single Natures double name,
> Neither two nor one was called.
> Reason in it selfe confounded,
> Saw Diuision grow together,
> To themselves yet either neither,
> Simple were so well compounded.
> That it cried, how true a twaine,
> Seemeth this concordant one,
> Loue hath Reason, Reason none,
> If what parts, can so remaine.

Any other poem, I sometimes think, would have made **Reason** cry

> How true a one
> Seemeth this concordant twain.

But the poem goes the further step, makes *Reason in it selfe confounded* speak in character and show itself to be confounded.

Very Shakespearean, this dramatic actuality!

> Whereupon it made this *Threne*
> To the *Phoenix* and the *Doue*,
> Co-supremes and starres of Loue,
> As *Chorus* to their Tragique Scene.

Note that Reason is the singer

THRENOS

> Beautie, Truth, and Raritie,
> Grace in all simplicitie,
> Here enclosde, in cinders lie.
> Death is now the *Phoenix* nest,
> And the *Turtles* loyall brest,
> To eternitie doth rest,

To the Phoenix, death is now a nest, a symbol of rebirth, but to

> the *Turtles* loyall brest,

it is a place of final repose.

> Leauing no posteritie,
> Twas not their infirmitie,
> It was married Chastitie.

What these

> Co-supremes and starres of Loue

have been concerned with has not been offspring. Besides, there
can be but the one Phoenix, although in this poem, we may
imagine, the sacrifice, the devotion of a Dove is needed for each
new regeneration or reincarnation.

> The intellect of man is forced to choose
> Perfection of the life or of the work,

wrote W. B. Yeats. Must poets give up their lives so that poetry
may be renewed?

> Truth may seeme, but cannot be,
> Beautie bragge, but tis not she,
> Truth and Beautie buried be.

As a poem may be something beyond anyone's reading or
apprehension of it?

> To this vrne let those repaire,
> That are either true or faire,
> For these dead Birds, sigh a prayer.

This prayer is wordless; it is sighed only, not spoken. What it
might have said is what the whole poem has been conveying, an
endeavor to apprehend a mystery. And it is no good asking what
this mystery is apart from this endeavor itself.

We may say if we like that this mystery is the mystery of
being, which is forever dying into cinders and arising to flame
and die anew; and always, perhaps, demanding a sacrifice of
constancy for the sake of that to which it is loyal and true. But
no remarks on this poem can be more than snapshots of some-

thing someone has thought he saw in it: helpful maybe to some but merely curiosities of opinion to others.

There are two remarks I would like, however, to make before inviting the reader to read the poem again straight through.

Beautie, Truth, and Raritie.

The truth celebrated in the poem is chiefly loyalty, faithfulness, and constancy, which, as with Troilus, the true knight, the true lover, is truth spelled *Troth*. At first sight troth may not seem to have very much to do with the ways in which a statement in a science may be true (or false), or evidence offered in a law court may be true (or false), or philosophical or critical or historical or literary views may be true (or false). And yet, for all of these, if we search and imagine faithfully enough, we will find that the statement or opinion, whatever it is, hangs in the midst of and is dependent upon a vast network of loyalties toward everything that may be relevant. Its truth is a matter of inter-inanimations and co-operations among loyalties, among troths.

And very significant parallels to all this hold for beauty.

This poem, one may well think, is not about any such high and remote abstractions but about two people; two people, who may be thought to have been "the very personifications, the very embodiments," as we lightly say, of beauty and truth, though they are spoken of in the poem as two birds. That is how the poem feels, no doubt about it. But, as certainly, there is a religious quality in its movement, a feeling in it as though we were being related through it to something far beyond any individuals. This Phoenix and this Turtle have a mythic scale to them, as though through them we were to become participants in something ultimate. All this, however, is so handled that it seems as easy and as natural and as necessary as breathing.

Let us read the poem again with a wider and more relaxed attention. Was it Mr. Eliot who remarked: "There is such a thing

as page fright as well as stage fright"? The very greatness of a
poem can stupefy the reader.

. . . .
To this vrne let those repaire . . .

No one who repairs to this urn will think there can be any end
to wondering about it.

8. The Representation of Nature
in Contemporary Physics*

WERNER HEISENBERG

THE PROBLEMS of modern art, so frequently and passionately discussed in our time, force us to examine those foundations which form the presupposition for every development of art, foundations which at other times are taken as self-evident. Indeed, the question has been raised whether the relation of modern man toward nature differs so fundamentally from that of former times that this difference alone is responsible for a completely different point of departure for the fine arts in contemporary culture. Certainly the relation of our period toward nature hardly finds its expression, as it did in earlier centuries, in a developed natural philosophy; rather, it is determined mainly by modern science and technology.

For this reason it is worthwhile to consider the view of nature held by modern science, and in particular by contemporary physics. From the start, however, a reservation must be made: there is little ground for believing that the current world view of science has directly influenced the development of modern art or could have done so. Yet we may believe that the changes in the

* By permission of the author and the publisher, R. Oldenbourg, Munich; from the Year Book of the Bavarian Academy of Fine Arts, Vol. III (1954), Die Kunste im Technischen Zeitalter. Original translation by O. T. Benfey, Earlham College, Richmond, Indiana.

foundations of modern science are an indication of profound transformations in the fundamentals of our existence, which on their part certainly have their effects in all areas of human experience. From this point of view it may be valuable for the artist to consider what changes have occurred during the last decade in the scientific view of nature.

I

First, let us consider the historical roots of recent science. When this science was being established in the seventeenth century by Kepler, Galileo, and Newton, the medieval image was at first still unbroken: man saw in nature God's creation. Nature was thought of as the work of God. It would have seemed senseless to people of that time to ask about the material world apart from its dependence on God. The words with which Kepler concluded the last volume of his *Harmony of the World* may be cited as a document of that era:

I thank thee, O Lord, our Creator, that thou hast permitted me to look at the beauty in thy work of creation; I exult in the works of thy hands. See, I have here completed the work to which I felt called; I have earned interest from the talent that thou hast given me. I have proclaimed the glory of thy works to the people who will read these demonstrations, to the extent that the limitations of my spirit would allow.

In the course of a few decades, however, this relation of man toward nature altered fundamentally. As the scientist immersed himself in the details of natural processes, he recognized that it was in fact possible, following Galileo's example, to separate out individual processes of nature from their environment, describe them mathematically, and thus "explain" them. At the same time, it certainly became clear to him what an endless task was thus presented to the infant science. Newton could no longer see the world as the work of God, comprehensible only as a whole. His position toward nature is most clearly circumscribed by his well-known statement that he felt like a child playing at the seashore, happy whenever he found a smoother pebble or a more beautiful sea shell than usual, while the great ocean of truth lay unexplored before him. This transformation in the attitude of the scientist toward nature may perhaps be better understood when we consider that, to some Christian thought of the period, God in heaven seemed so far removed from earth that it became meaningful to view the earth apart from God. Thus there may even be justification in speaking of a specifically Christian form of godlessness in connection with modern science. This would explain why such a development has not taken place in other cultures. It is certainly no coincidence that precisely in that period, nature becomes the object of representation in the arts independent of religious themes. The same tendency comes to expression in science when nature is considered not only independent of God, but also independent of man, so that there is formed the ideal of an "objective" description or explanation of nature. Nevertheless, it must be emphasized that for Newton the sea shell is significant only because it comes from the great ocean of truth. Observing it is not yet an end in itself; rather, its study receives meaning through its relation to the whole.

In the subsequent era, the method of Newton's mechanics was successfully applied to ever wider realms of nature. This period attempted to separate out details of nature by means of experiments, to observe them objectively, and to understand the laws underlying them. It attempted to formulate interrelations mathematically and thus to arrive at "laws" that hold without qualification throughout the cosmos. By this path it finally succeeded in making the forces of nature serve our purposes through technology. The magnificent development of mechanics in the eighteenth century and of optics, heat theory, and heat technology in the nineteenth century bears witness to the power of this innovation.

In proportion to the success of this kind of science, it spread beyond the realm of daily experience into remote regions of nature that could only be disclosed with the aid of technology, which developed in conjunction with science. Newton's decisive realization was that the laws which govern the fall of a stone also determine the orbit of the moon around the earth and thus are applicable in cosmic dimensions also. In the years that followed, natural science began its victory march on a broad front into those remote regions of nature about which we may obtain information only by the detour of technology—that is, by using more or less complicated apparatus. Astronomy used the improved telescope to master ever more remote cosmic regions. Chemistry attempted to understand processes at the atomic level from the behavior of substances in chemical reactions. Experiments with the induction machine and the Voltaic pile gave the first insight into electrical phenomena that were still hidden from the daily life of that era. Thus the meaning of the word "nature" as an object of scientific research slowly changed; it became a collective concept for all those areas of experience into which man can penetrate through science and technology, whether or not they are given to him "naturally" in direct experience. The term *description* of nature also progressively lost its original significance as a representation intended to convey the most alive and imaginable picture possible of nature; instead, in increasing measure a mathematical description of nature was implied—that is, a collection of data concerning interrelations according to law in nature, precise and brief yet also as comprehensive as possible.

The expansion of the concept of nature that had half unconsciously been completed in this development did not yet have to be considered as a fundamental departure from the original aims of science; the decisive basic concepts were still the same for the expanded area of experience and for the original direct experience of nature. To the nineteenth century, nature appeared as a lawful process in space and time, in whose description it was possible to ignore as far as axioms were concerned, even if not in practice, both man and his interference in nature.

The permanent in the flux of phenomena was taken to be matter unchangeable in mass and capable of being moved by forces. Since chemical phenomena from the eighteenth century on had been successfully organized and interpreted through the atomistic hypothesis taken over from antiquity, it seemed plausible to consider the atoms, in the sense of classical natural philosophy, as the truly real, as the unchangeable building stones of matter. As in the philosophy of Democritus, sensual qualities of matter were taken as appearance; smell and color, temperature and toughness were not intrinsic properties of matter, but originated as interactions between matter and our senses and thus had to be explained through the arrangement and motion of the atoms and the effects of this arrangement on our senses. In this way the all-too-simple world view of nineteenth century materialism was formed: the atoms, as intrinsically unchangeable beings, move in space and time and, through their mutual arrangement and motion, call forth the colorful phenomena of our sense world.

A first inroad into this simple world picture, though one not too dangerous, occurred in the second half of the last century through the development of electrical theory in which not matter but rather the force field had to be taken as the intrinsically real. Interactions between fields of force without a substance as carrier of the forces were less easily understandable than the materialistic conception of reality in atomic physics. An element of abstraction and lack of visualizability was brought into the otherwise apparently so obvious world view. That is why there was no dearth of attempts to return to the simple conception of matter in materialistic philosophy through the detour of a material ether that would carry these fields of force as elastic tensions. Such attempts, however, never quite managed to succeed. Nevertheless it was possible to be consoled by the fact that changes in fields of force could be considered as occurrences in space and time, describable objectively—that is, without consideration of the means of observation. Thus they corresponded to the generally accepted ideal of a process operating according to law in space and time. It was further possible to think of the force fields, since they can only be observed through their interaction with atoms, as called forth by the atoms, and thus to use them in a certain sense only in explaining the motions of atoms. To that extent, the atoms remained after all the intrinsically real; between them was empty space, which at most possessed a certain kind of reality as carrier of the force fields and of geometry.

For this world view it was not too significant that after the discovery of radioactivity near the end of the last century, the atoms of chemistry could no longer be taken as the final indivisible building blocks of matter but were themselves found to be composed of three types of basic building blocks, which we today call protons, neutrons, and electrons. This realization led in its practical consequences to the transmutation of the elements and to nuclear technology, and thus became tremendously important. As far as fundamental questions are concerned, however, nothing has changed now that we have recognized protons, neutrons, and electrons as the smallest building blocks of matter and interpret these as the intrinsically real. For the materialistic world view, it is important only that the possibility remains of taking these smallest constituents of the atoms as the final objective reality. On this foundation rested the coherent world view of the nineteenth and early twentieth centuries. Because of its simplicity it preserved for several decades its full powers of persuasion.

Precisely at this point profound changes in the foundations of atomic physics occurred in our century which lead away from the reality concept of classical atomism. It has turned out that the hoped-for objective reality of the elementary particles represents too rough a simplification of the true state of affairs and must yield to much more abstract conceptions. When we wish to picture to ourselves the nature of the existence of the elementary particles, we may no longer ignore the physical processes by which we obtain information about them. When we are observing objects of our daily experience, the physical process transmitting the observation of course plays only a secondary role. However, for the smallest building blocks of matter every process of observation causes a major disturbance; it turns out that we can no longer talk of the behavior of the particle apart from the process of observation. In consequence, we are finally led to believe that the laws of nature which we formulate mathematically in quantum theory deal no longer with the particles themselves but with our knowledge of the elementary particles. The question whether these particles exist in space and time "in themselves" can thus no longer be posed in this form. We can only talk about the processes that occur when, through the interaction of the particle with some other physical system such as a measuring instrument, the behavior of the particle is to be disclosed. The conception of the objective reality of the elementary particles has thus evaporated in a curious way, not into the fog of some new, obscure, or not yet understood reality concept, but into the transparent clarity of a mathematics that represents no longer the behavior of the elementary particles but rather our knowledge of this behavior. The atomic physicist has had to come to terms with the fact that his science is only a link in the endless chain of discussions of man with nature, but that it cannot simply talk of nature "as such." Natural science always presupposes man, and we must become aware of the fact that, as Bohr has expressed it, we are not only spectators but also always participants on the stage of life.

II

Before we can speak of the general implications arising out of this new situation in modern physics, it is necessary to discuss a development which is more important for practical purposes, namely the expansion of technology which has proceeded hand in hand with the growth of science. This technology has carried natural science from its origin in the West over the face of the earth and helped it to a central position in the thought of our time. In this process of development during the last two hundred years technology has always been both presupposition and consequence of natural science. It is presupposition because an extension and deepening of science often can take place only through a refinement of the means of observation. The invention of the telescope and microscope and the discovery of X-rays are examples. Technology, on the other hand, is also a consequence of science, since the technical exploitation of the forces of nature is in general only possible on the basis of a thorough knowledge of the natural laws of that particular realm of science.

Thus in the eighteenth and early nineteenth centuries there first developed a technology based on the utilization of mechanical processes. The machine at that stage often only imitated the actions of man's hand, whether in spinning and weaving or in the lifting of loads or the forging of large pieces of iron. Hence this form of technology was initially seen as an extension of the old crafts. It was understandable and obvious to the onlooker in the same way as the work of the craftsman, whose fundamental principles everyone knew even if the detailed techniques could not be copied by all. Even the introduction of the steam engine did not fundamentally change this character of technology; however, from this time on the expansion of technology could progress at a formerly unknown rate, for it now became possible to place the natural forces stored in coal in the service of man to perform his manual work for him.

A decisive transformation in the character of technology probably began with the technical utilization of electricity in the second half of the last century. It was hardly possible to speak any longer of a direct connection with the earlier crafts. Natural forces were now exploited that were almost unknown to people in direct experience of nature. For many people, even today, electricity has something uncanny about it; at the least it is often considered incomprehensible, though it is all around us. The high-voltage lines which one must not approach admittedly give us a kind of conceptual lesson concerning the force field employed by science, but basically this realm of nature remains foreign to us. Viewing the interior of a complicated electrical apparatus is sometimes unpleasant in the same way as watching a surgical operation.

Chemical technology also might be seen as a continuation of old crafts such as dyeing, tanning, and pharmacy. But here also the extent of the newly developed chemical technology from about the turn of the century no longer permits comparison with the earlier circumstances. Nuclear technology, finally, is concerned with the exploitation of natural forces to which every approach from the world of natural experience is lacking. Perhaps this technology, too, in the end will become as familiar to modern man as electricity, without which man can no longer conceive his environment. But the things that are daily around us do not for that reason become a part of nature in the original sense of the word. Perhaps, in the future, the many pieces of technical apparatus will as inescapably belong to man as the snail's house to the snail or the web to the spider. Even then, however, these machines would be more parts of our human organism than parts of surrounding nature.

Technology thus fundamentally interferes with the relation of nature to man, in that it transforms his environment in large measure and thereby incessantly and inescapably holds the scientific aspect of the world before his eyes. The claim of science to be capable of reaching out into the whole cosmos with a method that always separates and clarifies individual phenomena, and thus goes forward from relationship to relationship, is mirrored in technology which step by step penetrates new realms, transforms our environment before our eyes, and impresses our image upon it. In the same sense in which every detailed question in science is subordinate to the major task of understanding nature as a whole, so also does the smallest technical advance serve the general goal, that of enlarging the material power of man. The value of this goal is as little questioned as the value of natural knowledge in science, and the two aims coalesce in the banal slogan "Knowledge is Power." Probably it is possible to demonstrate in the case of every technical process its subservience to this common goal; it is, on the other hand, characteristic for the whole development that the individual technical process is bound to the common goal in such an indirect way that one can hardly view it as part of a conscious plan for the accomplishment of this goal. Technology almost ceases to appear at such times as the product of conscious human effort for the spreading of material power. Instead it appears as a biological process on a large scale, in which the structures that are part of the human organism are transferred in ever larger measure to man's environment. Such a biological process would be outside man's control, for man can indeed do what he wills, but he cannot will what he wills.

III

It has often been said that the profound changes in our environment and our way of life in the technical age have also transformed our thinking in a dangerous way. Here, we are told, is the root of the crises by which our era is shaken—and by which modern art is shaped. But this objection is older than the technology and science of our time; technology and machines in a more primitive form have existed in much earlier times, so that men were forced to think about such questions in periods long past. Two and a half thousand years ago, the Chinese sage Chang Tsi spoke of the dangers to man of using machines. I would like to quote a section from his writings that is important for our subject:

When Tsi Gung came into the region north of the river Han, he saw an old man busy in his vegetable garden. He had dug ditches for watering. He himself climbed into the well, brought up a container full of water in his arms, and emptied it. He exerted himself to the utmost, but achieved very little.

Tsi Gung spoke: "There is an arrangement with which it is possible to fill a hundred ditches with water every day. With little effort much is accomplished. Wouldn't you like to use it?" The gardener rose up, looked at him and said, "What would that be?"

Tsi Gung said, "A lever is used, weighted at one end and light at the other. In this way water can be drawn, so that it gushes out. It is known as a draw-well."

At that, anger rose up in the face of the old man and he laughed, saying, "I have heard my teacher say: 'When a man uses a machine he carries on all his business in a machine-like manner. Whoever does his business in the manner of a machine develops a machine heart. Whoever has a machine heart in his breast loses his simplicity. Whoever loses his simplicity becomes uncertain in the impulses of his spirit. Uncertainty in the impulses of the spirit is something that is incompatible with truth.' Not that I am unfamiliar with such devices; I am ashamed to use them."

That this ancient tale contains a considerable amount of truth, everyone of us will agree; "uncertainty in the impulses of the spirit" is perhaps one of the most telling descriptions we can give to the condition of man in the present crisis. Nevertheless, although technology, the machine, has spread over the world to an extent that the Chinese sage could not have imagined, two thousand years later the world's finest works of art are still being created and the simplicity of the soul of which the philosopher spoke has never been completely lost. Instead, in the course of the centuries it has shown itself, sometimes weakly, sometimes powerfully, and it has borne fruit again and again. Finally, the ascent of man has, after all, occurred through the development of tools; thus technology cannot carry the whole blame for the fact that the consciousness of this interconnection has in many places been lost.

Perhaps we will come nearer the truth if the sudden and—measured by earlier changes—unusually swift diffusion of technology in the last fifty years is held responsible for the many difficulties. The speed of technological transformation, in contrast to that of earlier centuries, leaves no time to mankind in which to adjust to the new conditions of life. But even this is probably not the correct or the complete explanation of why our time seems to face a new situation, hardly without analogy in history.

We have already mentioned that the changes in the foundations of modern science may perhaps be viewed as symptoms of shifts in the fundamentals of our existence which then express themselves simultaneously in many places, be it in changes in our way of life or our usual thought forms, be it in external catastrophes, wars, or revolutions. When one attempts to grope one's way from the situation in modern science to the fundamentals that have begun to shift, one has the impression that it is not too crude a simplification of the state of affairs to assert that for the first time in the course of history man on earth faces only himself, that he finds no longer any other partner or foe. This observation applies first of all in a commonplace way in the battle of man against outward dangers. In earlier times he was endangered by wild animals, disease, hunger, cold, and other forces of nature, and in this strife every extension of technology represented a strengthening of his position and therefore progress. In our time, when the earth is becoming ever more densely settled, the narrowing of the possibilities of life and thus the threat to man's existence originates above all from other people, who also assert their claim to the goods of the earth. In such a confrontation, the extension of technology need no longer be an indication of progress.

The statement that in our time man confronts only himself is valid in the age of technology in a still wider sense. In earlier epochs man saw himself opposite nature. Nature, in which dwelt all sorts of living beings, was a realm existing according to its own laws, and into it man somehow had to fit himself. We, on the other hand, live in a world so completely transformed by man that, whether we are using the machines of our daily life, taking food prepared by machines, or striding through landscapes transformed by man, we invariably encounter structures created by man, so that in a sense we always meet only ourselves. Certainly there are parts of the earth where this process is nowhere near completion, but sooner or later the dominion of man in this respect will be complete.

This new situation becomes most obvious to us in science, in which it turns out, as I have described earlier, that we can no longer view "in themselves" the building blocks of matter which were originally thought of as the last objective reality; that they refuse to be fixed in any way in space and time; and that basically we can only make our knowledge of these particles the object of science. The aim of research is thus no longer knowledge of the atoms and their motion "in themselves," separated from our experimental questioning; rather, right from the beginning, we stand in the center of the confrontation between nature and man, of which science, of course, is only a part. The familiar classification of the world into subject and object, inner and outer world, body and soul, somehow no longer quite applies, and indeed leads to difficulties. In science, also, the object of research is no longer nature in itself but rather nature exposed to man's questioning, and to this extent man here also meets himself.

Our time has clearly been given the task of coming to terms with this new situation in all aspects of life, and only when this is accomplished will man be able to regain that "certainty in the impulses of the spirit" talked of by the Chinese sage. The way to this goal will be long and arduous, and we do not know what stations of the cross are still ahead. But if indications are sought as to the nature of the way, it may be permissible to consider once more the example of the exact sciences.

In quantum theory, we accepted the described situation when it became possible to represent it mathematically and when, therefore, in every case we could say clearly and without danger of logical contradiction how the result of an experiment would turn out. We thus resigned ourselves to the new situation the moment the ambiguities were removed. The mathematical formulas indeed no longer portray nature, but rather our knowledge of nature. Thus we have renounced a form of natural description that was familiar for centuries and still was taken as the obvious goal of all exact science even a few decades ago. It could also be said for the present that we have accepted the situation in the realm of modern atomic physics only because our experience can in fact be correctly represented in that area. As soon as we look at the philosophical interpretations of quantum theory, we find that opinions still differ widely; the view is occasionally heard that this new form of natural description is not yet satisfying since it does not correspond to the earlier ideal of scientific truth, and hence is to be taken only as another symptom of the crisis of our time, and in any case is not the final formulation.

It will be useful to discuss in this connection the concept of scientific truth in somewhat more general terms and to ask for criteria as to when an item of scientific knowledge can be called consistent and final. For the moment, a more external criterion: As long as any realm of the intellectual life is developing steadily and without inner break, specific detailed questions are presented to the individual working in this area, questions that are in a sense problems of technique, whose solution is certainly not an end in itself but appears valuable in the interest of the larger relationship that alone is important. These detailed problems are presented to us, they do not have to be sought, and working on them is the presupposition for collaborating at the larger relationship. In the same sense, medieval stone masons endeavored to copy as accurately as possible the folds of garments, and the solution of their special problem was necessary because the folds of the garments of the saints were part of the large religious relationship that was the real aim. In a similar way, special problems have always presented themselves in modern science, and work on these is the presupposition for the understanding of the large relationship. These questions presented themselves, also, in the development of the last fifty years; they did not have to be sought. And the aim was always the same: the large interrelatedness of the laws of nature. In this sense, purely from the outside, there seems to be no basis for any break in the continuity of exact science.

With respect to the finality of the results, however, we should remember that in the realm of exact science final solutions are continually being found for certain delimited areas of experience. The problems, for instance, which could be studied with the concepts of Newtonian mechanics found their final answer for all time through Newton's laws and the mathematical deductions drawn from them. These solutions, to be sure, do not extend beyond the concepts and questions of Newtonian mechanics. Thus electrical theory, for instance, was not accessible to analysis by these concepts. New systems of concepts emerged in the exploration of this new realm of experience with whose help the laws of electricity could be mathematically formulated in their final form. The word "final" in connection with exact science evidently means that we will always find closed, mathematically describable systems of concepts and laws that fit certain areas of experience, are valid in them anywhere in the universe, and are incapable of modification or improvement. It cannot, however, be expected that these concepts and laws will later be suitable for the representation of new realms of experience. Only in this limited sense, therefore, can the concepts and laws of quantum theory be designated as final, and only in this limited sense can it ever happen that scientific knowledge finds its final fixation in mathematical or any other language.

Similarly, certain philosophies of justice assume that justice always exists but that, in general, in every new legal case justice must be found anew, that at all events the written law always covers only limited areas of life and therefore cannot be everywhere binding. Exact science also goes forward in the belief that it will be possible in every new realm of experience to understand nature, but what the word "understand" might signify is not at all predetermined. The natural knowledge of earlier epochs, fixed in mathematical formulas, might be "final," but not in any sense always applicable. This state of affairs makes it impossible to base articles of belief that are to be binding for one's bearing in life on scientific knowledge alone. The establishment of such articles of faith could only be based on such "fixed" scientific knowledge, a knowledge only applicable to limited realms of experience. The assertion often found at the beginning of creeds originating in our time that they deal not with belief but with scientifically based knowledge, thus contain an inner contradiction and rests on a self-deception.

Nevertheless, this realization must not mislead us into underestimating the firmness of the ground on which the edifice of exact science has been built. The concept of scientific truth basic to natural science can bear many kinds of natural understanding. Not only the science of past centuries but also modern atomic physics is based on it. Hence it follows that one can come to terms with a knowledge situation in which an objectification of the process of nature is no longer possible, and that one should be able to find our relation to nature within it.

When we speak of a picture of nature provided by contemporary exact science, we do not actually mean any longer a picture of nature, but rather a picture of our relation to nature. The old compartmentalization of the world into an objective process in space and time, on the one hand, and the soul in which this process is mirrored, on the other—that is, the Cartesian differentiation of *res cogitans* and *res extensa*—is no longer suitable as the starting point for the understanding of modern science. In the field of view of this science there appears above all the network of relations between man and nature, of the connections through which we as physical beings are dependent parts of nature and at the same time, as human beings, make them the object of our thought and actions. Science no longer is in the position of observer of nature, but rather recognizes itself as part of the interplay between man and nature. The scientific method of separating, explaining, and arranging becomes conscious of its limits, set by the fact that the employment of this procedure changes and transforms its object; the procedure can no longer keep its distance from the object. The world view of natural science thus ceases to be a view of "natural" science in its proper sense.

The clarification of these paradoxes in a narrow segment of science has certainly not achieved much for the general situation of our time, in which, to repeat a simplification used earlier, we suddenly and above all confront ourselves. The hope that the extension of man's material and spiritual power always represents progress thus finds a limit, even though it may not yet be clearly visible. The dangers are the greater, the more violently the wave of optimism engendered by the belief in progress surges against this limit. Perhaps the nature of the danger here discussed can be made clearer by another metaphor. With the seemingly unlimited expansion of his material might, man finds himself in the position of a captain whose ship has been so securely built of iron and steel that the needle of his compass no longer points to the north, but only toward the ship's mass of iron. With such a ship no destination can be reached; it will move aimlessly and be subject in addition to winds and ocean currents. But let us remember the state of affairs of modern physics: the danger only exists so long as the captain is unaware that his compass does not respond to the earth's magnetic forces. The moment the situation is recognized, the danger can be considered as half removed. For the captain who does not want to travel in circles but desires to reach a known—or unknown—destination will find ways and means for determining the orientation of his ship. He may start using modern types of compasses that are not affected by the iron of the ship, or he may navigate, as in former times, by the stars. Of course we cannot decree the visibility or lack of visibility of the stars, and in our time perhaps they are only rarely visible. In any event, awareness that the hopes engendered by the belief in progress will meet a limit implies the wish not to travel in circles but to reach a goal. To the extent that we reach clarity about this limit, the limit itself may furnish the first firm hold by which we can orient ourselves anew.

Perhaps from this comparison with modern science we may draw hope that we may here be dealing with a limit for certain forms of expansion of human activity, not, however, with a limit to human activity as such. The space in which man as spiritual being is developing has more dimensions than the one within which he has moved forward in the preceding centuries. It follows that in the course of long stretches of time the conscious acceptance of this limit will perhaps lead to a certain stabilization in which the thoughts of men will again arrange themselves around a common center. Such a development may perhaps also supply a new foundation for the development of art; but to speak about that does not behoove the scientist.

9. Uses of Symbolism*

A. N. WHITEHEAD

THE ATTITUDE of mankind towards symbolism exhibits an unstable
mixture of attraction and repulsion. The practical intelligence,
the theoretical desire to pierce to ultimate fact, and ironic critical
impulses have contributed the chief motives towards the repulsion from symbolism. Hard-headed men want facts and not
symbols. A clear theoretic intellect, with its generous enthusiasm
for the exact truth at all costs and hazards, pushes aside symbols
as being mere make-believes, veiling and distorting that inner
sanctuary of simple truth which reason claims as its own. The
ironic critics of the follies of humanity have performed notable
service in clearing away the lumber of useless ceremony symbolizing the degrading fancies of a savage past. The repulsion
from symbolism stands out as a well-marked element in the
cultural history of civilized people. There can be no reasonable
doubt but that this continuous criticism has performed a necessary service in the promotion of a wholesome civilization, both
on the side of the practical efficiency of organized society, and on
the side of a robust direction of thought.

No account of the uses of symbolism is complete without this
recognition that the symbolic elements in life have a tendency to
run wild, like the vegetation in a tropical forest. The life of

* Reprinted from A. N. Whitehead, *Symbolism, Its Meaning and Effect*.
Copyright 1958 by The Macmillan Company and used with the publisher's
permission.

humanity can easily be overwhelmed by its symbolic accessories. A continuous process of pruning, and of adaptation to a future ever requiring new forms of expression, is a necessary function in every society. The successful adaptation of old symbols to changes of social structure is the final mark of wisdom in sociological statesmanship. Also an occasional revolution in symbolism is required.

There is, however, a Latin proverb upon which, in our youth, some of us have been set to write themes. In English it reads thus:—Nature, expelled with a pitchfork, ever returns. This proverb is exemplified by the history of symbolism. However you may endeavor to expel it, it ever returns. Symbolism is no mere idle fancy or corrupt degeneration: it is inherent in the very texture of human life. Language itself is a symbolism. And, as another example, however you reduce the functions of your government to their utmost simplicity, yet symbolism remains. It may be a healthier, manlier ceremonial, suggesting finer notions. But still it is symbolism. You abolish the etiquette of a royal court, with its suggestions of personal subordination, but at official receptions you ceremonially shake the hand of the Governor of your State. Just as the feudal doctrine of a subordination of classes, reaching up to the ultimate overlord, requires its symbolism; so does the doctrine of human equality obtain its symbolism. Mankind, it seems, has to find a symbol in order to express itself. Indeed 'expression' is 'symbolism.'

When the public ceremonial of the State has been reduced to the barest simplicity, private clubs and associations at once commence to reconstitute symbolic actions. It seems as though mankind must always be masquerading. This imperative impulse suggests that the notion of an idle masquerade is the wrong way of thought about the symbolic elements in life. The function of these elements is to be definite, manageable, reproducible, and also to be charged with their own emotional efficacy: symbolic transference invests their correlative meanings with some or all of these attributes of the symbols, and thereby lifts the meanings into an intensity of definite effectiveness—as elements in knowledge, emotion, and purpose,—an effectiveness which the meanings may, or may not, deserve on their own account. The object of symbolism is the enhancement of the importance of what is symbolized.

In a discussion of instances of symbolism, our first difficulty is to discover exactly what is being symbolized. The symbols are specific enough, but it is often extremely difficult to analyze what lies beyond them, even though there is evidently some strong appeal beyond the mere ceremonial acts.

It seems probable that in any ceremonial which has lasted through many epochs, the symbolic interpretation, so far as we can obtain it, varies much more rapidly than does the actual ceremonial. Also in its flux a symbol will have different meanings for different people. At any epoch some people have the dominant mentality of the past, some of the present, others of the future, and others of the many problematic futures which will never dawn. For these various groups an old symbolism will have different shades of vague meaning.

In order to appreciate the necessary function of symbolism in the life of any society of human beings we must form some estimate of the binding and disruptive forces at work. There are many varieties of human society, each requiring its own particular investigation so far as details are concerned. We will fix attention on nations, occupying definite countries. Thus geographical unity is at once presupposed. Communities with geographical unity constitute the primary type of communities which we find in the world. Indeed the lower we go in the scale of being, the more necessary is geographical unity for that close interaction of individuals which constitutes society. Societies of the higher animals, of insects, of molecules, all possess geographical unity. A rock is nothing else than a society of molecules, indulging in every species of activity open to molecules. I draw

attention to this lowly form of society in order to dispel the
notion that social life is a peculiarity of the higher organisms.
The contrary is the case. So far as survival value is concerned,
a piece of rock, with its past history of some eight hundred
millions of years, far outstrips the short span attained by any
nation. The emergence of life is better conceived as a bid for
freedom on the part of organisms, a bid for a certain independence of individuality with self-interests and activities not to be
construed purely in terms of environmental obligations. The
immediate effect of this emergence of sensitive individuality has
been to reduce the term of life for societies from hundreds of
millions of years to hundreds of years, or even to scores of
years.

The emergence of living beings cannot be ascribed to the
superior survival value either of the individuals, or of their societies. National life has to face the disruptive elements introduced by these extreme claims for individual idiosyncrasies. We
require both the advantages of social preservation, and the contrary stimulus of the heterogeneity derived from freedom. The
society is to run smoothly amidst the divergencies of its individuals. There is a revolt from the mere causal obligations laid
upon individuals by the social character of the environment.
This revolt first takes the form of blind emotional impulse; and
later, in civilized societies, these impulses are criticized and
deflected by reason. In any case, there are individual springs of
action which escape from the obligations of social conformity.
In order to replace this decay of secure instinctive response,
various intricate forms of symbolic expression of the various
purposes of social life have been introduced. The response to the
symbol is almost automatic but not quite; the reference to the
meaning is there, either for additional emotional support, or for
criticism. But the reference is not so clear as to be imperative.
The imperative instinctive conformation to the influence of the
environment has been modified. Something has replaced it, which

by its superficial character invites criticism, and by its habitual use generally escapes it. Such symbolism makes connected thought possible by expressing it, while at the same time it automatically directs action. In the place of the force of instinct which suppresses individuality, society has gained the efficacy of symbols, at once preservative of the commonweal and of the individual standpoint.

Among the particular kinds of symbolism which serve this purpose, we must place first Language. I do not mean language in its function of a bare indication of abstract ideas, or of particular actual things, but language clothed with its complete influence for the nation in question. In addition to its bare indication of meaning, words and phrases carry with them an enveloping suggestiveness and an emotional efficacy. This function of language depends on the way it has been used, on the proportionate familiarity of particular phrases, and on the emotional history associated with their meanings and thence derivatively transferred to the phrases themselves. If two nations speak the same language, this emotional efficacy of words and phrases will in general differ for the two. What is familiar for one nation will be strange for the other nation; what is charged with intimate associations for the one is comparatively empty for the other. For example, if the two nations are somewhat widely sundered, with a different fauna and flora, the nature-poetry of one nation will lack its complete directness of appeal to the other nation— compare Walt Whitman's phrase,

"The wide unconscious scenery of my land"

for an American, with Shakespeare's

". . . this little world,
This precious stone set in the silver sea,"

for an Englishman. Of course anyone, American or English, with the slightest sense for history and kinship, or with the slightest sympathetic imagination, can penetrate to the feelings conveyed by both phrases. But the direct first-hand intuition, derived from earliest childhood memories, is for the one nation that of continental width, and for the other nation that of the little island world. Now the love of the sheer geographical aspects of one's country, of its hills, its mountains, and its plains, of its trees, its flowers, its birds, and its whole nature-life, is no small element in that binding force which makes a nation. It is the function of language, working through literature and through the habitual phrases of early life, to foster this diffused feeling of the common possession of a treasure infinitely precious.

I must not be misunderstood to mean that this example has any unique importance. It is only one example of what can be illustrated in a hundred ways. Also language is not the only symbolism effective for this purpose. But in an especial manner, language binds a nation together by the common emotions which it elicits, and is yet the instrument whereby freedom of thought and of individual criticism finds its expression.

My main thesis is that a social system is kept together by the blind force of instinctive actions, and of instinctive emotions clustered around habits and prejudices. It is therefore not true that any advance in the scale of culture inevitably tends to the preservation of society. On the whole, the contrary is more often the case, and any survey of nature confirms this conclusion. A new element in life renders in many ways the operation of the old instincts unsuitable. But unexpressed instincts are unanalyzed and blindly felt. Disruptive forces, introduced by a higher level of existence, are then warring in the dark against an invisible enemy. There is no foothold for the intervention of 'rational consideration'—to use Henry Osborn Taylor's admirable phrase. The symbolic expression of instinctive forces drags them out into the open: it differentiates them and delineates them. There is then opportunity for reason to effect, with comparative speed, what otherwise must be left to the slow operation of the centuries amid ruin and reconstruction. Mankind misses its opportunities, and its failures are a fair target for ironic criticism. But the fact that reason too often fails does not give fair ground for the hysterical conclusion that it never succeeds. Reason can be compared to the force of gravitation, the weakest of all natural forces, but in the end the creator of suns and of stellar systems:— those great societies of the Universe. Symbolic expression first preserves society by adding emotion to instinct, and secondly it affords a foothold for reason by its delineation of the particular instinct which it expresses. This doctrine of the disruptive tendency due to novelties, even those involving a rise to finer levels, is illustrated by the effect of Christianity on the stability of the Roman Empire. It is also illustrated by the three revolutions which secured liberty and equality for the world—namely the English revolutionary period of the seventeenth century, the American Revolution, and the French Revolution. England barely escaped a disruption of its social system; America was never in any such danger; France, where the entrance of novelty was most intense, did for a time experience this collapse. Edmund Burke, the Whig statesman of the eighteenth century, was the philosopher who was the approving prophet of the two earlier revolutions, and the denunciatory prophet of the French Revolution. A man of genius and a statesman, who has immediately observed two revolutions, and has meditated deeply on a third, deserves to be heard when he speaks on the forces which bind and disrupt societies. Unfortunately statesmen are swayed by the passions of the moment, and Burke shared this defect to the full, so as to be carried away by the reactionary passions aroused by the French Revolution. Thus the wisdom of his general conception of social forces is smothered by the wild unbalanced conclusions which he drew from them: his greatness is best shown by his attitude towards the American Revolution. His more general reflections are contained first, in his youthful work *A Vindication of Natural Society*, and secondly, in his *Reflections on the French Revolution*. The earlier work was meant ironically; but, as is often the case with genius, he prophesied unknowingly. This essay is practically written round the thesis that advances in the art of civilization are apt to be destructive of the social system. Burke conceived his conclusion to be a *reductio ad absurdum*. But it is the truth. The second work—a work which in its immediate effect was perhaps the most harmful ever written—directs attention to the importance of 'prejudice' as a binding social force. There again I hold that he was right in his premises and wrong in his conclusions.

Burke surveys the standing miracle of the existence of an organized society, culminating in the smooth unified action of the state. Such a society may consist of millions of individuals, each with its individual character, its individual aims, and its individual selfishness. He asks what is the force which leads this throng of separate units to co-operate in the maintenance of an organized state, in which each individual has his part to play—political, economic, and aesthetic. He contrasts the complexity of the functionings of a civilized society with the sheer diversities of its individual citizens considered as a mere group or crowd. His answer to the riddle is that the magnetic force is 'prejudice,' or in other words, 'use and wont.' Here he anticipates the whole modern theory of 'herd psychology,' and at the same time deserts the fundamental doctrine of the Whig party, as formed in the seventeenth century and sanctioned by Locke. This conventional Whig doctrine was that the state derived its origin from an 'original contract' whereby the mere crowd voluntarily organized itself into a society. Such a doctrine seeks the origin of the state in a baseless historical fiction. Burke was well ahead of his time in drawing attention to the importance of precedence as a political force. Unfortunately, in the excitement of the moment, Burke construed the importance of precedence as implying the negation of progressive reform.

Now, when we examine how a society bends its individual members to function in conformity with its needs, we discover

that one important operative agency is our vast system of in-
herited symbolism. There is an intricate expressed symbolism
of language and of act, which is spread throughout the community, and which evokes fluctuating apprehension of the basis
of common purposes. The particular direction of individual
action is directly correlated to the particular sharply defined
symbols presented to him at the moment. The response of action
to symbol may be so direct as to cut out any effective reference
to the ultimate thing symbolized. This elimination of meaning
is termed reflex action. Sometimes there does intervene some
effective reference to the meaning of the symbol. But this meaning is not recalled with the particularity and definiteness which
would yield any rational enlightenment as to the specific action
required to secure the final end. The meaning is vague but insistent. Its insistence plays the part of hypnotizing the individual
to complete the specific action associated with the symbol. In the
whole transaction, the elements which are clear-cut and definite
are the specific symbols and the actions which should issue from
the symbols. But in themselves the symbols are barren facts
whose direct associative force would be insufficient to procure
automatic conformity. There is not sufficient repetition, or sufficient similarity of diverse occasions, to secure mere automatic
obedience. But in fact the symbol evokes loyalties to vaguely
conceived notions, fundamental for our spiritual natures. The
result is that our natures are stirred to suspend all antagonistic
impulses, so that the symbol procures its required response in
action. Thus the social symbolism has a double meaning. It
means pragmatically the direction of individuals to specific action;
and it also means theoretically the vague ultimate reasons with
their emotional accompaniments, whereby the symbols acquire
their power to organize the miscellaneous crowd into a smoothly
running community.

The contrast between a state and an army illustrates this
principle. A state deals with a greater complexity of situation

than does its army. In this sense it is a looser organization, and in regard to the greater part of its population the communal symbolism cannot rely for its effectiveness on the frequent recurrence of almost identical situations. But a disciplined regiment is trained to act as a unit in a definite set of situations. The bulk of human life escapes from the reach of this military discipline. The regiment is drilled for one species of job. The result is that there is more reliance on automatism, and less reliance on the appeal to ultimate reasons. The trained soldier acts automatically on receiving the word of command. He responds to the sound and cuts out the idea; this is reflex action. But the appeal to the deeper side is still important in an army; although it is provided for in another set of symbols, such as the flag, and the memorials of the honorable service of the regiment, and other symbolic appeals to patriotism. Thus in an army there is one set of symbols to produce automatic obedience in a limited set of circumstances, and there is another set of symbols to produce a general sense of the importance of the duties performed. This second set prevents random reflection from sapping automatic response to the former set.

For the greater number of citizens of a state there is in practice no reliable automatic obedience to any symbol such as the word of command for soldiers, except in a few instances such as the response to the signals of the traffic police. Thus the state depends in a very particular way upon the prevalence of symbols which combine direction to some well-known course of action with some deeper reference to the purpose of the state. The self-organization of society depends on commonly diffused symbols evoking commonly diffused ideas, and at the same time indicating commonly understood actions. Usual forms of verbal expression are the most important example of such symbolism. Also the heroic aspect of the history of the country is the symbol for its immediate worth.

When a revolution has sufficiently destroyed this common

symbolism leading to common actions for usual purposes, society can only save itself from dissolution by means of a reign of terror. Those revolutions which escape a reign of terror have left intact the fundamental efficient symbolism of society. For example, the English revolutions of the seventeenth century and the American revolution of the eighteenth century left the ordinary life of their respective communities nearly unchanged. When George Washington had replaced George III, and Congress had replaced the English Parliament, Americans were still carrying on a well-understood system so far as the general structure of their social life was concerned. Life in Virginia must have assumed no very different aspect from that which it had exhibited before the revolution. In Burke's phraseology, the prejudices on which Virginian society depended were unbroken. The ordinary signs still beckoned people to their ordinary actions, and suggested the ordinary common-sense justification.

One difficulty of explaining my meaning is that the intimate effective symbolism consists of the various types of expression which permeate society and evoke a sense of common purpose. No one detail is of much importance. The whole range of symbolic expression is required. A national hero, such as George Washington or Jefferson, is a symbol of the common purpose which animates American life. This symbolic function of great men is one of the difficulties in obtaining a balanced historical judgment. There is the hysteria of depreciation, and there is the opposite hysteria which dehumanizes in order to exalt. It is very difficult to exhibit the greatness without losing the human being. Yet we know that at least *we* are human beings; and half the inspiration of our heroes is lost when we forget that *they* were human beings.

I mention great Americans, because I am speaking in America. But exactly the same truth holds for the great men of all countries and ages.

The doctrine of symbolism developed in these lectures enables us to distinguish between pure instinctive action, reflex action, and symbolically conditioned action. Pure instinctive action is that functioning of an organism which is wholly analyzable in terms of those conditions laid upon its development by the settled facts of its external environment, conditions describable without any reference to its perceptive mode of presentational immediacy. This pure instinct is the response of an organism to pure causal efficacy.

According to this definition, pure instinct is the most primitive type of response which is yielded by organisms to the stimulus of their environment. All physical response on the part of inorganic matter to its environment is thus properly to be termed instinct. In the case of organic matter, its primary difference from inorganic nature is its greater delicacy of internal mutual adjustment of minute parts and, in some cases, its emotional enhancement. Thus instinct, or this immediate adjustment to immediate environment, becomes more prominent in its function of directing action for the purposes of the living organism. The world is a community of organisms; these organisms in the mass determine the environmental influence on any one of them; there can only be a persistent community of persistent organisms when the environmental influence in the shape of instinct is favorable to the survival of the individuals. Thus the community as an environment is responsible for the survival of the separate individuals which compose it; and these separate individuals are responsible for their contributions to the environment. Electrons and molecules survive because they satisfy this primary law for a stable order of nature in connection with given societies of organisms.

Reflex action is a relapse towards a more complex type of instinct on the part of organisms which enjoy, or have enjoyed, symbolically conditioned action. Thus its discussion must be postponed. Symbolically conditioned action arises in the higher organisms which enjoy the perceptive mode of presentational immediacy, that is to say, sense-presentation of the contemporary world. This sense-presentation symbolically promotes an analysis of the massive perception of causal efficacy. The causal efficacy is thereby perceived as analysed into components with the locations in space primarily belonging to the sense-presentations. In the case of perceived organisms external to the human body, the spatial discrimination involved in the human perception of their pure causal efficacy is so feeble, that practically there is no check on this symbolic transference, apart from the indirect check of pragmatic consequences—in other words, either survival value, or self-satisfaction, logical and aesthetic.

Symbolically conditioned action is action which is thus conditioned by the analysis of the perceptive mode of causal efficacy effected by symbolic transference from the perceptive mode of presentational immediacy. This analysis may be right or wrong, according as it does, or does not, conform to the actual distribution of the efficacious bodies. In so far as it is sufficiently correct under normal circumstances, it enables an organism to conform its actions to long-ranged analysis of the particular circumstances of its environment. So far as this type of action prevails, pure instinct is superseded. This type of action is greatly promoted by thought, which uses the symbols as referent to their meanings. There is no sense in which pure instinct can be wrong. But symbolically conditioned action can be wrong, in the sense that it may rise from a false symbolic analysis of causal efficacy.

Reflex action is that organic functioning which is wholly dependent on sense-presentation, unaccompanied by any analysis of causal efficacy *via* symbolic reference. The conscious analysis of perception is primarily concerned with the analysis of the symbolic relationship between the two perceptive modes. Thus reflex action is hindered by thought, which inevitably promotes the prominence of symbolic reference.

Reflex action arises when by the operation of symbolism the organism has acquired the habit of action in response to immediate sense-perception, and has discarded the symbolic enhancement of causal efficacy. It thus represents the relapse from the high-grade activity of symbolic reference. This relapse is practically inevitable in the absence of conscious attention. Reflex action cannot in any sense be said to be wrong, though it may be unfortunate.

Thus the important binding factor in a community of insects probably falls under the notion of pure instinct, as here defined. For each individual insect is probably such an organism that the causal conditions which it inherits from the immediate past are adequate to determine its social actions. But reflex action plays its subordinate part. For the sense-perceptions of the insects have in certain fields of action assumed an automatic determination of the insects' activities. Still more feebly, symbolically conditioned action intervenes for such situations when the sense-presentation provides a symbolically defined specification of the causal situation. But only active thought can save symbolically conditioned action from quickly relapsing into reflex action. The most successful examples of community life exist when pure instinct reigns supreme. These examples occur only in the inorganic world; among societies of active molecules forming rocks, planets, solar systems, star clusters.

The more developed type of living communities requires the successful emergence of sense-perception to delineate successfully causal efficacy in the external environment; and it also requires its relapse into a reflex suitable to the community. We thus obtain the more flexible communities of low-grade minds, or even living cells, which possess some power of adaptation to the chance details of remote environment.

Finally mankind also uses a more artificial symbolism, obtained chiefly by concentrating on a certain selection of sense-perceptions, such as words for example. In this case, there is a chain of derivations of symbol from symbol whereby finally the local relations, between the final symbol and the ultimate meaning, are entirely lost. Thus these derivative symbols, obtained as it were by arbitrary association, are really the results of reflex action suppressing the intermediate portions of the chain. We may use the word 'association' when there is this suppression of intermediate links.

This derivative symbolism, employed by mankind, is not in general mere indication of meaning, in which every common feature shared by symbol and meaning has been lost. In every effective symbolism there are certain æsthetic features shared in common. The meaning acquires emotion and feeling directly excited by the symbol. This is the whole basis of the art of literature, namely that emotions and feelings directly excited by the words should fitly intensify our emotions and feelings arising from contemplation of the meaning. Further in language there is a certain vagueness of symbolism. A word has a symbolic association with its own history, its other meanings, and with its general status in current literature. Thus a word gathers emotional signification from its emotional history in the past; and this is transferred symbolically to its meaning in present use.

The same principle holds for all the more artificial sorts of human symbolism:—for example, in religious art. Music is particularly adapted for this symbolic transfer of emotions, by reason of the strong emotions which it generates on its own account. These strong emotions at once overpower any sense that its own local relations are of any importance. The only importance of the local arrangement of an orchestra is to enable us to hear the music. We do not listen to the music in order to gain a just appreciation of how the orchestra is situated. When we hear the hoot of a motor car, exactly the converse situation arises. Our only interest in the hoot is to determine a definite locality as the seat of causal efficacy determining the future.

This consideration of the symbolic transference of emotion raises another question. In the case of sense-perception, we may ask whether the æsthetic emotion associated with it is derivative from it or merely concurrent with it. For example, the sound waves by their causal efficacy may produce in the body a state of pleasurable æsthetic emotion, which is then symbolically transferred to the sense-perception of the sounds. In the case of music, having regard to the fact that deaf people do not enjoy music, it seems that the emotion is almost entirely the product of the musical sounds. But the human body is causally affected by the ultra-violet rays of the solar spectrum in ways which do not issue in any sensation of colour. Nevertheless such rays produce a decided emotional effect. Also even sounds, just below or just above the limit of audibility, seem to add an emotional tinge to a volume of audible sound. This whole question of the symbolic transfer of emotion lies at the base of any theory of the æsthetics of art. For example, it gives the reason for the importance of a rigid suppression of irrelevant detail. For emotions inhibit each other, or intensify each other. Harmonious emotion means a complex of emotions mutually intensifying; whereas the irrelevant details supply emotions which, because of their irrelevance, inhibit the main effect. Each little emotion directly arising out of some subordinate detail refuses to accept its status as a detached fact in our consciousness. It insists on its symbolic transfer to the unity of the main effect.

Thus symbolism, including the symbolic transference by which it is effected, is merely one exemplification of the fact that a unity of experience arises out of the confluence of many components. This unity of experience is complex, so as to be capable of analysis. The components of experience are not a structureless collection indiscriminately brought together. Each component by its very nature stands in a certain potential scheme of relationships to the other components. It is the transformation of this potentiality into real unity which constitutes that actual concrete fact which is an act of experience. But in transformation from potentiality to actual fact inhibitions, intensifications, directions of attention toward, directions of attention away from, emotional outcomes, purposes, and other elements of experience may arise.

Such elements are also true components of the act of experience; but they are not necessarily determined by the primitive phases of experience from which the final product arises. An act of experience is what a complex organism comes to, in its character of being one thing. Also its various parts, its molecules, and its living cells, as they pass on to new occasions of their existence, take a new colour from the fact that in their immediate past they have been contributory elements to this dominant unity of experience, which in its turn reacts upon them.

Thus mankind by means of its elaborate system of symbolic transference can achieve miracles of sensitiveness to a distant environment, and to a problematic future. But it pays the penalty, by reason of the dangerous fact that each symbolic transference may involve an arbitrary imputation of unsuitable characters. It is not true, that the mere workings of nature in any particular organism are in all respects favorable either to the existence of that organism, or to its happiness, or to the progress of the society in which the organism finds itself. The melancholy experience of men makes this warning a platitude. No elaborate community of elaborate organisms could exist unless its systems of symbolism were in general successful. Codes, rules of behavior, canons of art, are attempts to impose systematic action which on the whole will promote favorable symbolic interconnections. As a community changes, all such rules and canons require revision in the light of reason. The object to be obtained has two aspects; one is the subordination of the community to the individuals composing it, and the other is the subordination of the individuals to the community. Free men obey the rules which they themselves have made. Such rules will be found in general to impose on society behavior in reference to a symbolism which is taken to refer to the ultimate purposes for which the society exists.

It is the first step in sociological wisdom, to recognize that the major advances in civilization are processes which all but wreck the societies in which they occur:—like unto an arrow in the

hand of a child. The art of free society consists first in the maintenance of the symbolic code; and secondly in fearlessness of
revision, to secure that the code serves those purposes which
satisfy an enlightened reason. Those societies which cannot combine reverence to their symbols with freedom of revision, must
ultimately decay either from anarchy, or from the slow atrophy
of a life stifled by useless shadows.

Notes on Contributors

KENNETH BURKE, of the Bennington College Literature Department, was born in 1897 in Pittsburgh, Pa. He has been a prolific writer of stories, translations, critical articles; book reviewer and music critic; and lecturer on the practice and theory of literary criticism and on the psychology of the literary form. He spent the past academic year at the Center for Advanced Study in the Behavioral Sciences, and is teaching this summer at the School of Letters, Indiana University. His books include *Counter-Statement, Permanence and Change, Attitudes Towards History, Philosophy of Literary Form—Studies in Symbolic Action, A Grammar of Motives,* and *A Rhetoric of Motives.*

WERNER HEISENBERG was born in Würzburg, Germany, in 1901. He has been Director of the Max Planck Institute for Physics since 1941, and Professor of Theoretical Physics at the University of Göttingen since 1946. He received the Nobel Prize in Physics in 1932 for his researches in atomic physics. In addition to articles and books on atomic and nuclear physics, he has published contributions to the philosophy of science.

ERICH KAHLER was born in Prague, Czechoslovakia, in 1885. He has been on the faculties of The New School for Social Research, Black Mountain College and Cornell University. In 1955, he gave the Christian Gauss Seminars for Criticism at Princeton University. He has been a member of the Institute for Advanced Study at Princeton, N. J. since 1949, and is at present a Visiting Professor at Ohio State University. His publications include *Man the Measure* and *The Tower and the Abyss.*

ROLLO MAY was born in Ohio, in 1909, and received his Ph. D. from Columbia University in 1949. A practicing analyst in New York City, Dr. May is a Fellow and Member of the Faculty of the William Alanson White Institute of Psychiatry, Psychology and Psychoanalysis, a Fellow of the American Psychological Association and Past President of the New York State Psychological Association. He is the author of *The Meaning of Anxiety* (1950) and *Man's Search for Himself* (1953), and editor of *Existence: A New Dimension in Psychiatry and Psychology* (1958).

TALCOTT PARSONS, born in Colorado Springs in 1902, is Professor of Sociology at Harvard University where he has been since 1927. For the past academic year, he has been a Fellow at the Center for Advanced Study in the Behavioral Sciences at Stanford, California. He has translated Max Weber's *Protestant Ethic and Spirit of Capitalism*, and has authored *Structure of Social Action, Toward a General Theory of Action, The Social System, Essays in Sociological Theory*, and other books.

I. A. RICHARDS was born in Cheshire, England, in 1893, and educated at Cambridge University. He has been a Fellow of Magdalene College, Cambridge, since 1926. At Harvard University since 1939, he has been University Professor since 1944. His writings include *The Meaning of Meaning, Principles of Literary Criticism, Practical Criticism, Coleridge on Imagination, Mencius on the Mind, Philosophy of Rhetoric, How to Read a Page, A Leak in the Universe* (verse play), and *Speculative Instruments*. His first volume of poems, *Good-bye Earth*, appears in September.

NATHAN A. SCOTT, JR., Associate Professor of Theology and Literature at the University of Chicago, was born in Cleveland, Ohio, in 1925. He is the author of *Rehearsals of Discomposure: Alienation and Reconciliation in Modern Literature* (1952) and of *Modern Literature and the Religious Frontier* (1958); and he is the editor of *The Tragic Vision and the Christian Faith*. He has been at the University of Chicago since 1955. Previously he was Associate Professor of the Humanities and director of the General Education Program in the Humanities at Howard University.

PAUL TILLICH, born in Starzeddel, Prussia, in 1886, has been University Professor at Harvard University since 1955. He was educated at the Universities of Berlin, Tübingen, and Halle, and served as professor of theology and philosophy in Germany until 1933. From 1933 to 1955, he was Professor of Philosophical Theology at the Union Theological Seminary, New York. He is the author of *The*

*Protestant Era, Systematic Theology, The Courage to Be, Biblical
Religion and the Search for Ultimate Reality, Love, Power, and
Justice, Dynamics of Faith,* and others.

ALFRED NORTH WHITEHEAD was born in Ramsgate, England in 1861.
He was a Fellow of Trinity College at the University of Cambridge
and Professor of Philosophy at Harvard University. A renowned
philosopher and mathematician, Professor Whitehead was the author
of such well-known books as *Science in the Modern World, The
Aims of Education, Adventures of Ideas,* and *Introduction to
Mathematics.*

AMOS N. WILDER, born in 1895 in Madison, Wisconsin, has been
Hollis Professor of Divinity at Harvard Divinity School since 1956.
His principal field of interest is New Testament interpretation. His
publications include *Arachne: Poems, Eschatology and Ethics in the
Teaching of Jesus, Spiritual Aspects of the New Poetry, The Healing
of the Waters: Poems, Modern Poetry and the Christian Tradition,*
and *Otherworldliness and the New Testament.*